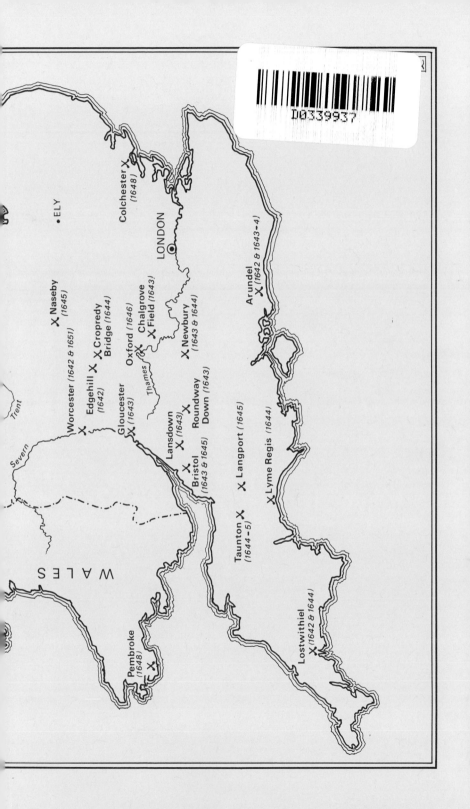

WALES

Severn

Trent

•ELY

Colchester X
(1648)

LONDON ⊙

X Naseby
(1645)

Worcester X (1642 & 1651)

Edgehill X (1642)

X Cropredy
Bridge (1644)

Oxford (1646) X X Chalgrove
Field (1643)

Thames

X Newbury
(1643 & 1644)

Gloucester X (1643)

Lansdown X (1643)
Roundway
Down (1643)

Arundel
X (1642 & 1643-4)

Bristol X
(1643 & 1645)

Taunton X
(1644-5)

X Langport (1645)

X Lyme Regis (1644)

Pembroke X
(1648)

Lostwithiel
X (1642 & 1644)

The Cavaliers

King Charles I on horseback, c.1635 by Van Dyck

MARK BENCE-JONES

The Cavaliers

CONSTABLE
LONDON

First published in Great Britain 1976
by Constable and Company Limited
10 Orange Street London WC2H 7EG
Copyright © 1976 by Mark Bence-Jones

ISBN 0 09 461260 9

Set in 11pt Monotype Garamond
Printed in Great Britain by
Ebenezer Baylis & Son Limited
The Trinity Press, Worcester, and London

Contents

Illustrations

A*   ix

Between pages 20 and 21

Richard Lovelace
(*Dulwich College Picture Gallery*)

Edmund Waller, after Riley
(*National Portrait Gallery, London*)

Between pages 148 and 149

James Butler, Duke of Ormonde
(*By permission of Sir Ralph Verney*)

Queen Henrietta Maria, by van Dyck
(*National Portrait Gallery, London*)

The Earl and Countess of Derby, by van Dyck
(*The Frick Collection, New York*)

James Graham, Earl of Montrose, after Honthorst
(*National Portrait Gallery, London*)

Sir Hugh Cholmley, by Janssen
(*By permission of C. D. Cholmeley Harrison Esq.*)

John Cleveland, attributed to Dobson
(*By permission of the Duke of Sutherland*)

Dr. Gilbert Sheldon, studio of Lely
(*National Portrait Gallery, London*)

Dr. John Fell
(*Christ Church, Oxford*)

Dr. Richard Sterne, from his effigy in York Minster
(*Photo: A. F. Kersting*)

Dr. Richard Dolben, from his effigy in York Minster
(*B. T. Batsford Ltd.*)

Sir Charles Lucas, by Dobson
(*By permission of Lord Methuen*)

George, Lord Digby, and William, Lord Russell, by van Dyck
(*By permission of Earl Spencer*)

Prince Rupert with two Cavalier officers, by Dobson
(*Private collection*)

Acknowledgements

I would like to express my deep gratitude to Mr T. Charles-Edwards and Mr B. H. G. Wormald, both of whom were of the greatest help to me in suggesting sources, as well as most kindly reading my typescript, giving me the benefit of their tremendous knowledge of seventeenth-century history. And I must also say how much my chapter on Edward Hyde, Earl of Clarendon, owes to Mr Wormald's authoritative work, *Clarendon, Politics, History and Religion, 1640-1660.*

In the same way, I must, like everyone else who writes about the Civil War period, make a special acknowledgement to the works of Dame Veronica Wedgwood, OM, DBE. Of all the other modern historians whose works I have consulted and have listed in the Select Bibliography at the end of this book, I feel most grateful to G. M. Young for his classic, *Charles I and Cromwell,* and to Bernard Fergusson (now Lord Ballantrae, GCMG, GCVO, DSO, OBE) for his admirable little biography, *Rupert of the Rhine.*

I use modern spelling throughout when quoting from seventeenth-century sources; and in the case of personages whose style changed during the course of their careers owing to their having inherited, or been given, peerages, I endeavour to refer to them consistently by their best-known style. Thus, I speak of Thomas Wentworth, Earl of Strafford, as 'Strafford', even though he was, for most of his career, Viscount Wentworth. I have, however, made an exception in the case of Edward Hyde, Earl of Clarendon; referring to him as 'Hyde' or 'Clarendon', depending on what stage of his career is being dealt with. On the other hand, when speaking of his literary works, I consistently refer to him as 'Clarendon'.

Introduction

To say, as Clarendon did, that England in the late 1630s 'enjoyed the greatest measure of felicity that it had ever known' might be something of an exaggeration; yet the country was then probably more peaceful and prosperous than anywhere else in contemporary Europe. Nobody at the time would have imagined that civil war was imminent, and that the conflict, which involved Scotland and Ireland as well as England, would last on and off until 1660. The war was unexpected because it was not fought along any obvious divisions of class or race, but over political and religious differences which, in the case of the vast majority of the belligerents, were not so very great. The Royalists or Cavaliers fought for the King, the Parliamentarians or Round-heads for Parliament; but few of the King's supporters would have wished to see Parliament abolished, while apart from what would now be called the extreme Left, the Roundheads were perfectly good monarchists. The Cavaliers fought for the Church of England, the Roundheads for Puritanism; but only the High Anglicans and their Catholic allies among the Cavaliers and the extreme Puritan zealots among the Roundheads were really separated in their religious beliefs.

In fact, both sides in the Civil War claimed to be fighting for the same thing: to maintain the fundamental laws of England against a usurped and arbitrary power, and to defend the Protestant religion. While nobody would have been able to say for certain what those fundamental laws were, as they did not really exist, the Royalists had the better claim to be maintaining them, since they were fighting to maintain the constitution as it then stood; whereas Parliament aimed at overthrowing the English Church as established by law—abolishing the bishops who were one of the Estates of the Realm—and usurping powers which constitutionally belonged to the King. The King, for his part, had encroached on the rights of Parliament, but his Royal Prerogative entitled him to do so in certain circumstances; it was simply a question of whether or not these circumstances had arisen—something which could be argued both ways. The Tudors used the Royal Prerogative far more tyrannically than the Stuarts ever did; but they—and, in particular, Elizabeth I—had the statesmanship necessary to carry Parliament and the country with them. Not only did James I and Charles I lack statesmanship, but they were singularly tactless in their handling of the Royal Prerogative, making their subjects conscious of it; whereas under the Tudors it had been taken for granted. James I even dressed it up in the doctrine of Divine Right, formerly exclusive to popes and emperors, according to which the King held his power of God. This doctrine was to a certain extent necessary in order to maintain the Reformation position against the Papacy, and it was believed by plenty of reasonable people. But its logical inference was that to disobey the King was to disobey God's will.

The first two Stuart kings faced a Parliament that had grown greatly in stature during the past century, even though it was still only called at the accession of a sovereign or during a crisis—throughout the forty-five years of Elizabeth I's reign, it was only in session for a total of twenty-two months. Not only did the Tudors strengthen the constitutional position of Parliament by making full use of it as a backing to their rule; but their social, economic, religious and foreign policy had enriched the country gentry and merchant classes, giving a new importance to the House of Commons. Almost inevitably, there would have been some kind of clash between the Early Stuarts and Parliament, but the conflict might never have assumed the proportions it did if they and the Commons had not been on opposite sides in the religious controversies which loomed so large in seventeenth-century Britain.

At the beginning of the century, the Church of England was predominantly Calvinistic, or Puritan, with a small Arminian or High Church party led by Lancelot Andrewes. Having had all too much experience of the Presbyterians in Scotland, James I did not take kindly to Puritanism, even in its milder English form. 'A Scottish Presbytery agreeth as well with a monarchy as God and the Devil,' he exclaimed angrily after hearing the English Puritan point of view at the conference which he called at Hampton Court in 1604; and for the rest of his reign he was on the side of the Arminians. Charles I went further in his espousal of the High Church cause, not merely through a distaste for Puritanism, as had been largely the case with his father, but because he sincerely believed in the teachings of Andrewes and of Andrewes's more celebrated disciple, William Laud, whom he made Archbishop of Canterbury in 1633.

With Charles's whole-hearted approval, Laud set out to make the Church of England uniformly Arminian. Just as the King had a legal justification for exercising the Royal Prerogative, so were Laud's church reforms justified by the Prayer Book. But—again like the King—he was exceedingly tactless in the way he carried them out, causing widespread resentment. And in harking back to the glories of the medieval church, Laud made himself still more disliked by claiming that the bishops had power over the laity: it was the ecclesiastical equivalent of the Royal Prerogative and Divine Right. The fact that Laud's sacramental and ritualistic Anglicanism was associated with Charles, whose Queen, Henrietta Maria, was a Catholic, meant that the opposition to both the Archbishop and the King was reinforced by the fear of Popery. The triumph of the forces of Catholicism on the Continent during the first phase of the Thirty Years War—which reached its height in 1629, the year that Charles I began his period of personal rule—made the Popish bogey seem particularly real to English Protestants.

The Early Stuarts were chronically short of money, owing to the increase in the cost of government as well as their own extravagance; they kept up a far larger household than that of Elizabeth I, and made substantial purchases of jewels, plate and works of art. The permanent revenue of the Crown was not enough to meet their expenses—particularly on account of a very severe inflation which halved the value of money during the course of James I's reign. They were thus obliged to call Parliament frequently, in order to ask for subsidies. These frequent sittings gave Parliament plenty of opportunities to criticize the King's government and in particular to demand the redress of grievances in the ecclesiastical field.

To avoid being confronted with such grievances, Charles I

managed without Parliament for eleven years, from 1629 to 1640. During this period, he was fortunate in having a minister of the greatest ability, energy and integrity: Thomas Wentworth, afterwards Earl of Strafford. But Charles I wasted Strafford's talents; instead of keeping him at the centre of affairs, he sent him first to York, as President of the Council of the North, and then to Ireland as Lord Deputy. Strafford was an austere character, no respecter of persons: he made a host of enemies. But his rule in York and Dublin was fair as well as effective: as proof of its popularity, the country round York was, in the Civil War, predominantly Royalist. In particular, he protected the poor and under-privileged against the rich vested interests. The nineteenth-century Whig view of history makes it seem as if Parliament defended the ordinary people against the oppression of Charles I: in fact, Charles I came closer to being a champion of the ordinary people than Parliament, which represented, and was largely composed of, the propertied classes.

During the eleven years that Charles I ruled without Parliament, he raised money by imposing taxes by Royal Prerogative. Considering how the country had grown in wealth under Elizabeth I and continued to grow richer throughout the Stuart period—with the East India and Levant Companies capturing the trade of distant parts of the world—the scale of taxation during Charles's reign was absurdly low, even by the standards of the time; so that the King was justified in attempting to make people pay more. But Prerogative taxation was regarded by the gentry and merchants as a tyrannical attack on the rights of property; it created further grievances to be stored up for when Parliament was next called, and enabled John Hampden to become a popular hero through his stand against the tax levied by Charles to subsidize his navy, known as Ship Money.

Charles's personal rule—known by supporters of the regime as the 'Rule of Thorough' and by its opponents as 'The Eleven Years' Tyranny'—ended when he became embroiled in two wars with Scotland, in 1639 and 1640, caused by his unfortunate policy of imposing Arminianism on the Scottish Church. Presbyterianism was not only far more deeply entrenched in Scotland than Puritanism in England, but the Scots nobles were unruly. As a result of these wars, Charles was so much in need of money that he was obliged to call Parliament, which carried through a programme of constitutional reform and sent Strafford to his death by passing a Bill of Attainder against him.

Parliament might never have gained the ascendancy it did but for the purposeful, energetic and none too scrupulous leadership of John Pym, which contrasted with Charles's undecided and rather erratic policy during the months that followed. Towards the end of 1641 however, Pym and his party overplayed their hand. Like so many others of their kind, they were not content to stop at reform, but went on to revolution. They attacked the bishops and the Established Church; they launched the fierce assault on the authority of the Crown known as the Grand Remonstrance. As a result, Parliament was split, and the moderate reformers, who believed that the Royal Prerogative had been sufficiently curbed by the legislation which had already been passed, went over to the King.

The dispute between King and Parliament might now have ended peacefully had it not been for the outbreak of the Irish rebellion, an outstanding instance of the Stuart's notorious ill-luck; and for the affair of the Five Members, a no less striking example of Charles's political ineptitude. By attempting to arrest five members of the Commons whom he had heard were planning to impeach the Queen, Charles played into the hands of Pym, who was able to convince Parliament that the King could not be trusted to observe the reforms to which he had given his consent unless his power were curtailed still further; in fact the affair was so disastrous to the King's cause that one would be justified in believing it to have been a trap set by Pym himself. The Irish rebellion made it necessary for an army to be raised with which to fight the rebels. Pym and the other leaders of the Commons feared that if the King controlled this army, he would use it against Parliament; so they attempted, by the Militia Ordinance of March 1642, to get control of the army themselves. The King refused to give his consent to the Militia Ordinance, which he rightly regarded as a wholly unprecedented usurpation of his powers. So Parliament raised an army without the Royal consent and the King, who had retired to York, raised troops of his own so as to prevent himself from becoming, as he put it, 'but the outside, but the picture, but the sign of a King' in the face of the all powerful Parliament. Civil war thus became inevitable.

Although the Civil War was not a class war, most of the Cavaliers came from the higher ranks of society: of the 120 peers, ninety supported the King. The gentry who were not peers—the class which produced Pym, Hampden and Cromwell—tended to support Parliament, though many Cavaliers came from the ranks of the gentry, particularly from among the smaller squires. The merchants, tradesmen and artisans in the towns provided Parliament with some of its staunchest champions; though again, there were Cavaliers among the urban middle classes. The country people usually followed their local squire; apart from the independent yeomen farmers who were one of the most revolutionary elements in Cromwell's army. In the West Country, towards the end of the war, there were risings of armed peasants known as Clubmen, who were exasperated by the depredations of both sides and attacked Cavaliers and Roundheads indiscriminately.

Allegiance in the Civil War was more likely determined by religion than by class. It would be safe to say that all High Anglicans and all Catholics—except for a few Catholic soldiers of fortune—were Cavaliers, and that all extreme Puritans were Roundheads. On the other hand, there were plenty of moderate Puritans among the Cavaliers. Largely on account of the prevailing religious climate, some parts of the country were predominantly Cavalier and others largely Roundhead. Thus, the strongly Protestant eastern counties and London were for Parliament; the north and west was for the King. But again, there were Cavaliers who came from the most Puritan towns of East Anglia, Roundheads from the hills and dales of Yorkshire.

Of the Cavaliers—men and women—portrayed in this book, some were staunch to the King all through; others joined him after the Grand Remonstrance; others again came over to his side during the course of the war, having started by fighting against him. Some of them fought for the King in the literal sense, others gave him moral support, or suffered on account of their loyalty to him. Most of them were English, though they include a Scot, an Irishman and three foreigners. Most of them were Anglican, but some were Catholic and at least three were Calvinist, Puritan or Presbyterian. But while they may have varied in many respects, they were alike in their loyalty to the King. It may not have been loyalty which made them espouse the

Royalist cause in the first place, but having fought for Charles I or suffered on his account, they invariably ended by feeling an intense devotion for him. That unsatisfactory yet strangely attractive monarch is the subject of the first of the succeeding chapters, in order to show what manner of man it was who inspired the Cavaliers depicted in the chapters that follow.

King Charles I

When Bernini was making his statue of Charles I, he was sent a portrait of the King without being told who the subject was. After looking intently at the portrait, he said that he had never seen a face 'which showed so much greatness, and, withal, such marks of sadness and misfortune'. Certainly we can see sadness in Charles's features, even in portraits dating from the years before his troubles began, when he described himself as the happiest King in Christendom. But can we see greatness? It would be nearer the mark to say, with the eighteenth-century historian, David Hume, that Charles I was a good, rather than a great man, who, had he been born either an absolute prince or a constitutional monarch, would have enjoyed a happy and successful reign; but whose misfortune it was to be King at a time when people were questioning the prerogative which he had inherited from his predecessors, and which he regarded as sacred.

It was, in fact, his misfortune that he ever became King, owing to the untimely death of his brilliant and popular elder brother, Prince Henry. Having been sickly as a child—some believe him to have been a victim of polio—he had been kept rather in the background, so was naturally shy; and while as a man he enjoyed remarkably good health, he was undersized, and suffered from an impediment in his speech. These physical disadvantages, however, were far less of a handicap to him than his weakness of character. Like so many weak men, he was obstinate, and when he found himself in a difficult position, he would resort to duplicity. And though irresolute and vacillating in his policies, he was unbending as regards the two central principles of his life, his prerogative and his religion.

These two principles were inextricably tied up with his idea

9

of kingship. His duty to uphold them was something for which he felt answerable to God; it was part of his sacred trust as an anointed king. But while he stood resolutely by his principles, he gave no thought as to their effect on the minds of other men. He was totally uninterested in politics, which meant that, having lacked political experience when he came to the throne at the age of twenty-four, he did nothing to make good this deficiency.

His failure to learn the art of government would not have mattered so much had he been the sort of monarch who prefers pleasure to duty; but in all other respects he took his kingship very seriously. Having become a king by accident and at an age when he was not yet ready to bear the burdens of his lofty position, he was determined, from the start, to be a great king. He more than made up for his diminutive stature by his dignity; he overcame his stammer, so that his low voice was notably attractive. He quickly put an end to the rackety palace life of his father's reign, so that his court became the most formal and elegant in Europe. His own taste was impeccable; to create a setting worthy of him both as a king and as a perfectionist, there was no shortage of talent. Ben Jonson was his Poet Laureate, Van Dyck his court painter. Laniere and Ferabasco conducted the music for his Chapel Royal and for the masques which were the favourite diversion of his Queen, their costumes and scenery designed by Inigo Jones. More enduring works by this first great architect of the English Renaissance were mostly beyond Charles's exchequer; his plan to replace the Tudor rabbit-warren of Whitehall with a palace twice the size of the Escurial never got further than the drawing-board. There was, however, Inigo Jones's more modest palace at Greenwich, the Queen's House, as well as his Banqueting House at Whitehall with its ceiling painted by Rubens, who, like Van Dyck, settled in England under the King's patronage. Charles could afford to patronize artists, if not architects, and he built up a collection of pictures which, had it survived intact, would now be the greatest in the world.

Though Charles fitted so perfectly into the setting of his court —a small, exquisite, darkly-clad figure moving with measured tread across a floor of white and tawny marble, against a background of classical columns and cloth of gold—he was not really of it in the way that, say, Charles II identified himself with the vast concourse of people that surrounded him. His sense of being an anointed king, and also his shyness, kept him apart. After the murder of Buckingham, the worthless Royal favourite inherited from his father, he was never really intimate with anybody, except for the Queen. His friends and courtiers did not really know him. Even Archbishop Laud, whom Charles not only revered as the personification of the High Anglicanism which he loved so dearly, but liked for his grave conversation, was rather scared of him. If he seemed distant to his associates, he was, to the rest of his subjects, remote. Apart from his journeys to Scotland, he did not travel very much about his kingdom before the Civil War, mostly doing the rounds of his palaces and deer parks in the Home Counties to indulge his passion for hunting. He lacked Elizabeth's gift of captivating people with a word or two. Though he listened with courteous attention to those whom he received in audience, it was necessary to have more than just an occasional meeting with him to fall under his spell; he was too cold, too aloof, too short of humour to make anything like an instant impression.

Charles might have been closer to his subjects had he been prepared to be always on view, in the manner of Louis XIV; it would, after all, have been consistent with his ideas of kingship. But his fondness for family life, more characteristic of the monarchs of later centuries than those of his own day, meant that, whenever he could, he retired into quiet domesticity. He was a devoted husband and father. His marriage, after a bad start, had turned out to be blissfully happy; which was fortunate for him, since his religion and his high moral principles would never have permitted him to seek love elsewhere. The Queen, Henrietta Maria—known to Charles and his subjects as Mary—was a small, exquisite figure like her husband, with a liveliness in her dark eyes which made her attractive even after she had lost her bloom through childbearing. For all her gaiety and love of pleasure—which served as a perfect foil to Charles's stateliness— she was a woman of intelligence and resolution; she had inherited a Gallic shrewdness from her father, Henri IV, and a flair for statecraft from her mother's family, the Medici. As the only person to whom the King really opened his mind, it was natural that she should have influenced him; and had she been Queen of any other country but England, her influence would have been beneficial. But given the peculiar temperament and institutions of the English, whom she never really understood, her solution to her husband's problems, which was that he should support his position by military strength, was not necessarily the right one. On the other hand, it was probably not as wrong as Whig historians would have us believe; for if Charles had possessed an army at the beginning of 1642, there would have been no Civil War. Charles would have done better to have followed his wife's advice entirely, instead of just enough to bedevil the plans of his other advisers; but however remote he may have been from his subjects, he was closer than she was to their way of thinking.

As well as being unable to understand the English, the Queen was a poor judge of character, a fault she shared with her husband, who relied too much on first impressions. Her friends served the King badly, in particular the gifted but inept George, Lord Digby. She favoured Catholics, cosmopolitans and court gallants regardless of their actual worth; regardless, too, of the fact that these were just the sort of people Parliament and the majority of the nation mistrusted. It must, however, in fairness be said that these were also just the sort of people most likely to be attracted to her, as much as she to them: the people who, for her husband's sake, she should have cultivated were on the whole too Protestant and too xenophobic to be at ease in her company. And it must be remembered that she favoured people not necessarily through having taken a fancy to them, but on account of their services. This was something in which she differed radically from Charles, who tended to take people's services for granted, regarding them as no more than what every subject owed to his anointed King. His servants were not the same as his friends; and while to his friends he was almost invariably faithful, his servants could, at a moment's notice, be dismissed and forgotten. Even when in favour, a servant could not rely on Charles's whole-hearted trust.

This was particularly true of the greatest of Charles's servants, Thomas Wentworth, Earl of Strafford. Charles never really liked him, so failed to give him the support which he deserved. No king stood more in need of a strong and able minister than Charles; with such a minister, he could have been a popular and successful monarch. Strafford was just such a minister, but instead of keeping him in London, Charles relegated him to York and Dublin. With a strong man like Strafford at the centre of affairs, Charles's period of Prerogative rule might have lasted far longer than eleven years; for though it came to be known as the Eleven Years' Tyranny, it failed because it was not strong enough.

Having assured Strafford of his safety, Charles was obliged to sacrifice him to the wrath of Parliament, something for which he never forgave himself. To forget an old servant was all too easy for him, but to have sent an innocent man to the scaffold for reasons of expediency went against his conscience as a Christian. Strafford was the victim of Charles's lack of statecraft, as much as of his weakness. When the Bill of Attainder for sending him to his death came before the House of Lords, Charles made the fatal mistake of announcing that, if it were passed, he would not give it the Royal Assent. This meant that the Lords were able to pass it and avoid incurring the wrath of the Commons and the populace, which they would have suffered had they thrown it out; confident that, in the end, Strafford's life would be spared by the King. Whereas, by keeping the Lords in doubt as to whether or not he would give his assent to the Bill, Charles could have made them feel that the question as to whether Strafford lived or died really did depend on their vote; and in that case, they would almost certainly have voted for him to live. When the Lords had passed the Bill, Charles failed in his resolve not to give it his assent. He was scared into signing Strafford's death-warrant by the fury of the London mob—not that he himself was afraid of the apprentices and shop-boys, but he feared for the safety of the Queen.

If his fear for the Queen's safety was the cause of Charles's betrayal of Strafford, the most shameful action of his life, it was also the cause of his greatest political blunder, which occurred at the beginning of 1642: his spectacular attempt to arrest the Five Members for treason, descending in person on the House of Commons only to find that the birds had flown. He acted as he did on the advice of Digby, having heard that the Members were bent on the Queen's impeachment: it could well be said in Charles's defence that the very thought of Henrietta Maria being in danger drove him so frantic that he hardly knew what he was doing.

The attempt on the Five Members threw away the advantage which the King had gained in the weeks following the Grand Remonstrance. Pym's scare-tactics appeared to be justified; the Parliamentary leaders themselves were more than confirmed in their mistrust of the King's intentions. Apart from their expressed fears that Charles would repudiate the constitutional reforms which Parliament had achieved during the previous year, Pym and his friends were afraid for their own lives; if the King regained control of the situation, who could say that they would not be charged with treason?

So all hopes of a reconciliation between King and Parliament were at an end. It was to no avail that the King's ministers were now popular statesmen like Lord Falkland, Sir John Culpeper and Edward Nicholas, the first two being in fact strongly committed to moderate constitutional reform; nor was it any use when Charles, either of his own accord or following the advice of an even more dedicated Parliamentarian, the lawyer Edward Hyde, granted numerous concessions. Pym and his friends were determined to have no settlement with the King unless they could dictate to him from a position of strength.

With this in mind, they attempted to get control of the Militia, the army which was about to be raised for use against the Irish rebels. 'By God, not for an hour!' exclaimed the King, when asked by a deputation of Parliamentary peers whether he would be prepared to allow Parliament to control the Militia at any rate for a limited period. 'You have asked that of me in this, which was never asked of a king, and with which I will not trust my wife and children.' Nevertheless, from the letters written to him by the Queen, who was now in Holland, it seems that he began to waver on this vital point. Certainly, knowing him as well as she did, she did not trust him to keep to his resolution; and so threatened to retire to a convent if he gave way: 'I can never *trust myself* to those *persons* who would be *your directors.*' It was unkind of her to add to Charles's worries by threatening to leave him, yet she made up for it by constantly assuring him of her love: 'I can no longer live as I am without you', she declared in one of her letters at this time. There is no doubt that she genuinely loved him; and if her letters contained advice that was unfortunate, one cannot but admire her wifely efforts to instil a little commonsense into her vague and wayward husband: 'Delays have always ruined you ... once again I remind you to take care of your pocket and not let our cypher be stolen.'

In fact, after the attempt on the Five Members, the Queen's advice was probably more realistic than Hyde's. Certainly after the Militia Ordinance, by which Parliament took control of the Militia without the King's consent, there was no course open to Charles except to meet force with force; and in May he issued a proclamation forbidding the Militia from acting in obedience to the Ordinance. By now, he had established himself at York; he had left London in January, only to return seven years later as a prisoner.

Despite Charles's proclamation, the Parliamentary leaders, with the wealth of London behind them, were able to raise troops. They were confident that they could force the King to terms, for they had an army and he had not. But within a few months, the King was able to build up an army of his own, the number of his followers being greatly swelled by those who came over to his side, either because his proclamations convinced them of the justice of his cause or because they could no longer stand the tyranny of 'King' Pym's Puritan dictatorship. So instead of surrendering, as Parliament expected him to do, he set up his standard at Nottingham on a stormy day in August.

The raising of his standard made Charles 'very melancholy': he was by nature humane, and the prospect of civil war filled him with horror, though his enemies were later to call him 'Charles Stuart, that man of blood'. On the other hand, he was extremely reluctant to make a final offer of peace to Parliament, which his advisers urged him to do, not in any hope that it would be accepted, but in order that the Parliamentary leaders 'would make themselves the more odious to the people' by rejecting it. Having been at last prevailed upon to make the offer, he burst into tears and was so overwrought that he hardly slept that night. Parliament replied to the King's offer by insisting that he should withdraw his protection from those of his supporters who had 'been voted by both Houses to be delinquents'; a condition to which he could not possibly have agreed, though the Queen seems to have feared that he might have been weak enough to abandon his friends in this way. She hastened to remind him of the folly and injustice of such a course: 'If you do not take care of those who suffer for you, you are lost.' Her knowledge of Charles told her that he might have all too easily forgotten his friends and forgiven his enemies.

Charles's consideration for his enemies caused him to make the first of three strategic errors which lost him the war. After the battle of Edgehill in the autumn of 1642, his nephew, Prince Rupert, proposed to make a quick dash to London, which was then virtually undefended, a plan which might have won the King an early victory. But having been told by courtiers ill-disposed towards Rupert that the Prince would 'set the town on fire' if he reached London ahead of his uncle, Charles restrained him; so that the march on the capital was postponed until it was too late.

Charles's second great mistake was to write to Rupert in 1644 urging him to fight the armies of the Scots and the English Roundheads at York, which led to the disastrous battle of Marston Moor; he seems to have written the fatal letter in the heat of the moment, when he was himself in difficulties, being chased by the Roundhead general, Sir William Waller, in Worcestershire. To make him more than ever distracted, the Queen was gravely ill following her last confinement; she was not expected to live. A few weeks earlier he had written the Royal physician a brief but heart-rending note: 'Mayerne, for the love of me, go to my wife.'

In 1645, Charles made his third major error of strategy by deciding, against the advice of both Rupert and another brilliant commander, Lord Goring, to fight the battle of Naseby, in which he was so utterly defeated that his cause was irretrievably lost. On this occasion, as in the affair of the Five Members, he allowed himself to be influenced by Digby, who on the Queen's advice he had made Secretary of State. Almost as fatal to his cause as his strategic blunders was his tendency to be swayed by Digby's charm. Digby—and, indeed, the Queen herself—influenced him against Rupert, who was his best general.

If Charles had no head for strategy, he showed a certain ability for tactics; in the heat of battle, away from the conflicting influences of the court, he could think for himself. It was mostly in the winter months that he held court at Oxford; during the campaigning season he spent as much time as he could with his troops, sharing their hardships and dangers. The exquisite, art-loving monarch was also remarkably tough, thanks to his love of hunting and other outdoor sports: one has only to look at some of his later portraits to see how his features, which are generally supposed to have been over-refined and almost effeminate, as they were in his youth, had by middle age turned rugged. And in what was essentially a cavalry war, his superlative horsemanship stood him in good stead. He took part in several major battles, including two notable Royalist successes: the victory over Waller at Cropredy Bridge, near Banbury, in the summer of 1644 and the action at Lostwithiel in Cornwall later that year, when a more important though less able Roundhead commander, the Earl of Essex, was cornered with his army on the Fowey peninsula. In that battle Charles very much directed operations himself; and when it was over, he rode in person about the field giving strict orders to his officers to ensure that none of the defeated enemy was plundered.

Charles's bad strategy was all but redeemed by his bravery in the field. At Edgehill, in a black velvet cloak lined with ermine, the blue ribbon of the Garter across his gleaming breastplate, he rode along the lines encouraging his men, looking and speaking as became a chivalrous monarch. 'Your King is both your cause, your quarrel and your Captain!' he had told his principal officers in his tent. At Naseby, resplendent in gilt armour, he tried to lead a last charge which might have saved the day. But even here, there was a courtier at hand ready to thwart him. 'Will you go upon your death in an instant?' exclaimed the Earl of Carnworth with 'two or three full-mouthed Scots oaths'; and seizing the King's bridle, he turned his horse's head. The troops behind took this as a sign that they should turn also, and before Charles realized what was happening, they had galloped off to the right in some confusion.

Charles lost the war at Naseby, though he campaigned for a few months longer, moving restlessly from place to place so that the account of his wanderings reads like the report of a royal tour in the Court Circular. But while his enemies were triumphant, he was now far more popular with the nation as a whole than he had been when the war started. He had lost his kingdom and his army, but had gained immeasurably in stature. If he was not yet Charles the Martyr, he was, at any rate, Charles the hero; the King for whom so many had died and for whom

many more had sacrificed their property. People who had joined
his cause because they were convinced of its justice, or because
they could not stand the tyranny of Parliament, now felt an
intense personal loyalty to him. The war enabled him to get
through to his subjects in a way he had never managed to do
when hedged in with the trappings of Whitehall. Even his
friends and courtiers had found him something of a mystery in
the years of peace; but his goodness, his piety and his courage
made an unforgettable impression on those who were close to
him during the vicissitudes of the conflict. Few of his followers
deserted him as his fortunes declined; on the contrary, a great
many people were to come over to him from the winning side
after his defeat.

Contemplating his position in the spring of 1646, after the
surrender of the last effective Royalist force at Stow-on-the-Wold,
Charles had no reason to give up hope. The victors were overwhelmingly in favour of monarchy and much more sympathetic
towards him now that he was beaten. They were also by no
means united; the kingdom was in the hands of three distinct
powers. These were Parliament, backed by the City of London;
the victorious New Model Army, commanded by Sir Thomas
Fairfax and Oliver Cromwell; and the Scots, who had invaded
England as the allies of Parliament at the beginning of 1644
and still occupied the northern counties. Parliament and the
Scots were Presbyterian; the army, on the other hand, was mostly
composed of Puritans of different sects, known as Independents.

The King chose to throw in his lot with his fellow-country-
men, the Scots. Riding secretly out of Oxford, he made his way
to their army at Newark and was taken by them to Newcastle.
As a condition for restoring him to the throne, the Scots insisted
that he and all his subjects should take the Covenant; which
meant that the Church of England would be replaced by Presbyterianism. Charles was willing to go so far as to agree to Presbyterianism being legally established, provided Anglicanism could
be allowed to exist alongside it, but the Scots would accept no
such compromise. The negotiations foundered, as did subsequent
moves for Charles's restoration, on the rock of his devotion to

Anglicanism. Had he been willing to abandon his church, he would certainly have preserved his throne as well as his life; but the church was one thing on which he would not give way. Even the Queen, who was now in France, could not shake his resolve, though she made every effort to do so; never having quite realized how much the Church of England meant to him. It has thus been widely held that Charles died for his religion: until 1859, the Church of England venerated him as King Charles the Martyr, and kept the anniversary of his death as a day of solemn prayer and fasting.

To what extent Charles also died for his Prerogative is not so clear; for although his Prerogative would have been severely curbed had he accepted the terms which Parliament put forward following the breakdown of his negotiations with the Scots, and repeated at various times until shortly before his death, it was not for this reason that he refused those terms, but because they inevitably included the 'utter abolishing and taking away' of the Anglican hierarchy. He did, however, also hesitate to accept the terms put forward by the army leaders which affected the Prerogative but not the church; and while to have agreed to these terms might not necessarily have regained him his throne, it would almost certainly have saved his life.

In January 1647, the Scots handed Charles over to the Parliamentary Commissioners and he was brought south. His journey was almost a triumphal progress; crowds cheered and bells rang in every town and village through which he passed. It was now the army's turn to make him an offer. Though the men who had fought under Fairfax and Cromwell included republicans, Anabaptists, Levellers and others of what would now be called the extreme Left, these were only a minority. Most of the army was monarchist, including its leaders, and in particular, Cromwell's influential son-in-law, the grim and steely Henry Ireton. And what was more important, the army leaders were less strongly opposed to Anglicanism than either Parliament or the Scots; provided they could have toleration for their own sects, it did not matter much to them whether the Established Church was Anglican or Presbyterian. As well as agreeing in principle to a restoration, Fairfax and Cromwell regarded the King as a trump card to be played against Parliament, which had failed to pay the army its arrears and was thought to be planning to oust the present leaders from their command.

Having been politely abducted by Cornet Joyce and his troopers, Charles was brought to Newmarket where he met the leaders of the army. He was treated with every courtesy, and Ireton produced a formula for his restoration which was known as the Heads of Proposals. After some successful bargaining on Charles's part, these terms were modified so that, in effect, they required no more of him than that he should give up control of the Militia for ten years, and abolish the coercive power of the bishops. In all other respects, the church was to be left undisturbed. In that summer of 1647, as Cromwell and Ireton negotiated with the King, it seemed that a restoration was very near. The King, though still a prisoner, was installed in his palace at Hampton Court; Mrs Cromwell and Mrs Ireton were said to be already fancying themselves as peeresses.

Charles, however, still could not bring himself to agree to the Heads of Proposals, but continued to play for time, hoping for a restoration which would preserve his authority intact. He realized, too, that the terms put forward by the army leaders would not necessarily be supported by the army as a whole. And, much to his credit, he was resolute in insisting on an amnesty for all his followers; whereas under the Heads of Proposals, five of the leading Cavaliers were to be excepted from the general pardon.

Everything was thrown into the melting pot when the Heads of Proposals were rejected by Parliament, even though the army commanders had taken the precaution of marching on London and purging the Commons of some of the more extreme Presbyterians. Having been repudiated by Parliament, Ireton's formula was repudiated by the rank-and-file of the army, in which the radicals grew daily more powerful. Meanwhile, the Scots reopened negotiations with the King, this time without insisting on the Covenant; and in December he concluded a secret treaty with them. By then he was no longer under any obligation to the army leaders, who had failed to get the Heads of Proposals accepted by Parliament. It was also clear to him that Cromwell had moved over to the side of the radicals, in order to keep the army under control. 'I appeal to all indifferent men to judge, if I have not just cause to free myself from the hands of those who

King Charles I and Queen Henrietta Maria, by Mytens

William Cavendish,
Duke of Newcastle,
by Samuel Cooper

(*Left*) Margaret Cavendish,
Duchess of Newcastle,
engraving after
Diepenbeck

(*Right*) Lucius Cary,
Viscount Falkland,
attributed to van Dyck

(*Above*) Dr. William Juxon, Bishop of London

(*Left*) Prince Rupert, after van Dyck

D: Logan ad vium sculp:

Honoratissimus Illustrissimusqᵉ Dominus D. EDOARDUS HIDE. Eques Auratus, CLARENDONIÆ Comes, Cornburiæ Vicecomis, Baro HIDE de Hindon, Summus Angliæ, nec non almæ Oxoniensis Academiæ Cancellarius, ac sacræ Maᵗⁱˢ regiæ à secretioribus Consilijs.

(*Above*) The Earl of Newport, and George, Lord Goring, by van Dyck

(*Left*) Edward Hyde, Earl of Clarendon

Sir John Suckling, by van Dyck

Sir William Davenant

Richard Lovelace

Edmund Waller, after Riley

change their principles with their condition,' Charles wrote in
November, when attempting to justify his recent escape from
Hampton Court to Carisbrooke Castle in the Isle of Wight.

On the other hand, it seems likely that Charles began to negotiate with the Scots before the Heads of Proposals were rejected
by Parliament. Even if we discount Cromwell's story of how a
letter from Charles to the Queen proving this, was intercepted
and brought to him sewn in a saddle, we know that the Scots
Commissioners in London paid frequent visits to Hampton Court
from the moment the King arrived there. In view of Charles's
concept of kingship, he would have felt obliged to continue bargaining with all sides in order to get the best terms: an anointed King
could never be bound by a formula which only gave him back
a part of his rightful Prerogative, but must forever strive to
recover it all. It was a duty which he owed to God and his
people.

As a result of their agreement with Charles, the Scots invaded
England in the following year, only to be defeated by Cromwell
at Preston. The risings of the English Royalists known as the
'Second Civil War', which anticipated the Scots invasion, were
no more successful. By the autumn of 1648 the army was in as
strong a position as ever; and its leaders, with the notable
exception of Fairfax, had more or less decided that Charles must
die. The radicals had made up their mind even before the Second
Civil War that no mercy could be shown to the 'Man of Blood'.
Parliament, however, had one more try at persuading the King
to take the Covenant, and it seems likely that if this had been
successful, Cromwell would have gone back to supporting a
restoration. There was also an attempt by Fairfax to revive
the Heads of Proposals; but Charles was now even less favourably inclined towards them than he had been in the previous
year, as though adversity made him more than ever conscious
of his rights and duties as King. He thus sealed his own fate;
for on finding that he had never really taken their Proposals
seriously, Cromwell and Ireton, who had already contemplated
putting him to death for reasons of expediency, were fired by
righteous indignation to go through with the deed.

It was for reasons of expediency that Charles had to die.
The Second Civil War had convinced the army leaders that
there could be no peace so long as he was alive; and it was also

necessary to placate the republicans and Anabaptists in the army, who were clamouring for his head. But Cromwell and his friends had to dress up their act of judicial murder to look as though Charles were being justly punished for his tyranny and for making war against his people. Having gained control of Parliament by means of another purge—carried out by Colonel Thomas Pride—the army leaders staged a show trial, in which, since no English lawyer of repute could be found who was willing to do so, the evidence against the King was prepared by a Dutchman, Isaac Dorislaus.

In Westminster Hall, surveying the sixty-seven judges who sat facing him on benches hung with scarlet, Charles asked one of his attendants who they were; he was so out of touch with his chief opponents that he knew hardly any of them by sight. When the Lord President, John Bradshaw, called on him to reply to the charge, he merely challenged the authority of the court. He continued to challenge its authority on the succeeding days, and when pressed to answer the charge, he said firmly: 'I know that I am pleading for the liberties of the people of England more than any of you ... if Power without Law may make Law, I do not know a subject in England who can be sure of his life or anything he can call his own.' Now that Parliament had been reduced by Pride's purge to a mere unlawful assembly, Charles alone stood for the laws and liberties of his people, just as he was the only constitutional authority left in the land. Now, on trial for his life, he felt more than ever a King.

Before pronouncing sentence, Bradshaw declared that the King was being charged 'in the name of the people of England'. 'Not a half, not a quarter of them!' cried one of the ladies in the gallery. She spoke the truth: Charles was tried not by the people but by the ruling military clique. He himself made this point as he stood on the scaffold outside the Banqueting House at Whitehall on that cold January afternoon in 1649: 'And so I die a martyr for my people, and I pray that God will not lay it to their charge.'

Charles's execution caused horror, indignation and dismay throughout Britain and all over Europe. There was widespread grief at the loss of so excellent a prince, particularly after people had read *Eikon Basilike*, which purported to be his apologia, and which, though almost certainly not by him, contained sentiments very much his own. As the Royal Martyr, Charles did more for kingship and the English Church than either the sword of Rupert or the pen of Hyde. If he fell short of greatness during most of his life, he certainly attained it at his trial and in the brave and dignified manner in which he faced death.

Newcastle

The borders of Nottinghamshire and Derbyshire are to this day dominated by the personality of William Cavendish, the Cavalier Duke of Newcastle. His castle at Bolsover still rises from its cliff in that strange, broken country bordered by the moors and high hills, just as it does in the plates of his book on horsemanship where its turrets and cupolas form the background to illustrations of himself performing *caprioles* and *balottades* on his noble Spanish mares. Below the castle, his ridinghouse remains as a monument to his passion for the *haute école*, as does his other riding-house at Welbeck, a few miles to the east in Sherwood Forest; though there the mansion itself has changed from the irregular, gabled structure of his time. At Bolsover, too, there is the great gallery, now roofless, which he built to entertain Charles I and Henrietta Maria; more like the palace of a Renaissance princeling than part of an English country house.

Newcastle was very much a Renaissance figure, who aspired to the ideal of the 'Complete Man', of Castiglione's Courtier. He was a gentleman of fine appearance and perfect manners, who danced well and excelled not only in riding, but in fencing and all other manly sports. Such was his love of music that in his youth he paid £50 for a 'singing boy'; an extravagance which his father had applauded, saying that 'if he should find his son to be so covetous, that he would buy land before he was twenty years of age'—as a young relative had just done—'he would disinherit him'. He had a talent for literature and a knowledge of philosophy and science, so that as well as being the patron of Ben Jonson and William Davenant, he was the friend of Hobbes.

And yet, for all his Renaissance culture, there was something of the knight-errant about him, as can be seen from his portrait; his face is amiable and quixotic, though his eyes have the challenging gleam usually born of the conviction that one is always right. He dreamed the same dreams of chivalry which inspired his father to build the fantasy castle at Bolsover. Chivalry played no small part in Newcastle's 'signal fidelity to the Crown', which he saw in terms of the loyalty due from a knight to his liege lord; declaring, after he had suffered exile and enormous losses in the Royalist cause, that 'if the same wars should happen again, and he was sure to lose both his life and all he had left him, yet he would most willingly sacrifice it for His Majesty's service.'

It was, however, chivalry reinforced with gratitude. There was the gratitude felt towards the monarchy by families such as the Cavendishes which had grown rich and powerful under the Tudors, and which made them, with notable exceptions, loyal to Charles I—though as the son of a younger son, Newcastle had himself inherited little of the Cavendish fortune, his great estates having come to him from his wife, his mother and his grandmother, the redoubtable Bess of Hardwick. And Newcastle felt a personal gratitude to the Stuarts, having been a favourite at court since the age of sixteen. He was made a viscount by James I, who cannily charged him £4,000 for the honour, and Earl of Newcastle by Charles I in 1628. Then, after much angling, he obtained the coveted post of Governor to the seven-year-old Prince of Wales, in which capacity he was responsible for such homely details of the young Prince's life as making him take his physic, as well as educating him to be King. Living as he did in the reflected glory of the crown, Newcastle had no desire to see that glory diminished; and unlike some of his fellow-peers, who took up arms against Charles I in much the same spirit as that in which the over-mighty subjects of medieval kings had rebelled against them, he believed that the interests of the nobility were best served by a strong monarch.

There are other factors, too, which combined to make Newcastle a natural Cavalier. He was on friendly terms with Strafford, who had been his contemporary at that most loyal of Cambridge colleges, St John's: an important consideration, since Newcastle's influence extended into Yorkshire, where Strafford held sway as President of the Council of the North. Being 'indifferent' in

matters of religion, while favouring Episcopacy for the support
which it afforded to the established order, he had no sympathy
with the religious zeal of the Puritans, whom he hated with the
hatred of one who loved plays and masques and all the other
things which they regarded as sinful.

Newcastle was able to give full rein to his love of beauty and
splendour and at the same time demonstrate his loyalty when
the King visited him at Welbeck in 1633 on the way to being
crowned in Scotland; and again in the following year when
the King and Queen came to Bolsover. The Puritans were not
alone in being shocked at the prodigiousness of these two entertainments, which cost £9,000 and £15,000 respectively: Clarendon,
in his *History*, rather primly thanks God that nobody was tempted
to imitate them. The money spent on the Royal visit to Bolsover
must have included the cost of building the great gallery, in
which the masque *Love's Welcome*, written specially for the
occasion by Ben Jonson and with costumes and stage setting
by Inigo Jones, was performed. For two days the vast rooms,
with their huge classical doorways of stone, were crowded with
the ladies and gentlemen of the court and filled with the sound
of poetry, of singing and lute music; and after that they were
hardly, if ever, used again. Now that the gallery is deserted and
roofless, it seems like some temporary pavilion, put up for that
one occasion only: as temporary as the masque itself—that most
transient of art-forms—so well expressing the dream-like quality
of life in those years before the Civil War.

When war threatened, the King sent Newcastle to Northumberland with a secret commission to secure the town of Newcastle,
which, with Hull and Scarborough both in Parliamentary hands,
was the only possible port for bringing in supplies from the
Continent. Such was Newcastle's influence in Northumberland,
where he had large estates inherited from his mother, that he
quickly secured Newcastle for the King, as well as the county
and the neighbouring County Palatine of Durham. He set to
work constructing fortifications, and in order that the inhabitants
might not be exposed to subversive influences, he employed an
Arminian divine 'to view all sermons that were to be preached,
and suffer nothing in them that in the least reflected against His
Majesty's person and Government'.

At the outbreak of war, Newcastle was appointed General of

all the King's forces north of the Trent, with power to confer
knighthoods, coin money and raise men. He performed the last
part of the commission with great zeal, and having started by
raising troops from among his own tenants and friends, he had,
by the autumn of 1642, built up a formidable army which he
equipped with the help of a shipload of arms and ammunition
sent by the King of Denmark. At the beginning of December
he marched southwards with six thousand men to the relief of
York, which was threatened by a Parliamentary army raised in
Yorkshire by Lord Fairfax and his son, Sir Thomas. Newcastle's
march saved York and obliged the Fairfaxes to withdraw into
the West Riding, which effectively reduced their strength, since
the North Riding regiments disbanded themselves rather than
go with them.

Newcastle established his headquarters at York, which, with
his flair for splendour, he made into an oasis of elegance and
civilization, particularly during the weeks in 1643 when the Queen
held her court here, having crossed from Holland and landed
at Bridlington Bay. It was all too easy for his enemies in the
Royalist camp to represent him as a sybarite who neglected his
duties: 'a sweet General', who 'lay in bed until eleven o'clock
and combed till twelve' as one of the Queen's ladies is alleged to
have called him; though whether she actually did is doubtful,
since we only hear of it from behind the Parliamentary lines.
Clarendon, while paying tribute to the way in which Newcastle
always endeavoured to be in the thick of the fighting—exposing
himself fearlessly in the face of danger so that there were times
when the fortunes of the day were changed through his men
taking fresh heart at the sight of him—tells us that no sooner
was an action over than 'he retired to his delightful company,
music, or his softer pleasures, to all which he was so indulgent,
and to his ease, that he would not be interrupted upon what
occasion soever; insomuch as he sometimes denied admission
to the chiefest officers of the army.'

Then there were those who criticized Newcastle for his
'romantic spirit', to which the Roundhead general, Lord Fairfax,
alluded sarcastically when challenged by him to follow 'the
examples of our heroic ancestors' and engage in a pitched battle,
replying that he refused 'to follow the rules of Amadis de Gaul,
or the Knight of the Sun'. Newcastle's 'misfortune'—as the

King's confidant, Sir Philip Warwick, regarded it—of being something of a poet, was held against him when he appointed a fellow-poet, William Davenant, as his Lieutenant-General of Ordnance. With Davenant and other congenial souls attending his councils of war, these gatherings were reported as being more notable for their wit than for their strategy and tactics.

All this was unfair to Newcastle, who, far from entrusting the conduct of the war to a band of poets, made good his own total lack of military experience by relying on professional soldiers, such as the gaunt and austere Yorkshire Catholic, Sir Marmaduke Langdale, the brilliant if erratic George Goring and, above all, Lord Eythin, a Scot who had served in the Swedish army and who became his right-hand man. He himself acted not so much as a general but as an energetic and conscientious war leader, the equivalent of the modern wartime prime minister; putting heart into the Yorkshire Royalists, raising troops, organizing taxes, gingering up the populace by the occasional show of force, such as when he sent soldiers to the town hall at York to secure the re-election of a Mayor 'of much loyalty and discretion'. The Roundheads took him seriously enough to exclude him whenever they offered the Royalists a general pardon and to launch a propaganda campaign against him, calling his army the 'Queen's Army' or the 'Catholic Army' in order to bring it into disrepute, accusing him of planning to overthrow the Protestant religion on the grounds that he gave commissions to Catholics.

At first, Newcastle's military operations were successful, if somewhat slow, considering his superior numbers. He succeeded in driving the Parliamentarians out of the West Riding, but only at the third attempt, in June 1643, when he had his desire and fought a pitched battle against the Fairfaxes, beating them soundly. After the battle, Sir Thomas Fairfax's wife was captured by the Royalists; but Newcastle courteously sent her in his own coach to join her husband at Hull, where he and his father had fled. Hull was now the only stronghold in Yorkshire left to Parliament. The King proposed that Newcastle should leave it behind him and march southwards on London, through Norfolk and the other counties of the so-called Eastern Association, while he himself approached the capital by way of Sussex and Kent. Charles's strategy was all too often disastrous; but this plan of his might have won the war, even if the combined attack on London had not been carried out. For Newcastle to have invaded the Eastern Association in the late summer of 1643 would have been to strike at the very heart of Puritan England while its army was not yet ready, with the gallant Royalist rising at Lynn as evidence that the people were growing restive under the Parliamentary yoke.

Newcastle marched into Lincolnshire, but after a month returned to Yorkshire. His reason for disobeying the King was that most of his officers, who were Yorkshiremen, refused to leave their county until Hull was captured. In later years, Newcastle would speak as though he had been in complete agreement with the King's plan, but at the time there were those who suspected him of being no less anxious than his officers to return to Yorkshire, because he did not wish to lose his independent command. He was encouraged to follow his own inclinations in the matter by the Queen, who had formed a high opinion of his leadership during her stay at York; even though she once described him as 'fantastic and inconstant'.

From the moment Newcastle returned to Yorkshire, his luck ran out. His siege of Hull was a fiasco, for supplies could always reach the garrison by sea: Fairfax had opened the dykes and flooded the surrounding country, and in October a successful sally and a high tide obliged the Royalists to withdraw, leaving some of their cannon stuck in the mud. Then, in the following January, the Scots entered the war on the side of Parliament, and Newcastle found himself caught between two hostile armies. He hurried northwards to meet the invaders, marching through the deep snow of that cruel winter. At first it looked as though he would have to stand siege in Newcastle, which was not yet properly fortified; but he succeeded in beating the enemy off. The Queen wrote to say how glad she was that he had 'not yet eaten rats'; one suspects that she was teasing him, knowing his fondness for good living. She added: 'Provided that the Scotch do not eat "Yorkshire oat cakes" all will go on very well.' But while the town of Newcastle was for the time being safe, the Scots continued to move slowly southwards, in spite of being severely harassed by Langdale's cavalry. Newcastle hoped to engage them in battle before they could join up with the army of the Fairfaxes, but they outmanœuvred him.

There was great dissatisfaction in the Royalist camp at Newcastle's failure to stop the Scots. Unable as he was to stand up to much public criticism, he thought of resigning his command. The King dissuaded him: 'Remember all courage is not in fighting, constancy in a good cause being the chief, and the despising of slanderous tongues and pens being not the least ingredient.' In fact, it is hard to see how Newcastle could have done any better. The Scots vastly outnumbered him, and he was threatened in the rear by the Yorkshire Parliamentarians. In April, he felt he had no option but to fall back on York, which would otherwise have been captured by Sir Thomas Fairfax, even though this meant leaving the way open for the Scots.

For nearly two months, Newcastle and his troops were closely besieged in York by the combined forces of the Scots, the Fairfaxes and the Earl of Manchester, who had advanced from Lincolnshire with Oliver Cromwell as his second-in-command. Newcastle and Eythin organized the defence and the rationing, which does not appear to have been very stringent; there was never any need to eat rats. The enemy trained cannon on to the city wall and by springing a mine made a breach which they entered; but Newcastle's own regiment attacked, killing them in great numbers, and the breach was quickly mended.

At the end of June, Prince Rupert came to Newcastle's help with an army; as he approached, the enemy raised the siege and retired in confusion. Newcastle wrote a letter of rather fulsome congratulations to Rupert, who was encamped to the north of York, ending: 'Neither can I resolve anything since I am made of nothing but thankfulness and obedience to Your Highness's command.' This is just how one would have expected an old courtier to address the King's nephew, but Rupert took it literally, and assumed that Newcastle was putting himself entirely at his disposal and could tell him nothing about the movements of the enemy. So, having decided on an immediate battle, in accordance with what he took to be the King's wish, he did not bother to consult Newcastle, but ordered him rather peremptorily to march with his troops against the enemy at four o'clock next morning.

In this way Rupert not only offended Newcastle, who once again threatened to resign—he was, after all, twice the Prince's age, used to being respected and inclined to be touchy—but never gave himself a chance of hearing Newcastle's view of the situation until it was too late. Newcastle knew that the enemy forces were about to separate, owing to jealousies between the English Roundheads and the Scots, so that there was every reason for not fighting them immediately. But he was not able to tell this to Rupert until the impetuous young Prince had already marched towards the enemy at Long Marston and thus committed himself to a battle; for he met him not at four in the morning but at nine. The reason for his delay was that his troops, having endured two months of siege, were on the point of mutiny at being ordered into battle without first being allowed a little rest. He had in fact come out ahead of them, leaving Eythin to follow with them later in the day. Rupert wished to attack without waiting for them, knowing that the enemy was not yet in battle order, but Newcastle was for waiting, and Rupert unfortunately deferred to him. By the time Eythin and the army from York arrived, the enemy was fully drawn up and singing psalms.

In the ensuing battle, Newcastle held no command, but fought as a private gentleman at the head of a company of volunteers. As he rode up to them, he said: 'You have done me the honour to choose me as your Captain, and now is the fittest time that I may do you service; wherefore if you follow me, I shall lead you on the best I can, and show you the way to your own honour.' He then led them to attack a Scots regiment of foot, which they charged and routed; he himself killed three of the enemy with his page's half-leaden sword, having lost his own—he had refused to take one from any of his gentlemen.

If Newcastle fought bravely, so did his tenants—'stout and faithful men' from the moorlands of his northern estates—who made up his own regiment of foot. They were known as 'Newcastle's Lambs' from their white woollen clothing. There had been a shortage of red cloth when he recruited them, so he had obtained white cloth, intending to have it dyed; but his men asked to have it 'un-dyed as it was, promising they themselves would dye it in the enemy's blood'. But on the morning after the battle they were found to have coloured their uniforms with their own life's blood, for they lay dead in their ranks; the regiment having been virtually wiped out.

On that morning after Marston Moor, Newcastle was faced not only with the loss of his regiment, but with the destruction of his entire army. It was more than he could stand, and he decided at once to lay down his command and leave the country. To Prince Rupert, who tried to persuade him to stay and rally his broken forces, he said: 'I will not endure the laughter of the court.' Though he was physically brave, Newcastle lacked moral courage. And having laboured for two years in what Clarendon calls an 'undelightful condition of life' to raise and preserve the army which had been 'in a moment cast away and destroyed', he had not the heart to start all over again.

As he sailed towards Germany, Newcastle, who was a widower, may have consoled himself in his misfortunes with thoughts of marriage. He had been asked to look after the sister of Sir John Lucas, one of his officers, who was a maid-of-honour at the Queen's court in Paris and exposed to dangers on account of her beauty. Newcastle had a weakness for beautiful women and his interest was aroused, though he was fifty-two and Margaret Lucas only twenty. When he met her early in the following year—having travelled from Hamburg to Paris in a coach drawn by nine Holstein horses, which he had bought on credit—he found that she came up to her brother's description; in fact she was a very remarkable woman. She was beautiful, with soulful eyes and a well-shaped mouth; she was a poet and a writer and was interested in philosophy and science. If she had little or no sense of humour, the same could be said of him. The marriage took place and, founded as it was on mutual admiration, proved a great success.

During the years of exile they were chronically short of money, for Newcastle's estates had all been confiscated by the Roundheads. Margaret went over to England to try and obtain some income from them, the wives and children of forfeited Royalists being generally allowed to claim in this respect; but she was told by the Parliamentary authorities that she could expect nothing, since her husband had been 'the greatest traitor of England'. The Queen gave them £2,000, but they mostly had to live on credit. Once, when the creditors grew tired of paying, Newcastle's steward came to him and told him that there would be no dinner. It looked as though Margaret would have to pawn her clothes, but in the end her husband spoke to the creditors himself, and was so polite and persuasive that they let him have more money. There were numerous other occasions when Newcastle had to use his charm to extend his credit.

Having lived for a while in Paris, they went, at the request of the Queen, to attend on the Prince of Wales in Holland; but when they arrived there, they found he had gone to sea. Newcastle, once again the knight-errant, resolved to follow him but was dissuaded by Margaret, who was, as she put it, 'unwilling that My Lord should venture upon so uncertain a voyage and (as the proverb is) seek a needle in a bottle of hay'. Eventually they settled in Antwerp, in a house belonging to Rubens's widow. While he was still in Paris, Newcastle had spent much of his hard-won credit on buying a pair of Barbary horses, 'resolving for his own recreation and divertissement to exercise the art of *manège*'. At Antwerp he increased his stable to eight horses, which he trained and rode so brilliantly that Spaniards, watching him perform, would cross themselves and cry '*Miraculo!*' His celebrated work on horsemanship was written during his years in exile. This was not his only literary effort at this time; he also wrote two plays and a treatise on kingship for the benefit of his former charge, now Charles II, in which, among other advice, he recommended the banning of all books of controversy, unless they were in Latin: 'the Bible in English under every weaver's and chambermaid's arm hath done us much hurt.'

Margaret, who had no horses to ride, found herself with even more time on her hands than her husband, so turned to literature with an enthusiasm that exceeded his own. Her *Philosophical Fancies* was published in 1653, the year that also saw the appearance of her first book of poems. Two years later she published a book of essays called *The World's Olio*. As she remarked with innocent pride in the preface to one of her works, her scientific and philosophical views were all her own; she pleaded total ignorance of other writers, and admitted that she understood no language except for colloquial English. One wonders how she acquitted herself when Newcastle entertained his friend and fellow-exile, Hobbes, and particularly on the occasion in Paris when Descartes and Gassendi, as well as Hobbes and the poet Edmund Waller, dined at his table.

On the King's Restoration, Newcastle was so impatient to return to England that he sailed in 'an old rotten frigate', leaving Margaret 'in pawn' to the Antwerp creditors. He landed at Greenwich, 'where his supper seemed more savoury to him than any meat he had hitherto tasted', so glad was he to be back in his native land; and 'the noise of some scraping fiddlers he thought the pleasantest harmony that ever he had heard'. Margaret joined him as soon as the debts had been paid, and after a brief look at Restoration London, which was not much to her taste, they retired to Welbeck. The great house was empty of furniture, but the place was not devastated like most of Newcastle's other seats, thanks to the timely action of his brother, Sir Charles Cavendish, who, having been allowed during the Commonwealth to redeem his own estates by 'compounding', or paying a fine, was able to buy back Welbeck and Bolsover before the vandalistic new owners had done their worst, though not until part of Bolsover had been pulled down. From the rest of Newcastle's many estates, there came an unvarying tale of felled woodlands, broken fences, ruined houses and plundered furnishings—of the hundred and fifty sets of tapestry hangings which he had possessed before the war, only ten or twelve had been saved. His losses in the service of Charles I and Charles II were reckoned at just under a million sterling, for which he received no compensation apart from the dukedom which the King granted him in 1662—he had already been made a marquess in 1643. Like other Royalists, he only received back those estates of his which had been confiscated by the Roundheads, and not those which he had been obliged to sell to meet his expenses during the war.

He set to work to put his estates into some order; and although there were so many more essential things that needed doing, he managed to find the money to build a new riding-house at Bolsover. He also continued to devote himself to literature, and between his return to England and his death, at the age of eighty-four in 1676, he wrote numerous poems as well as two more plays and an English version of his book on horsemanship. But he was overshadowed as a literary lion by Margaret, who became so compulsive a writer that she made her young ladies sleep in a room next to her own, 'ready, at the call of her bell, to rise any hour of the night, to write down her conceptions, lest they should escape her memory'. Her output was prodigious, and although much of what she wrote is of little value, there is some genuine literature buried in the mountain of pseudo-scientific and philosophical speculation; notably her auto-biography, and her biography of her husband—despite its somewhat daunting title, which is *The Life of the Thrice Noble, High and Puissant Prince, William Cavendish, Duke, Marquess and Earl of Newcastle; written by the Thrice Noble, Illustrious and Excellent Princess, Margaret, Duchess of Newcastle, his Wife.*

With that appealing mixture of vanity and honesty which characterizes all her numerous self-revelations, she admitted that her ambition was to achieve fame. She certainly succeeded in this respect; she has a place among the immortals, though later generations have tended, rather unfairly, to regard her as eccentric to the point of madness. In her lifetime, when men of learning showed a proper deference to duchesses, her works were widely acclaimed.

She also has the distinction of being the first English woman writer, as well as being a pioneer—perhaps the originator—of what in these days is called the personality cult. Thanks to her writings—in which she even goes so far as to employ the now familiar technique of telling her readers what her husband has for breakfast—the Newcastles came to be known by the English public in a way that no great nobleman and his wife had ever before been known. On Margaret's rare visits to London, her coach would be jostled by the coaches of people eager to catch a glimpse of her. With her 'extraordinary fanciful' clothes, and her 'antic' feathered head-dress, she was easily recognizable. Perhaps the most revealing comment on her appearance comes from Charles II, who when told at a masquerade of a strange woman who had just arrived, with 'at least sixty ells of gauze and silver tissue about her, not to mention a sort of pyramid upon her head, adorned with a hundred thousand baubles', exclaimed rather ungallantly: 'I bet that it is the Duchess of Newcastle!'

3

Falkland:
'That Incomparable Young Man'

The England of the last peaceful decade before the Civil War is
seen at its most delightful in the company of scholars, poets and
wits gathered at Great Tew, the country house in Oxfordshire of
Lucius Cary, second Viscount Falkland. It was described as a
'college situated in a purer air'; people came and went without
formality, and engaged in friendly disputations under the oaks
and limes, strolling in and out of the walled gardens with their
Renaissance doorways of golden stone. At the centre of this
charmed circle, which included the theologians Sheldon, Chillingworth and Hales, the lawyer Hyde and the poets Suckling and
Davenant, was Falkland himself: a young man of less than
average height, of no particular looks, his movements awkward
and his voice grating. Yet such was 'the wit and weight of all he
said', and 'his disposition and nature was so gentle and obliging,
so much delighted in courtesy, kindness and generosity, that all
mankind could not but admire and love him'.

Whilst he seems so much a flower of that Indian summer of the
sixteen-thirties, Falkland was in many ways a character out of his
period. It is significant that after suffering eclipse for two hundred
years he should have been rehabilitated by writers such as Bulwer
Lytton and Matthew Arnold, who admired him for his love of
liberty, his 'largeness of temper', his patriotism and his moderation; virtues which made him, in their eyes, a fellow-Victorian.
While believing less implicitly in progress than they did, one has
to admit that these virtues are more typical of the nineteenth
century than of the seventeenth; though one feels that Falkland
would have been more at home towards the end of the last
century, in the world of the 'Souls', than as a High Victorian.

Amidst the fierce controversies of his own lifetime, his moderation and largeness of temper made him a poor politician but an
exceptional person. That he was always so much more reasonable
than anybody else would explain the spell which he cast over his
contemporaries. From the best-known portrait of him, we can see
that the expression of sweet reason in his eyes would have given
his face a certain beauty even though it was one of those faces
which appear to have been slightly squashed from above, making
the features lopsided.

In seeking to explain why Falkland was so much loved and
admired, one must make some allowance for the fact that he was
a lord, yet different from other lords; treating the poets and
theologians and philosophers on equal terms as a friend, just as an
intellectual peer of the nineteenth century would have done,
rather than as a patron, which would have been more usual in the
seventeenth century when peers kept up a semi-royal state. But
though he was a lord, he was far from being one of the great
magnates of the kingdom. His father was an impecunious
courtier and soldier of fortune who became a rather unsuccessful
Lord Deputy of Ireland and was given a Scottish peerage—a
second-class honour, since he was an Englishman. His Oxfordshire estates of Great Tew and Burford came to him from the
family of his mother, a talented and courageous woman, who
braved her husband's wrath when he was Lord Deputy by
declaring herself a Catholic.

Most of her daughters followed her into the Catholic Church,
and four of them became nuns in France. Her change of religion
had a profound effect on Falkland, who was very much his
mother's son. Though her efforts to convert him were unsuccessful, they made him uncertain as to his own religious beliefs and
gave him his passion for theological speculation. Being on
affectionate terms with his mother—apart from when she caused
a temporary rift by spiriting away his two younger brothers so as
to bring them up in her adopted faith—he naturally learnt to
respect and tolerate Catholics, even though he could not be won
over by Catholicism. When he engaged them in controversy, he
always remained courteous; his *Discourse of Infallibility* is notable
for its 'sweetnesses and civilities so unexpected in a quarrelling
treatise' as one of his Catholic opponents admitted.

Uncertainty and toleration gave rise to his own attitude towards religion, whereby he favoured doctrinal simplicity and freedom of belief while recognizing the need for a State Church—and if there was to be a State Church, what better than the Church of England? 'In all decency and majesty of ceremonies, the King's chapel seems to me to equal the Queen's,' he once declared, when arguing against Catholicism. Along with this distaste for dogma and outward allegiance to Anglicanism went a strong sense of good and evil.

How much or how little he actually believed is debatable, though we can safely say that he believed in a personal God and an afterlife. 'He finds doubts and scruples better than resolves them,' lamented his friend John Earle, who was destined to become a Restoration bishop; and it would seem that Falkland himself would have liked to believe more, declaring that if God were to allow him any choice in the matter, he would prefer that the Infallibility of the Church of Rome were true rather than not. His attitude made him all things to all men. His opponents feared that his views might render the church unnecessary; he was rumoured to have become a convert to Socinianism, a Polish sect which denied the Trinity and the divinity of Christ. His friends and admirers, on the other hand, were convinced that someone as intelligent and reasonable as he must surely believe as they did; he was a High Anglican to High Anglicans like Hyde, and Catholics hoped he would go over to Catholicism sooner or later. Two centuries after his death, the Scottish liberal Presbyterian theologian, John Tulloch, maintained that Falkland was at heart a Calvinist, owing to his having been at Trinity College, Dublin, during the period when his father was Lord Deputy.

A more significant result of his Irish upbringing was that when he returned to England he did not have a ready-made circle of young men of his own class with whom he had been brought up, but was free to choose his own friends. He did so 'by other rules than were prescribed to the young nobility of that time' and joined 'the tribe of Ben', the writers and wits who gathered round Jonson at the Devil Tavern. He also formed a romantic friendship with a young man named Sir Henry Morison, who all too soon was struck down by smallpox; after which he turned his affections to Morison's sister, Lettice, and married her. In her portrait she looks a rather ordinary, pleasant, somewhat horse-faced English girl; but she was endowed with exceptional

qualities of character and mind. The marriage caused an estrange-
ment with his father, who had hoped for a more advantageous
match. In an attempt to be reconciled, he made a gesture which,
though nothing if not generous, shows an impetuosity surprising
in so rational a being as himself: he offered his father the estates
which he had inherited from his maternal grandfather, an offer
which his father was too angry to accept. Having thus failed to
obtain his father's pardon, he went with his young wife to
Holland, intending to be a soldier of fortune. He had long been
attracted to the profession of arms, having commanded his own
company of foot in Ireland from the age of fourteen.

Holland in the event provided no opening for a military career,
so he and Lettice returned to England. He continued, however,
to stay away from London, much as he loved it; not only because
his angry father was a prominent figure at court, but in order to
learn Greek. Having been thwarted in his dreams of military
glory, his ambition was now to excel as a scholar. Living as he
did within easy reach of Oxford, he became friendly with 'the
most polite and accurate men of that University', to whom he
kept open house. There was Earle and another High Anglican
divine, Gilbert Sheldon, Warden of All Souls and future Archbishop of Canterbury. There was George Morley, also destined to
be a bishop but inclining towards Calvinism; when asked by 'a
grave country gentleman' what the Arminians held, he replied
that 'they held all the best bishopricks and deaneries in England'.
There was the 'rational and solid' William Chillingworth, who
more than any of the others influenced Falkland's own religious
views; having embraced Catholicism for a period, he had returned to the Anglican fold, but as an Anglican whose beliefs
were limited to a few essentials.

The company at Great Tew (and at Falkland's other house,
Burford Priory, where he lived as much as at Tew until he sold
it to pay the debts left behind by his father, who died in 1633)
was by no means limited to Oxford dons. There were county
neighbours like the scholarly Sir Francis Wenman, and there were
many friends from London who willingly made the journey west-
wards to this 'club of wits'. Among the latter were poets like the
fashionable Sir John Suckling, who 'had the strange happiness to
make whatsoever he did become him'; the urbane Edmund
Waller and William Davenant, 'high and stately' if a little raffish

with his pox-eaten nose. There was the up-and-coming lawyer
Edward Hyde and the diminutive soldier, courtier, poet and wit,
'Little Cid' Godolphin. There was John Selden, the jurist and
antiquary, whose lack of religious feeling contrasted with the
pious Anglicanism of Lettice Falkland, Hyde and the High
Church divines. There was the even more godless Thomas
Hobbes.

Falkland's guests were not necessarily all male. It is yet another
instance of his being in advance of his time that he enjoyed
intellectual friendships with members of the opposite sex. This
inevitably gave rise to scandal, which was repeated by Roundhead pamphleteers during the Civil War, particularly regarding his
relations with Lady Sophia Murray and Lady Dungarvan; but
such slanders are disproved by his well-known purity and his
devotion to Lettice. The young women in question were not even
his 'mistresses' in the Elizabethan sense, adored beings to whom
lyrics were addressed, but friends whom he esteemed for their
gifts of the spirit.

All came and went as they pleased, so that Falkland never knew
what guests were staying until he met them at dinner or supper;
it must have taxed Lettice's housekeeping, though she was
unfailing in her hospitality. If they wanted exercise, they could
ride out into the pleasantly rolling countryside, though Sidney
Godolphin was so fussy about himself that when it rained or the
wind blew in his face he would, 'after a little pleasant murmuring',
turn his horse and head for home. If they wished to work, they
could find all the books they needed in their host's library.
Chillingworth wrote *The Religion of Protestants* while staying with
Falkland; and Falkland himself spent a great deal of his time
studying and writing. He used to say that he pitied unlearned
gentlemen on a rainy day. He wrote poems as well as theological
treatises, of which the best known is his *Discourse of Infallibility*.
None of his literary works lives; though he is said to have tried
out his prose on the chambermaids to make sure that it was clear
enough to be understood by them. It was as a talker, rather than
as a writer, that he excelled, despite his squeaky voice; he shone
as the brightest star in the 'happy and delightful conversation'
which was always the chief attraction of Burford and Tew. His
talk, as Clarendon, the former Edward Hyde, remembered it, was
'one continued *convivium philosophicum*, or *convivium theologicum*,

enlivened and refreshed with all the facetiousness of wit, and good humour, and pleasantness of discourse, which made the gravity of the argument itself (whatever it was) very delectable.' His conversation gained much from his wide reading and his prodigious memory, which Clarendon reckoned to be greater than that of any other man he had known.

The idyll of Great Tew was cut short by the outbreak of the first Scots war. Falkland answered the call to arms and went north with the King's forces, spurred on by his patriotism and by the thought of how this might be his long-awaited opportunity to prove himself in battle. 'Great is thy charge, O North; be wise and just, England commits her Falkland to thy trust,' sang Cowley; but the war ended before there was any real danger. The meeting of the 'Short' Parliament took Falkland to London as a member of the House of Commons, in which, having only a Scottish peerage, he was able to sit. It was as natural for him to enter Parliament as to fight for the King in the north; his friend Hyde also became a member, as did Wenman, Suckling and Waller. The Short Parliament of April 1640, which, unlike its successor, conducted itself with 'gravity and sobriety', made a very favourable impression on him, giving him a reverence for parliaments and convincing him that the country could not do without them. Its untimely dissolution did not improve his feelings towards the court, of which he already had a poorish opinion having seen his father waste a fortune there.

And so, when he returned to Westminster in the autumn of 1640 as a member of the 'Long' Parliament, he was, like Hyde, a supporter of the popular party. Like Hyde, who doubtless influenced him in this respect, he had a great regard for the laws of the land; it seemed intolerable to him that they should be broken for reasons of state. So he spoke against Ship Money, condemning those judges 'who should have been as dogs to defend the sheep' but instead had 'been as wolves to worry them'; and he joined in the attack on Lord Keeper Finch, accusing him of having 'used the Law not only against us, but against itself, making it, as I may say, *felo de se*'. Like so many moderates, he could be immoderate about certain issues, when his eyes would lose their look of tolerant forbearance and blaze with indignation. Nor did he fear to express his views. Once, when the Speaker invited the House to pay what he considered to be an unmerited compliment to a certain Member by taking off their hats to him, he rammed his own hat down on his head with both hands.

There was certainly nothing moderate about Falkland's attitude towards Strafford. In the words of the twentieth-century historian, Sir John Marriott, 'he pursued him to his death with a relentlessness almost as keen as that of Pym'; and like Pym he did so on the grounds of necessity, the very grounds on which Strafford had based his absolutism, with fatal results to himself. It was not, as with others, the settling of an old score against the fallen Minister, it was that he disliked Strafford's politics, as well as his personality.

In the same way, Falkland had a prejudice against Laud, though this was less extreme and went with a genuine regard for the Archbishop's learning and integrity; after all, he numbered several of Laud's disciples among his close friends. He objected to Laud's interference in affairs of state, and to the power which the Laudian bishops claimed to exercise over the laity, no less than he objected to Catholic Infallibility. When, in March 1641, the popular party fired its first salvo at the Established Church in the form of a bill to deprive the bishops of their vote in Parliament, Falkland supported it. He stood up and spoke in its favour immediately after it had been opposed by Hyde, who was sitting next to him, which caused a great stir in the House, since the two friends were usually of the same opinion. To the extremists, who saw Hyde moving away from their point of view, it seemed as though Falkland was moving closer to them.

Six months later, when a similar bill was introduced, its predecessor having been rejected by the Lords, Falkland was at one with Hyde in opposing it. To Hampden, who remarked on his change of opinion, he replied that 'he had been persuaded by that worthy gentleman to believe many things which he had since found to be untrue'. Historians critical to Falkland have taken this as showing that he had hardly a first-class mind, that he voted one way under the influence of Hampden, and the other under the influence of Hyde. Horace Walpole took it as a sign of weakness and Macaulay, with typical exaggeration, spoke of how 'he was always going backward and forward'.

In fact, Falkland never moved from his position as a moderate. Though he objected to the excesses of Arminianism, he was as strongly wedded to Episcopacy as Hyde was. Could it be wise, he asked the House, 'to abolish upon a few days' debate an order which hath lasted in most churches these sixteen hundred years, and in all from Christ to Calvin?' He feared the strength of the anti-Episcopal extremists—the 'Root and Branch Men'; they were only a minority, but the majority in favour of Episcopacy was lukewarm—or as he himself put it, 'they who hated bishops hated them worse than the devil' but 'they who loved them did not love them so well as their dinner'. Having been assured by Hampden at the beginning of 1641 that if the first bill depriving the bishops of their Parliamentary vote were passed, 'there would be nothing more attempted to the prejudice of the Chu.ch', he had deemed it expedient to support the bill, not feeling particularly strongly about the matter of the bishops' vote. But when, for all Hampden's assurances, the mild bill of March was followed two months later by the 'Root and Branch Bill' for 'the utter abolishing and taking away' of archbishops and bishops, it became clear to him that the enemies of Episcopacy were determined on its overthrow and would not be satisfied by any concessions. So he took his stand against them, well aware that if the Root and Branch Bill had become law, Episcopacy would merely have been replaced by a Scottish-type Presbyterianism coercing the laity with even more arrogance than Laud. It was the substitution of one infallible church for another, and he found Puritan dogmatism no less distasteful than the claims of Rome and Canterbury.

The attack on Episcopacy taught Falkland the lesson which moderates learn sooner or later, namely that radicals, once they have their head, will not stop at reform but will rush on to revolution. The lesson was repeated when Pym launched the fierce assault on the authority of the crown known as the Grand Remonstrance. Falkland had disliked the absolutism of Strafford, which as a conservative he regarded as an unwarranted innovation and as a patriot he considered a menace to the state; but he had no wish to see a diminution of what he believed to be the rightful and traditional Royal Prerogative. His devotion to the state was combined with a no less true devotion to the crown: to 'a monarchy without a Strafford', in Bulwer Lytton's phrase, just as he was true to 'a Church without a Laud'. So there was nothing inconsistent in the fact that having helped to condemn Strafford in the spring, he opposed the Grand Remonstrance when it was

43

debated by a fevered and unruly House in November; speaking so passionately that his high-pitched voice rose to a scream. In this, as in the matter of Episcopacy, he stood where he had always stood. He may have been impulsive, but he was not changeable; his character was summed up by a contemporary as 'quicksilver fixed'.

As Falkland's opposition to the extremists in Parliament grew stronger, he came to be regarded as an advocate for the court. This was not at all what he would have wished, for it might have given the impression that he was merely out for preferment. So he did all he could to prevent any Royal favour from coming his way, even being a little off-hand to the King himself. But Charles was too much in need of Falkland's services to be thus discouraged, and, very probably on Hyde's recommendation, made him a Privy Councillor and Secretary of State. Falkland only agreed to take office after much persuasion by Hyde and others, and in the thought that to have refused would have brought discredit to the King's cause and also would have appeared as if he were afraid of the dominant party in Parliament.

At the same time as Falkland became Secretary of State, another moderate, Sir John Culpeper, was made Chancellor of the Exchequer. Together with Hyde himself, who refused office, they formed a rudimentary cabinet, a 'responsible' ministry such as had been attempted earlier in the year under the Earl of Bedford and abandoned on account of that nobleman's death. The King promised to consult them on everything to do with the House of Commons, a promise which he broke almost immediately when he failed to inform them of his intention to arrest the Five Members.

As well as having to submit to the vagaries of his Royal master, Falkland had to face the bitter hostility of the prevailing party in the Commons, led by Pym. Going in and out of the House, he ran the gauntlet of Pym's allies, the London mob, whose leaders proclaimed him from a table-top as a 'person disaffected to the kingdom' in order that no opportunity would be missed to jostle and insult him. To Falkland, who, in the words of Bulwer Lytton, 'was a lover of liberty but liberty as her image would present itself to the mind of a scholar and the heart of a gentleman', the idea of coercion by the 'prentices and rabble would have been supremely distasteful. With a demagogue like

Pym as his adversary, he was at a disadvantage; he had neither the talent nor the inclination to use the same tactics and conjure up a rival mob in support of the King, which would not have been very difficult. This is just one instance of how his fastidiousness hampered him as a politician. He firmly refused to employ spies or open letters on suspicion, which were regarded as necessary expedients in carrying out the duties of his office.

While events moved rapidly in the direction of war, Falkland worked hard for peace, urging the King to be more conciliatory than even Hyde would have wished. He and his two colleagues remained in London for as long as they could, taking it in turns to sit in the House of Commons so that in the likely event of Pym's wrath falling upon them, they would not all three be arrested at once. When it was no longer safe for them to stay, they joined the King. Falkland paid a final visit to London on an eleventh-hour peace mission. On his way back he met Hampden, whom he still regarded as a friend and fellow-moderate; but now, to his distress, he found him full of 'violence and acrimony of spirit'.

It broke Falkland's heart to see his beloved country torn by civil strife; Clarendon tells us that from the outbreak of war 'his natural cheerfulness and vivacity grew clouded, and a kind of sadness and dejection of spirit stole over him'. But there was no doubt in his mind as to the justice of the King's cause, despite allegations made to the contrary by historians of the nineteenth-century neo-Cromwellian school. In a letter written after the early Royalist victory at Powicke Bridge, near Worcester, he spoke of dying Roundheads begging God's pardon for 'this great sin of rebellion', adding: 'their blood will lie heavy upon those *boute-feux* that have engaged them and others, and so many men to their ruin and destruction'. He sold some of his land to raise money for the King, and continued to serve devotedly as Secretary of State, his task being rendered all the more difficult by the numerous frictions and jealousies within the Royalist camp. No sooner had the war begun than he had to contend with the touchiness of Prince Rupert, who objected to receiving the King's orders from him instead of from the King himself. As a result there was a coolness between them, so that at Edgehill, Falkland chose to fight with Henry Wilmot's cavalry rather than with Rupert's.

Like so many others with a hatred of war, Falkland found it less unbearable in the thick of the fighting. Whenever there was an action, he 'forgot that he was Secretary of State and desired to be where there would probably be most to do'. At Edgehill, having taken part in a successful charge, he urged Wilmot to charge again against a party of Parliamentary horse under Sir William Balfour which had managed to escape the first charge and was doing great mischief to the Royalist infantry; but Wilmot replied: 'My lord, we have got the day, and let us live to enjoy the fruit thereof.' Had he listened to Falkland, the battle might have ended as a victory for the King instead of a draw; for it was Balfour's horse which saved the day for Parliament.

Falkland was depressed by the number of people who died at Edgehill, but hoped the battle might put a speedy end to the war. After the peace negotiations which followed it had broken down, and the King's army had returned from its march towards London, his depression grew into 'a perfect habit of uncheerfulness'. He looked pallid and abandoned his customary neatness in dress; and having formerly been so affable, he now received suitors with a brusqueness which made them imagine that he was conceited. Sitting with his friends, he would often, 'after a deep silence and frequent sighs', exclaim in 'shrill and sad' tones, 'Peace, peace!'

He was driven to desperate measures and entered into correspondence with Royalists in London who were plotting to seize the Tower and arrest the leaders of Parliament. To encourage the loyal Londoners in their design, they were given the King's commission empowering them to raise troops in his service; the document was smuggled to them in a box tied 'about the thighs' of Kate, Lady Aubigny, a lively young war-widow who slipped away from Oxford and managed to get through the Parliamentary lines. The plot was discovered. Falkland's friend, the poet Edmund Waller, who was in London and very much implicated in it, saved his own skin by testifying against his fellow-conspirators, two of whom were hanged. Lady Aubigny was imprisoned and so was Lady Sophia Murray, to whom Falkland had written a letter in cypher. The thought that a woman he so esteemed was suffering on account of his indiscretion must have added greatly to his misery. And he must have reproached himself bitterly for having connived at the plot, which had only served to strengthen the hand of Pym and the extremists, making the chances of a negotiated peace more than ever remote.

Yet while Falkland was mostly sunk in gloom during the spring and summer of 1643, he occasionally recovered something of his natural gaiety, such as when he and the King had a bet about whether or not it was always possible to recognize Hyde's prose style. At the siege of Gloucester, he had the company of his friends Chillingworth and Davenant; the three of them would sit together in 'a smoky hut', talking theology late into the night. Chillingworth hated the war even more than Falkland did and was hard at work inventing a siege engine which he hoped would bring the Royalists an early victory; but which was merely to land him in a Roundhead prison, where he died.

Falkland was spared the death of Chillingworth, which did not occur until after his own death, but he mourned for other friends. Suckling, in exile, had taken poison when down-and-out. Sidney Godolphin had fallen fighting bravely in Devonshire, having cheerfully endured the hardship of long winter marches—he who had so disliked going for a ride in the rain. Waller's shameful conduct made him worse than dead; while news came from London that Sophia Murray, who was consumptive, could not live much longer in her prison.

It was popularly believed that Falkland's grief for Sophia Murray made him deliberately court death. Historians critical of him have maintained that when he rode forward at Newbury to where the enemy bullets fell thickest, he was committing suicide—using this as further evidence of his moral weakness. But there is a world of difference between suicide and being careless with one's life when there appears to be nothing much to live for. And Falkland had a reason, other than a mere death-wish, for being foolhardy in battle: he did not want it to be thought that his well-known longing for peace stemmed from cowardice. At the siege of Gloucester, when his friends remonstrated with him for exposing himself unnecessarily, 'he would say merrily that his office could not take away the privileges of his age, and that a Secretary in war might be present at the greatest secret of danger.'

On the morning of that fatal first battle of Newbury, in September 1643, he was, as Clarendon tells us, 'very cheerful'. This statement, and a passage in the memoirs of the Parliamentarian, Bulstrode Whitlocke, based only on hearsay, which

47

tells of how on the morning of the battle he 'called for clean linen, as though expecting to be slain' and declared to his friends 'that he was weary of the times, foresaw much misery to his own country, and did believe he should be out of it ere night', have been used to support the suicide theory. But we know that Falkland was always cheerful when going into action. As for putting on a clean shirt, it was just the sort of thing a gentleman would have done; far from implying that he expected to be killed, it could have been a wise precaution, in case he was wounded. More difficult to explain is the remark about being 'out of it ere night', if indeed he ever made it. Sir John Marriott suggests that Whitlocke merely garbled a remark which Falkland made a few days before the battle, that he hoped its issue 'would put an end to the misery of the kingdom'; in other words, that he expected it to be conclusive.

On that September day, he put himself in the front rank of Sir John Byron's cavalry, which was advancing between hedges lined on both sides by Roundhead musketeers. They came to a gap, which Byron ordered to be widened; but before this could be done, Falkland spurred his horse through it, heedless of the murderous fire. Horse and rider were both instantly killed; his body was not found until next day, by which time it had been so mutilated as to be almost unrecognizable.

'Thus fell that incomparable young man, in the four and thirtieth year of his age.' Like Montrose, with whom he shares the honour of being regarded as the noblest of the Cavaliers, he was destined never to grow old. But in the words of Clarendon, he 'so much despatched the business of life that the oldest rarely attain to that immense knowledge, and the youngest enter not into the world with more innocence . . . whosoever leads such a life need not care upon how short warning it be taken from him.'

4

Prince Rupert

Rupert of the Rhine, the tall, impetuous young prince who led
cavalry charges as fearlessly as he commanded a buccaneering
fleet, is one of the two most romantic figures of the Civil War; the
other being Montrose. He has the face of a hero: thoughtful and
melancholy eyes, a classical nose, a resolute chin, a slightly super-
cilious upper lip and an expression that is stern yet not without
a certain gentleness. He might indeed be a hero of antiquity,
though at the same time there is something rather modern about
his clean-shaven good looks that goes with his interest in science
and mezzotint engraving.

If he does not seem quite to belong to the Civil War period, he
also did not quite belong to England, being a German who had
gained his early military experience on the Continent, though
England was to be the country of his adoption. He was a son of
Frederick, Elector Palatine, the 'Winter King', who was elected
King of Bohemia at the beginning of the Thirty Years War but
was driven out by the Imperial forces after a reign of only a few
months. His mother was Charles I's sister, Elizabeth, 'Queen of
Hearts', one of the most popular and attractive of all British
princesses. What is not generally realized about Rupert is that he
was, on his father's side, a Wittelsbach, a scion of the ruling house
of Bavaria. If at times he behaved unpredictably, it could be
attributed to his having inherited something of the Wittelsbachs'
erratic temperament along with much of their brilliance.

Rupert's childhood and youth were spent in Holland in comparative poverty, for his father, having lost Bohemia, was
deprived of the family territory, the Rhine Palatinate, as well.
He became a soldier of fortune at a very early age, serving with
the Prince of Orange at the Siege of Rheinberg in 1633 when he
was not yet fourteen. He fought with dash and courage at the

Siege of Breda in 1637, and in 1638 joined with a Swedish force against the Emperor, which led to his being captured by the Imperialists. For nearly three years he was a prisoner in the castle of Linz, overlooking the Danube. It was not a rigorous confinement; he made friends with his gaoler, Graf von Kuffstein, and had a romance with Kuffstein's daughter. His imprisonment was further beguiled by the gift of a 'beautiful white dog, of a breed so famous that the Grand Turk gave it in particular injunction to his ambassador to obtain him a puppy thereof'. This was Boy, destined to be more famous than the rest of his breed; Rupert's inseparable companion for the next five years.

While Rupert was at Linz, efforts were made to induce him to become a Catholic and take service under the Emperor, but he remained a staunch Calvinist. As the son of Frederick, a leading champion of the Protestant cause, he was looked on with favour by Protestants everywhere; doubly so by the English, since he was also the son of the much-loved and no less Protestant Elizabeth. During the months when he and his elder brother Charles-Louis visited England in 1636 and 1637, they were constantly fêted. Charles-Louis made himself especially popular with the Puritans, so that in years to come the possibility of replacing Charles I or Charles II with him or one of his brothers was actually mooted in some Roundhead circles. Had Rupert's Calvinism caused him to fight for Parliament instead of for the King, he might well have ended by usurping his uncle's or his cousin's throne; for though on that first visit to England his fondness for hunting and for masques and other gaieties had made him less acceptable to the Puritans than the grave Charles-Louis, his personality was so much stronger and more attractive than that of his unsatisfactory elder brother that he would have had no difficulty in surpassing him in the popular esteem.

But there is no question of Rupert having even for a moment entertained any such ideas. His loyalty to his uncle, whom he adored, was far stronger than either his Calvinism or his ambition; and as a Prince of one of the oldest Royal Houses in Europe, he saw the English conflict in simple terms as a rebellion against a rightful King. To him, as indeed to his uncle, there was an infinity of difference between kings and subjects.

And so, when the Civil War loomed, it was natural that Rupert should have offered his services to the King. As well as considering it his bounden duty to do so, he would have seen in an English war a providential chance of resuming his military career, which had come to a halt since he had been obliged to give an undertaking never again to bear arms against the Emperor as a condition for being released from Linz. And he was glad to be able to return to England, having fallen in love with the country when he visited it four years previously.

Charles made him General of the Horse, and he arrived in time to be present when the King's standard was raised at Nottingham. He immediately took command of his eight hundred ill-equipped cavalry, and set about teaching them the latest methods of warfare which he had learnt on the Continent. As an experienced soldier, with a high reputation for courage, Rupert was at first very welcome in the Royalist camp, but within a short time his presence began to cause jealousies and friction. For all his Royal blood, he was only a youth of twenty-three; and while most Cavalier generals could not approach him in military experience, there were a few professionals among them.

To make matters worse, Charles exempted him from taking orders from anybody but himself, and in the earlier stages of the war, he listened to him more readily than he listened to any of his other advisers. It was inevitable that Rupert should have made use of his privileged position for the benefit of his cavalry, which aroused the jealousy of the rest of the army.

Rupert's 'full inexperience of the customs and manners of England' did not help; nor did 'that roughness and unpolishedness of his nature which rendered him less patient to hear, and consequently less skilful to judge of those things which should have guided him'. These are the words of Clarendon, who as Edward Hyde had himself suffered from Rupert's high-handedness, so he would not have been wholly unprejudiced. But we know that Rupert also alienated other leading Royalists, including the commander-in-chief, the Earl of Lindsey, and Hyde's colleague in the King's 'cabinet', Sir John Culpeper; he even had a brush with the third member of the triumvirate, the tolerant Lord Falkland. He was not, however, wholly without friends among the best of the Cavaliers. His friendship with 'Honest Will' Legge, with that good old soldier Sir Jacob Astley who had once been his tutor, with Mr Secretary Nicholas and with the King's cousin, the Duke of Richmond, endured all the vicissitudes of the war, showing that he had it in him to recognize real worth.

The fact that Rupert incurred the enmity of some of the worst of the King's advisers can likewise be held to his credit as indicating that he was quick to detect charlatanism. Yet it would have been wiser for him to have placated these men while being on his guard against them, for as his enemies they were powerful enough to do him harm. In particular, he should have endeavoured to keep on good terms with his uncle's evil genius, George, Lord Digby. Charles was unfortunately fascinated by Digby's brilliance, and never learnt the lesson that it was fatal to take his advice. It did not much matter when Rupert was near the King, who tended to listen to him rather than to anybody else; but when he was away, Digby was able to influence Charles against him, with disastrous results both to his military career and to the Royalist cause.

As a further source of friction, there was Rupert's brave but boorish younger brother, Prince Maurice. Rupert was devoted to him, and encouraged his resentment at being only Lieutenant-General to the Marquess of Hertford. Neither Rupert nor Maurice appreciated that while Hertford was no soldier, he knew how to handle the civilian population much better than they did; and that it was just as vital for the King's cause to win and keep the goodwill of his subjects as to fight victorious actions. After being in England only a fortnight, Rupert showed his disregard for public opinion by demanding a loan of £2,000 from the rich and important town of Leicester, which had not yet decided for either King or Parliament, threatening retribution if the money was not handed over the very next day. The King, when he heard of this, was horrified, and hastened to smooth down the ruffled citizens.

Two weeks later, Rupert redeemed his good name with his uncle by routing a superior Parliamentary force at Powicke Bridge, near Worcester. The Roundheads, picked men sent by the Earl of Essex to surprise the city, nearly caught the Cavaliers napping, coming upon them when they were resting in a field after a long march. There was barely time for Rupert to get his men on to their horses, let alone marshal them into any sort of order, but somehow he managed to lead them in a devastating charge. Although the enemy did not suffer very serious losses in the action, their troops were so shaken by it that many of them went back to their homes and were never seen again. Rupert's victory caused dismay and consternation throughout the Roundhead camp, just as it gave great courage to the Royalists.

In the following month, at Edgehill, Rupert charged the Roundhead cavalry so furiously that some of them are said to have fled almost as far as London. But his impetuousness caused him to make a mistake which he was to repeat at Naseby: having put the enemy to flight, he was so carried away by the chase that he pursued them too far, leaving the Royalist infantry to be harried by a body of Parliamentary horse commanded by the Scotsman, Sir William Balfour, which had managed to stay in reserve. Had Rupert's cavalry returned to the battlefield in time to make a second charge against Balfour before he could do too much mischief, Edgehill might have been a Royalist victory instead of a draw.

Rupert's charge at Edgehill, following closely on his victory at Powicke, gave him the name of being well-nigh invincible. It proved the superiority of the swift, light cavalry tactics which he had learnt when attached to the Swedish army—the tactics of Gustavus Adolphus—over the more ponderous Dutch methods of warfare favoured by Lindsey. Edgehill, though inconclusive, was a severe setback for the Roundheads. Knowing this, and that the Parliamentary army under Essex had moved northwards leaving the road to London open, Rupert proposed making a quick dash to the capital while the morale of Parliament and the citizens was at its lowest following the news of the battle, seizing Westminster and Whitehall and holding them until the King came up with the remainder of the army. It was his first attempt at strategy and his most brilliant; if only the plan had been followed, the King might have won the war before the autumn was out. Unfortunately however Rupert's enemies at court, led by Digby's father, Lord Bristol, persuaded Charles that he would pillage the capital if he got there before the rest of the army. So instead of allowing Rupert to strike at London when it was virtually undefended, Charles preferred to advance slowly on the capital in the following month, by which time it was too late. Essex had overtaken him and put the Londoners into a state of defence; the trained-bands were ready and waiting.

Having thrown away the best chance he ever had of a quick

victory, Charles went into winter quarters in Oxford. A new strategic plan was adopted for 1643, by which Newcastle's army from the north and Sir Ralph Hopton's from the west were to advance on London simultaneously. Before the plan could be put into effect, it was necessary to deal with the Roundhead garrisons of Bristol, Birmingham and other towns in order to secure the lines of communication. This was a task for which Rupert was particularly suited, and throughout 1643 he enjoyed a spectacular run of success. Employing the tactics of the commando or flying column, he went 'like wildfire' from place to place. One by one the towns fell to him: Cirencester, Birmingham, Lichfield, Bristol. Nobody knew where he would strike next; he was always on the move, raising troops and levying contributions from townspeople of Roundhead sympathies when he was not summoning garrisons to surrender.

His very name struck terror in Puritan hearts. All kinds of legends grew up about him, and were broadcast by the Roundhead pamphleteers. He was said to have observed the strength of Essex's army by disguising himself as an apple vendor and peddling his fruit among the soldiers. Two Roundhead merchants who were brought before him at Henley and found him, for some reason, in bed with his clothes on, were quick to report that he had vowed never 'to undress or shift himself until he had re-seated King Charles at Whitehall'. He was invested with diabolical powers, and his white dog, Boy, was seen as his familiar spirit. The tales told about Boy surpassed those told about his master. He could prophesy, he could make himself invisible, he was endowed with the gift of languages. 'He is weapon-proof himself, and probably hath made his master so too . . . they lie perpetually in one bed, sometimes the Prince upon the Dog, and sometimes the Dog upon the Prince; and what this may in time produce, none but the close committee can tell.'

Other pamphlets accused Rupert of atrocities, and of behaving harshly to the civilian population. He was the 'Bloody Prince', 'fighting against religion, imprisoning and killing faithful ministers, shedding the blood of the Saints of God with all outrage and cruelty.' Woodcuts were published of a blazing town, purporting to be Birmingham, which when captured by Rupert had been partly fired, the inhabitants having put up an unusually stubborn resistance, being 'of as great fame for hearty, wilful, affected disloyalty to the King as any place in England'. Rupert and his troops were accused of rape no less than of arson; of slaughtering children, and of eating them too. Attempts were even made to cast doubt on Rupert's loyalty. 'If law and Parliament be destroyed, he may bid for the Crown, having possessed himself of so much power already by his German manner of plundering, and his active military disposition having won the hearts of many thousand soldiers of fortune and men of prey.'

Rupert took these various accusations seriously enough to publish a denial of them, while declaring that his 'known disposition' was 'so contrary to this scribbling age'. He challenged 'the most valiant and quick-sighted of that lying faction to name the time, the person or the house where any child or woman lost so much as a hair from their head by me, or any of our soldiers.' Though he had learnt his soldiering in the harsh school of the Thirty Years War, and while he might not have shown sufficient respect for the feelings of minor English dignitaries such as the Mayor of Leicester, Rupert was a humanitarian with a strong sense of chivalry. He had too high a regard for military discipline and the rules of war to have tolerated rape or plunder; when some of his soldiers tried to plunder the inhabitants of Bristol after it had surrendered to him, he and Maurice restored order by riding among the plunderers and 'hacking and slashing them' with their swords, as is testified by the Roundhead commander, Colonel Nathaniel Fiennes. The very strictness with which he enforced the rules often made him unpopular with the English, who were unused to professional soldiers and wished to fight the war according to rules of their own. When the Leicestershire trained-bands refused to go beyond the borders of their county, he and his staff rode up to them and ordered them to march, to which the spokesman for the soldiers said 'Nay!' Rupert treated this as mutiny and 'clapped his pistol' to the man's head, whereupon all the men laid down their arms, and the men of Nottinghamshire and Derbyshire did likewise in sympathy. When Rupert hanged thirteen Roundhead prisoners in retaliation for the hanging of thirteen Irish soldiers by the Roundheads, there was a tremendous outcry, and Parliament ordered Essex to inform Rupert 'that there was a very great difference between Englishmen and Irishmen'.

Having disapproved of the peace moves in the autumn of 1642,

Rupert, after nine months of fighting, was ready for a negotiated peace. This further antagonized the Queen, who since her return from Holland had ranged herself with Rupert's enemies, which made his position increasingly difficult. And it did no good to the war-effort for the King to be vacillating between the advice of his nephew and his wife.

At the beginning of 1644, the whole balance of the war changed when a Scots army invaded England in support of Parliament. With Newcastle caught between the Scots and a Parliamentary army, it was necessary for Rupert to go north to his help; particularly as the Roundheads were at the same time threatening other northern Royalists. The expedition was also intended to encourage the Welsh in the King's support, for which purpose Rupert was made President of Wales, just as he was created Duke of Cumberland to increase his standing in the north.

At first, in his northern campaign, Rupert's proverbial luck did not desert him. He relieved Newark and captured a useful stock of arms and ammunition into the bargain. As he approached Lancashire, the Roundhead besiegers of Lathom House (which had been gallantly defended for three months by Rupert's cousin, Charlotte de la Tremouille, Countess of Derby) retired to Bolton. This town, so Puritan as to be known as the 'Geneva of the North', was Rupert's objective, and after the garrison had put up a fanatical defence, he took it by storm. According to the rules of war, the garrison of a town that was taken by storm could expect no quarter, and Rupert on this occasion gave none. His blood was up: the Puritans of Bolton had repulsed him twice and defied him by slaughtering prisoners on the ramparts. And the knowledge of how they had treated Lady Derby, a lady who was half Royal and his cousin, cannot have made him any more inclined to show mercy.

Wigan and Liverpool fell easily to Rupert following the capture of Bolton, and after a week he was master of almost the whole of Lancashire. Had he given himself time to raise troops here and in loyal Wales, he could have increased his strength to twenty thousand men, making him more than a match for the armies of the Scots and the English Roundheads which were besieging Newcastle's army in York. But before he had finished with the Roundheads of Lancashire, he received a letter from the King which he interpreted as an order to march immediately to the relief of York and to engage the besieging armies in battle, even though they outnumbered him by three to two. He was to carry this letter with him for the rest of his life, as proof that he had had no option but to fight the fatal battle of Marston Moor.

Although the wording of the King's letter is somewhat involved, it is hard to see how Rupert could have taken it as anything less than a positive order. 'Before God you are undone, for upon this peremptory order he will fight, whatever comes on't,' exclaimed Culpeper to the King, having seen a copy of the letter after its dispatch. Digby and his clique, however, were to maintain that the letter only expressed the King's inclinations, leaving the actual decision to Rupert; but even if this were the case, Charles should have been sufficiently well acquainted with his nephew's psychology to know that inclinations expressed in such a way would almost certainly be taken by him as an order to fight.

Having received the King's letter, Rupert hurried to York, being joined by a force of Royalist cavalry under George Goring, which had escaped being bottled up with Newcastle. By a brilliant manœuvre he approached the city from the north, whereas the Parliamentary army was expecting him to appear from the west; finding he had outwitted them, the enemy retired in confusion. But now, after his initial success, Rupert made the mistake of marching straight towards the enemy at Long Marston without first consulting Newcastle, who would have told him that the enemy forces were about to separate; so that if he had waited, the Scots would soon have been so far from the English that neither army could have come to the other's assistance. He could then have attacked whichever army he chose. But by marching towards Long Marston, Rupert made it clear to the enemy that he was about to give battle, so that the English and Scots stayed together in readiness. Had Rupert waited, he would also have heard that the King's position had greatly improved following the action at Cropredy, so that it was no longer so urgent for him to fight.

Having committed himself to a battle, Rupert's inclination was to attack immediately, without waiting for Newcastle's troops who, being exhausted after the long siege, refused to come into action without being first allowed to rest; for he knew that the enemy was not yet in battle order. But Newcastle, who had joined

Rupert ahead of his men, was for waiting, and Rupert made his second mistake by deferring to him. By the time the army from York arrived, the enemy was drawn up and singing psalms. It was a formidable host, being made up of three armies: the Yorkshire Roundheads under Fairfax, the Scots, and the army of the Eastern Association under the Earl of Manchester. One of Manchester's commanders was Oliver Cromwell, the only cavalry leader on the Roundhead side whose fame approached that of Rupert himself. Rupert felt a boyish thrill at the prospect of fighting him; it was the first time he had done so.

Rupert's instinct was that they should attack as soon as Newcastle's troops arrived, though by then it was four in the afternoon. Up to now it had always been he who had attacked first; it was July and there were several hours of daylight left. Newcastle's second-in-command, the Scottish professional Lord Eythin who blamed Rupert's 'forwardness' for a defeat which they had suffered when fighting together in Germany, was for delaying until the following morning. Inexplicably Rupert gave in to him, forgetting that if he did not take the initiative, the Roundheads would. And take the initiative they did; so that Rupert, usually so clever at surprising the enemy, was himself surprised. At half-past seven, when he was at supper and Newcastle had gone to smoke a pipe in his coach, the Roundheads opened fire, the noise of their shooting being drowned by a great clap of thunder which was followed by torrential rain. Cromwell, who in charging would have been at a disadvantage owing to the ditch which separated the opposing cavalry, solved the problem by charging when the Royalists, confident that there would be no action that night, had broken their ranks.

Lord Byron, who commanded Rupert's front line in the Royalist right wing, quickly got his men into action; but after an initial success was driven back by the onslaught of the Ironsides, though Cromwell himself was wounded in the neck. Rupert galloped forward with his second line and managed to rally some of the front line who were already in disorder, but his charge was impeded by the Royalist musketeers. Soon Rupert's cavalry began to break and flee towards York; he himself was nearly captured as he tried in vain to keep some of them together, and he only escaped by putting his horse at a fence. Meanwhile the Roundheads were making short work of the Royalist foot. Only in the left wing was Goring's cavalry successful, but that was not enough to stem the tide of defeat. The battle was over in an hour; by dusk the field was thickly strewn with Royalist dead, so many corpses that even for a month after they had been buried, 'there was such a stench thereabouts that it almost poisoned them that passed over the Moor'. The north was lost to the King.

Rupert, joining the remnants of the Royalist army near York, still put on a brave face; when Newcastle and Eythin expressed their intention of leaving the country, he declared that he would rally his men. But he must have been sick at heart; in an hour's fighting on that damp July evening he had lost both his army and his reputation. And as though that were not enough, he also lost his beloved dog, Boy, who had been with him when he was eating supper and had followed him as he galloped into the fray. His carcase was found next morning among the dead. The Round-heads rejoiced, convinced that without his familiar spirit the Bloody Prince could no longer harm them. And indeed, after Marston Moor, Rupert's luck did not return.

The King showed that he still had confidence in Rupert by appointing him General-in-Chief in place of the Earl of Forth and Brentford, the old, deaf and drunken Scot who had suc-ceeded Lindsey; though he later undermined his nephew's authority by making the brilliant but erratic Goring a virtually independent commander in the west. During the winter that followed, Rupert endeavoured to build up the shattered Royalist army, while supporting the abortive peace negotiations. He also prevailed on Charles to march northwards in the spring and attack the Scots in Yorkshire who were no longer supported by Fairfax. This made good sense, even though Rupert may have been influenced as much by a desire to be avenged for Marston Moor as by strategy. But when, in May 1645, the King's army set out on its march, Goring and the best of the cavalry was sent into the West Country to prevent Taunton from being relieved. The Secretary to the Council of War, Sir Edward Walker, blamed this fatal division of the army on Rupert's jealousy of Goring. Whether or not Rupert allowed himself to be thus influenced by personal feelings—and Goring had also antagonized him by his intrigues for an independent command—the division of the army was one of those dreadful compromises which so frequently bedevilled the Royalist cause.

The march northwards at first brought the King a notable success: Rupert captured the rich town of Leicester, after an artillery barrage and a fierce assault. But then Charles followed the advice of Digby and turned back to Oxford, which was being besieged by Fairfax and Cromwell. At Daventry, it was learnt that Fairfax had raised the siege and was marching towards them. Cromwell was also on his way; the New Model Army was eager to engage the King in a battle which it was hoped would be decisive. Rupert was for continuing the march to the north and taking up a defensive position on the far side of the River Trent. In this way they could postpone giving battle until the enemy was at a disadvantage, and they would be able to wait for the arrival of Goring, who had been sent for by the King. Digby, ever the optimist, was for fighting the great battle immediately. The King hesitated, and one of his outposts, in the Northamptonshire village of Naseby, was surprised by Roundhead horse. Rupert was still for withdrawing northwards, but was overruled by the King, and so the battle which was to decide the Civil War was fought near Naseby on the windy morning of 14 June, the armies facing each other from opposing grassy ridges. The Roundheads outnumbered the colourful and glittering Royalist host by two to one.

This time, Rupert was able to attack first, charging the left wing of the Roundhead cavalry under Ireton. In the heady flush of success, with the greater part of Ireton's horse fleeing before him, he made the same mistake which he had made at Edgehill: he pursued his enemy too far, not realizing that some of the Round-head cavalry had managed to evade him and were causing havoc among the Royalist foot. Meanwhile, at the other end of the line, it was Cromwell, who, charging with the Roundhead right, scattered the Royalist left, but *he* did not make Rupert's mistake; he closed in on the Royalist foot, who thus found themselves encircled. It was an overwhelming defeat for the Royalists, the end of all hope for the King.

Rupert was blamed for Naseby, which was unfair, since the battle was fought contrary to his wishes. Even Digby had to admit as much, while hinting that he was to blame in other respects, which made Honest Will Legge accuse him of saying things to Rupert's prejudice 'not in an open and direct line, but obscurely and obliquely'. The clamour against Rupert grew in volume when, having assured the King that Bristol could hold out for four months against Fairfax who laid siege to it early in September, he surrendered the town to the Roundheads after only four days. Now he was charged not merely with ineptitude, but with cowardice and treachery. In fact, he was guilty of nothing worse than having been hopelessly over-sanguine in his estimate of how long Bristol could hold out; its defences were weak, the garrison was discontented and the town was infested with Roundhead agents. Faced with the overwhelming strength of Fairfax and Cromwell, his only course was to surrender on honourable terms. By now, too, he knew that the war was lost, and saw little point in continuing to fight.

The King took the surrender of Bristol so badly that he deprived Rupert of all military authority and ordered him to leave the country; writing at the same time to reproach his nephew for 'so mean an action'. Rupert in reply begged for an interview, so that he could justify himself; and when this request was ignored, he went without permission to see the King, who was at Newark. This entailed an adventurous dash through enemy-held country; at one stage he eluded the Roundheads through his knowledge of the back ways of the Leicestershire countryside, which he had acquired nine years before when hunting with the Earl of Rutland. Reaching Newark, he did not wait to be summoned into the Royal presence, but burst in on the King who was about to have supper. The King totally ignored him, but next day allowed him to state his case before a court-martial. As a result he was found 'not guilty of any of the least want of courage or fidelity'. At the same time, however, the King superseded the Governor of Newark, Sir Richard Willis, for siding too openly with Rupert. Rupert hastened to Willis's defence and in a fit of temper spoke disrespectfully to his uncle, who sighed and said: 'O Nephew!' Next day, he and Maurice left without apologizing. The King, watching from a window as they rode away, was seen to weep.

Rupert's friends—notably Will Legge, himself a sufferer from the King's vagaries—prevailed on him to apologize to his uncle, and the two of them were reconciled by the time that the King left Oxford in disguise to join the Scots. Rupert wished to accompany him, but the King feared that his height would give them away. Eventually he and Maurice left the country. Making his way to Paris, he entered the French service and was wounded while campaigning in Flanders.

In the summer of 1648 there was a mutiny in the Parliamentary navy, and some of the ships threw in their lot with the King. Rupert was put in command of these ships, and sailed with them to the harbour of Helvoetsluys in Holland, hotly pursued by the ships that were still under Roundhead control. For some weeks the two rival fleets confronted each other in the harbour, separated by a Dutch squadron, each trying to win over the crews of the other. Rupert managed to suppress two or three mutinies, in one of which he actually picked up the ringleaders with his strong arms and threw them overboard. At length the Roundhead ships departed, and in January 1649, with no experience of the sea other than a few crossings between England and the Continent, he embarked on a new career as a sailor.

Basing himself on Kinsale in the south of Ireland, he ran supplies to the Royalist garrison of the Scilly Isles and preyed on Commonwealth shipping in the Channel, until the Roundhead Admiral Blake drove him away. He then buccaneered in more southerly waters, sailing eventually to the West Indies. Near the Azores, his flagship, the *Constant Reformation*, sprang a leak; the weather grew stormy and all but one of the ship's boats were lost. When it was clear that she was foundering, the men insisted that Rupert should take the one surviving boat to transfer to another vessel, telling him that 'he was deferred and appointed for greater matters'. He indignantly refused to leave them, but they put him into the boat by force and he was rowed across to one of his other ships. Apart from a second boatload, it proved impossible to rescue any more of the *Constant Reformation*'s crew, three hundred and thirty-three of whom went down with her. Later, when the rest of the fleet had reached the West Indies, Rupert was dealt an even worse blow. Maurice, the brother who meant so much to him, was lost with his ship, which vanished without trace in a hurricane.

In 1653 Rupert arrived back in France, broken in health and with only one of his original ships left, but bringing treasure which the impoverished court in exile needed badly. Though at first he received a tremendous welcome from Charles II, the Queen and the court, he soon found himself involved in various wrangles, and left in disgust. He eventually settled down in Mainz, devoting himself to chemistry and to experiments in mezzotint engraving, of which he is said to have been the inventor.

After the Restoration, Rupert decided to make his home in England, having been invited to return by Charles II. He was given a pension of £6,000 a year and took an active part in public affairs, his particular concern being the navy. He also took an interest in overseas commercial ventures; his work on behalf of the Hudson's Bay Company is commemorated by the Rupert River in Canada. He was appointed to the Board which administered Tangier; he was a founder member of the Royal Society, and fascinated his colleagues with droplets of glass which exploded when their ends were broken off—they are still known as 'Prince Rupert's drops'.

During the Dutch War of 1665 he led the van of the Fleet in the battle of Solebay, after which he was given the joint command of the navy with the former Roundhead General Monck, now Duke of Albemarle. He and Albemarle worked well together, producing the 'Fighting Instructions' which anticipated the teachings of Nelson by almost a century and a half. He continued to go to sea until age and ill-health, the result of old wounds and recurring tropical fevers, made him unfit for active service. But though he beat the Dutch off the North Foreland and carried out a highly destructive raid on their coast, it was as an organizer rather than as a commander that he best served the navy and the kingdom. With his fiery temper, he was a terror on committees, and a particular scourge to the Secretary of the Navy, Samuel Pepys.

The dashing young prince had grown into a rather terrifying old man; even the King was said to be frightened of him. The astronomer, Thomas Streete, who told him he was 'no mathematician' when he made an assertion that was mathematically incorrect, was for ever afterwards pointed out as 'the man that huffed Prince Rupert'. Yet his popularity with the nation as a whole increased over the years. The somewhat alien cavalry leader had turned into a bluff English sea-dog. That he was not wholly immune to the pleasures of the Restoration court endeared him still more to people. It was good to see the 'natural fierceness' of this tall and stern figure 'brought down and greatly subdued' by the pretty young actress, Peg Hughes, with whom he fell violently in love. According to Grammont, his infatuation with her even made him forget his passion for science: *'adieu* alembics, crucibles, furnaces and all the black furniture of the forges; a complete farewell to all mathematical instruments and chemical speculations; sweet powder and essences were now the only ingredients that occupied any share of his attention.'

At last she became his mistress, and they were happy in each other's company until his death in 1682; she bore him a daughter, Ruperta. By his previous mistress, Frances Bard, he already had a son who followed him in the profession of arms and fell at the siege of Buda in 1686. Had this young man lived, he might one day have been a candidate for the throne, for there was a report that Rupert and Frances Bard were actually married. As it was, the son of Rupert's sister, Sophia, eventually succeeded to the throne of Great Britain as George I.

5

Bishop Juxon: 'That Good Man'

Archbishop Laud's finest hour was surely in 1636, when the
King and Queen, together with Charles-Louis of the Palatinate
and the court, came to see the new library quadrangle at St
John's College, Oxford. It had been built at the Archbishop's
own expense, and bore witness, in a flourish of golden stone
Baroque, to everything for which he stood. There was Divine
Right in the statues of Charles and Henrietta Maria which faced
each other from beneath pediments carried on Ionic and Corinthian columns; episcopal power in the numerous elaborately
carved cartouches of Laud's arms and his mitre. The learning
of the Laudian Church was symbolized by busts of Rhetoric,
Grammar and the other sciences between the arches of the
cloisters; its mysticism by a host of sculptured angels. To the
Royal visitors mounting the library stairs, it must have seemed
as if the College were endowed with a real angelic choir as well
as one of stone, for they were serenaded from above by singers
whose song was timed to last as many seconds as it took to make
the ascent.

As well as Laud, there was the Bishop of London, Dr William
Juxon, in attendance on Their Majesties that day. This second
great dignitary in lawn sleeves wore a very different expression
from the eager, penetrating gaze of the Archbishop. His big,
heavily-lidded eyes—which, like his other features, the prominent
nose, the thickish lips, had something vaguely Semitic about
them, particularly as he wore the fashionable pointed beard—
looked sleepy and melancholy. This impression, however, was
false, for he was not only industrious, but of a cheerful and
serene nature. He was particularly happy to see St John's raised
to its present glory from its former rustic insignificance among
the fields to the north-east of the university town, for he was

65

as devoted a son of the College as Laud himself, having followed Laud as President just as, more recently, he had succeeded him as Bishop of London. He had still been President of the College when the new buildings were begun, and it was very much thanks to his energy, his knowledge of architecture—for which he shared Laud's passion—and his talent for making money go a long way that they were such a success. It was also thanks to his love of hunting that the pillars were made of the beautiful Bletchington stone which polished like marble; for he had come upon this stone when out with his hounds.

In matters of church and state, no less than in his building schemes, Juxon was Laud's right-hand man. This had not always been so; in 1611 he had opposed the election of Laud as President of St John's. One would suspect that he was then not quite the Arminian which, through Laud's influence, he afterwards became. As a Londoner who had strong family ties with the Merchant Taylors' Company, and who before his ordination had read law at Gray's Inn, he belonged to a world that was predominantly Puritan; though he must have grown up with a respect for Episcopacy, since his father was Receiver-General of the See of Chichester. Whether or no' Laud approved of Juxon's theology in those early days, he saw in him 'a shrewd adversary' who 'might be a good friend'. And so the newly-elected President set out to win the friendship of the thirty-year-old Fellow and Vicar of St Giles, nine years his junior, who had already made a name for himself as a preacher. Juxon responded and proved indeed a good friend to Laud, who in return helped him up the ladder of preferment, so that his career reads as an ecclesiastical success-story: President of St John's, Vice-Chancellor, Prebendary of Chichester, Dean of Worcester, Chaplain to the King—this last appointment being, as Laud wrote, 'that I might have one that I might trust near His Majesty if I grow weak and infirm'. The next step was a Bishopric; at first Hereford, but after only a month he was moved to the far more important See of London, which had fallen vacant on Laud's elevation to Canterbury.

Laud saw in Juxon, as Clarendon put it, 'a man who would be vigilant to pull up those weeds which the London soil was too apt to nourish'. In other words, a fit successor to himself, who would continue his work of reform, just as at Oxford he had been Laud's chief agent for carrying out the reforms which resulted in the 'Laudian Code'. There, Juxon's tact had worked wonders, and he had even managed to remain on friendly terms with Laud's bitter opponent, Dr Rawlinson. But London, then 'in its height of giddiness and faction', was very different from Oxford. Not only did most Londoners detest Arminianism and all Laud's works and pomps, but they were noisier and more independent than any other people in the kingdom. For Juxon, a Laudian of the Laudians, zealously bent on enforcing the policy of his friend the Archbishop, the old red-brick riverside palace at Fulham promised anything but a quiet life.

But while in no way shrinking from his share of the Laudian task, Juxon proved universally popular as a Bishop, thanks to his patience, his humility and, above all, his sheer goodness. 'That good man' was how the King was wont to speak of him, and everybody else who had dealings with him spoke the same; though his virtues were, in the words of a contemporary, 'so modest that they hid themselves from others, and so humble that they were not known to himself'. Falkland used to say that 'he never knew anyone that a pair of lawn sleeves had not altered' but Juxon. Indeed, Juxon had nothing of the 'pompous piety' which all too many prelates were apt to affect, nor did he suffer from either ambition or greed: 'his preferments were his burden rather than his honour, advanced by him, rather than advancing him.' Nevertheless, he kept up such state as befitted his office, and maintained a suitably large household, including an excellent cook named Richard Hayward who had been recommended to him by the King's cook.

The extent to which Juxon managed to command obedience without giving offence—though the numbers of recalcitrant clergy in his diocese increased during the years immediately preceding the Civil War—makes one realize how much of the opposition to Charles I's Arminian policy was due to Laud's tactlessness, and how far easier it would have been for the King to carry out his church reforms given an Archbishop of different character. Juxon had 'a perfect command of his passion' and would always think carefully before he spoke, his eyes pensive beneath their heavy lids; whereas Laud would come out all too quickly with a stinging riposte. Juxon was also much more of a realist than Laud. He was fully aware of the difficulties of imposing Arminian reforms on Scotland. When writing to the Bishop of Ross about the new Scottish Canons, he good-humouredly predicted that they would 'make more noise than all the cannons in Edinburgh Castle'.

As if Juxon had not work enough with his spiritual cares, he was in 1636 appointed to the post of Lord High Treasurer, the highest secular office in the realm next to that of Lord Chancellor. Needless to say this was at the instigation of Laud, who rightly felt that Juxon's piety and his unmarried and childless state were safeguards against the temptation to enrich himself. The appointment caused much ill-feeling against Laud and the church, which was regarded as 'the gulf ready to swallow all the great offices'—there had not been a clerical Lord Treasurer since the reign of Edward IV—but from the point of view of the Treasury, Juxon was an inspired choice. Though the Lord High Treasurer was traditionally one of the most hated men in the kingdom, and though Juxon took up the office at a most difficult time when, after seven years of rule without Parliament, the Royal coffers were nearly empty, he not only kept his popularity but actually managed to improve the finances, so that the King might eventually have become solvent, had it not been for the Scots Wars.

Juxon achieved what he did by his energy, his economy and his ability to handle men: it was said of him that 'petitioners for money (when it was not to be had) departed well pleased with his denials, they were so civilly languaged'. As Lord High Treasurer, and holding the additional and still more unlikely office of Lord of the Admiralty, as well as being Commissioner for Colonies, Juxon was a member of the Committee of State, Charles I's cabinet—though at the time it was only called this by its enemies—and thus supervised all branches of government. Those who think of Charles I's personal rule as a tyranny are apt to forget that Juxon was one of its chief agents during its latter years. Had Charles's government been really tyrannical or arbitrary, Juxon's conscience—a conscience, in the words of a contemporary, 'bottomed on piety, not policy'—would not have allowed him to remain associated with it. As an instance of how Juxon was ready to incur the Royal displeasure rather than agree to something which he thought wrong, there is his opposition to the King's unhappy scheme for enlarging Richmond

Park by buying out the local landowners' and farmers' holdings.

When the Bill of Attainder against Strafford had been passed by the House of Lords, Juxon advised the King to follow his own conscience and spare the life of the fallen Minister; whereas with the exception of Archbishop Ussher of Armagh, the other bishops whom Charles consulted played safe and referred him to the judges. Laud would have been another exception, but by then he was himself a prisoner in the Tower. About the time of Strafford's execution, Juxon resigned the Treasurership. By now, Parliament was in full cry after the bishops, many of whom suffered impeachment and imprisonment—an imprisonment which for Laud was to end four years later on the scaffold. But amidst all the Parliamentary and popular clamour, not a word was heard against Juxon, who was allowed to stay on peacefully at Fulham.

He continued there throughout the Civil War, which showed considerable courage—as the historian, Thomas Fuller, writing in Juxon's lifetime, pointed out, comparing him with those other bishops who 'left their Bishoprics, flying into the King's quarters for safety'. Apart from being obliged to contribute £500 for the support of the Parliamentary army, he was unmolested and was even sometimes visited by the Roundhead 'Grandees', though he 'walked steadily in his old paths', never deviating from his Royalism. He corresponded frequently with the King, who consulted him on appointments to bishoprics and other matters. When negotiating with the Parliamentary Commissioners, the King summoned Juxon to ask his advice; though he once said that he would rather consult him through an intermediary, for then the advice would be all the more frank. 'I never got his opinion freely in my life,' he declared, 'but when I had it, I was ever the better for it.'

In the autumn of 1646, Juxon set the King's conscience at rest regarding the possibility of his tolerating Presbyterianism temporarily, while religious differences were being discussed; and in 1648 he was present at Newport in the Isle of Wight when Charles and Parliament negotiated for the last time. But it was after all these schemes had come to nothing that Juxon performed the service to his King for which he is best remembered. Having attended the King during his trial, he hardly left him after he had been sentenced, being the only divine Charles wished to see. When the colonel of the guard at St James's Palace decided to put two soldiers into the bedroom of the King, who submitted to this cruel indignity with a sigh, Juxon and Thomas Herbert, the King's page, pleaded with him until he agreed that the men should be withdrawn. On the morning of that cold and fatal thirtieth of January, Juxon read morning service to the King in his bedroom, which included St Matthew's account of the Passion; the King thanked him for choosing this particular chapter, to which Juxon replied that it was the proper lesson for the day. 'At which the King was much affected, and thought it a providential preparation for his death.' He then took Juxon's hand and said cheerfully: 'Let us go,' and they walked across the Park to Whitehall. When, after they had waited for a while in a room in the palace, the colonel of the guard came to tell the King that the time had come, Juxon fell to his knees, weeping. The King helped him up and the two of them walked on to the scaffold which had been erected outside the Banqueting House, above the crowded street.

There were many troops to keep back the crowd, so that the King, who had hoped to make a last speech to his people, contented himself with addressing those on the scaffold. When he spoke of his death as being an atonement for the death of Strafford—'an unjust sentence that I suffered to take effect is punished now by an unjust sentence upon me'—it must have afforded Juxon some small comfort to know that he had done his best to save Charles from that act of weakness for which he never forgave himself. While the King's hair was being put under his cap, Juxon said to him: 'There is but one stage more, which though turbulent and troublesome, yet it is a very short one; you may consider, it will soon carry you a very great way, it will carry you from Earth to Heaven, and there you shall find to your great joy the prize you hasten to, a Crown of Glory.' His last words to Charles were: 'You are exchanged from a temporal to an eternal crown, a good exchange,' and Charles, before putting his head on the block, said to Juxon: 'Remember!'

The groan of horror and dismay which went up from the crowd as the King's head, dripping with blood, was held up for all to see, would have but inadequately expressed the feelings of Juxon as he stood close by the headless trunk. To have some idea of how he felt, we must remind ourselves of the doctrine of Divine Right in which, as a pious Arminian divine, he would have passionately believed. He had not merely been present at the execution of his King and master, the head of his church, who was also his friend; he had witnessed a most abominable sacrilege, the murder of the Lord's Anointed.

Juxon was not allowed much time for sombre thoughts, for the army officers proceeded to interrogate him at length as to the King's last injunction to him; an ordeal through which he passed without revealing anything. After that, he had to concern himself with the funeral. Permission was refused for the burial to be in Henry VII's chapel at Westminster Abbey, but it was allowed to be at Windsor, provided the body was taken there 'without pomp or noise'. Juxon and a dozen of the King's gentlemen accompanied the coffin on its journey through driving snow; they were met at Windsor Castle by the only other mourners, four Lords of the Bedchamber headed by Charles's cousin, the Duke of Richmond, who had offered to be executed in his place. Even on this solemn occasion, there was an instance of the bureaucratic pettiness, more typical of the twentieth century than the seventeenth, for which so many Commonwealth functionaries showed a talent. The Governor of the Castle 'expressly, positively and roughly' refused to allow the King to be buried according to the rites of the Prayer Book, which Parliament had made illegal in 1645. So Charles, that most devoted son of the Church of England, was laid to rest without any of his church's prayers, 'without any words, or other ceremony than the tears and sighs of the few beholders'.

The newly-established Commonwealth did not show the forbearance towards Juxon which the Long Parliament had shown, and before the year of the King's death was out he had been ejected from his See, Fulham Palace and its lands being sold for £7,600 to a certain Colonel Edmund Harvey. Juxon said good-bye to his large household. His cook, Hayward, asked if it would be all right for him to enter the service of William Pierrepont, a wealthy Roundhead, to which Juxon replied: 'I will commend you to him as the best of Parliament men.' So Hayward went to cook for Pierrepont—who declared himself enchanted to have a servant 'that had served so noble a person

71

who was the best of bishops'—but only on condition that if Juxon were restored, he might be at liberty to return to his service.

Though he lost his See and his palace, Juxon was paid some arrears of his episcopal revenues that were due to him and was allowed to retire to his Gloucestershire manor of Little Compton, close to the Oxfordshire border, which he had bought a few years before. He lived quietly at the gabled Cotswold manor house adjoining Little Compton Church, where it was now illegal for him to officiate, so that he used to say his Sunday service at Chastleton, the house of a neighbouring Royalist squire. He devoted himself to helping the dispossessed clergy, and also—though he was a septuagenarian, in declining health —to hunting. On one occasion his hounds ran through Chipping Norton churchyard, the Bishop in full cry, just as a Puritan prayer meeting was taking place. The Men of God were scandalized, and sent one of their number to complain to Cromwell, who gave him short shrift. 'Do you think that the Bishop prevailed on the hare to run through the churchyard at that time?' he asked sarcastically. 'Get you gone, and let me hear no such frivolous complaints; whilst the Bishop continues not to give my government any offence, let him enjoy his diversion of hunting unmolested.'

The Restoration brought Juxon back to London, and set him up once more with a great episcopal household, including the faithful Hayward; but it was now at Lambeth instead of at Fulham, for he had, with nationwide approval, been made Archbishop of Canterbury. For all the rejoicings at his enthronement, Juxon was something of an anachronism in Restoration England, like the hammer-beamed hall which he built at Lambeth to replace the one demolished by the Roundheads. Charles II did not have the same regard for him as his father. He was also getting old, nearly eighty, and was tormented by the stone. He died in 1663, and was buried near Laud in the chapel of St John's College, Oxford. On the face of it, he achieved little during his brief Primacy. But his achievement lay in the mere fact of his being Primate; for it signified the triumph of Arminianism in the Restoration Church, which was in a large measure due to his tact and example.

6

Edward Hyde, Earl of Clarendon

The young lawyer Edward Hyde, the friend of Falkland and the advocate of moderation in the Long Parliament, tends to be overshadowed by the rich, all-powerful Clarendon who, with his military moustache and double chin, stares petulantly at us out of his later portraits—a seventeenth-century Colonel Blimp in Chancellor's robes. For this reason, Hyde cannot be seen in the same romantic light as the other Cavaliers who sacrificed their fortunes, if not their lives, in the King's cause. He, too, served the King, but in so doing he also served his own personal ambition, which was gratified beyond his wildest dreams; for, with the exception of Cromwell, no man rose higher as a result of the Civil War than he did. Yet the fact that he was more than adequately rewarded for them does not take away from the value of his services as chief political and legal adviser to Charles I throughout the Civil War, and to Charles II in the years that followed.

The very presence of Hyde in the King's camp during the war is a testimony to the legal right of the Royalist cause, for he was, above all, a constitutionalist. His lawyer's devotion to what he regarded as the ideal English constitution was one of the three guiding principles of his life, the others being his ambition and his attachment to the Church of England. He was, in fact, originally intended for the church, and read Divinity at Oxford; but when his elder brother died and he became heir to his father's small estate in Cheshire, where his family had been gentry for many generations, it was decided that the law would be a more suitable profession for him. So in 1627, when he was eighteen, he entered the Middle Temple. He disliked his studies there, preferring history and literature, though he did not follow the urge to write until he embarked on his *History of the Rebellion*

73

many years later—unless one counts the state papers which he wrote in the service of the King.

If, as a young man, he felt that his real talents were literary, he was no less talented in the law; for when marriage obliged him to take his profession seriously, he built up a highly lucrative practice, so that he soon found himself in the enviable position of being able to earn enough to live very comfortably, and to add to the family estate by 'convenient purchases of land' without having to work too hard. Forty years later, when writing his autobiography, the *Life of Edward, Earl of Clarendon*, he claimed to have had 'a contempt of money' but in view of the charges of rapacity made against him in the days of his power, one need not take this claim too seriously; one must remember, too, that he wrote the *Life* to justify himself after his fall from favour. Indeed, the *Life* betrays his vanity; such as when, looking back on his early career, he attributes his popularity in the legal world to 'the gaiety of his humour, and inoffensive and winning behaviour', though he goes on to admit that his fellow-lawyers also enjoyed his lavish hospitality, and hoped he would put in a word for them with the many 'persons of the best quality' who were his friends.

Hyde's friends in high places included Archbishop Laud, who had taken notice of him in the Court of Star Chamber. Through his friendship with Laud, which doubtless made him more than ever an Arminian, he met some of the other Ministers of the Crown. He was already on friendly terms with many of the younger nobility, having got to know them when sowing his wild oats in London after coming down from Oxford; it was at the time of the Cadiz expedition, when the town was full of young bloods hoping to be soldiers, so that even the prim Ned Hyde was, as he tells us, 'suddenly overwhelmed in that sea of wine and women and quarrels and gaming, which almost overspread the whole kingdom'. And though 'by God's immediate blessing' he 'disentangled himself from these labyrinths', he wisely kept in with the companions of his misspent youth, who would, in the normal course of events, grow into important peers and county magnates. Reading the *Life*, we see Hyde busily cultivating friendships to further his ambition, yet it is only fair to believe that he found it more amusing to dine with his fashionable friends than with the legal confraternity in Middle Temple

Hall; he used to say 'that he repaired himself with very good
company at dinner, for the ill company he had kept in the morning'. He was under the impression that civilized society had
taught him to overcome his 'pride and passion' and his quarrel-
some nature, but it cannot have done so to any great extent, for
throughout his life he antagonized people by his tactlessness, his
bad temper and his self-centred arrogance.

Hyde's closest friend among the nobility was, of course,
Falkland. In the enchanted world of Falkland's country houses at
Burford and Great Tew, he became friendly with some of the
most brilliant writers and thinkers of his time, which served to
broaden his mind. With Falkland himself he became inseparable;
so that later, when the two of them were travelling with the King,
they would sometimes share a bed—a circumstance which in
those days would not have carried the implications it does now,
any more than Falkland's habit of addressing Hyde in letters as
'Dear Sweetheart'. They must have been a strangely assorted
pair; Falkland, with his pinched, lopsided features lit up by sweet
reason; Hyde, full-faced, already, one imagines, running to a
double chin, for he admits to having been greedy about his food,
cheerful, confident, a little pugnacious. Falkland making his
points in his squeaky voice; Hyde rather pompous, speaking as he
wrote, in rolling periods. Hyde regarded this friendship as one of
the greatest blessings of his life; and it certainly is the best proof
we have that his virtues far exceeded his faults, for otherwise
Falkland would never have been as intimate with him as he
was.

In the House of Commons, of which they both became
members when Parliament was called in 1640, Hyde and Falkland
invariably sat next to each other. As a common lawyer, Hyde was
strongly opposed to Prerogative rule, and so he threw himself
heart and soul into Pym's programme of reform. Having given
up his legal practice when Parliament met, he was able to take an
active part in the day-to-day business of the House, acting as
chairman of several committees, notably of that which collected
evidence against the Council of the North. Like Falkland, he
spoke earnestly against Ship Money, and in the debate against the
Lord Keeper Finch; in fact, his speech is said to have been the
cause of Finch's hurried departure into exile.

In attacking the agents of Charles I's Prerogative rule it was natural that Hyde should have joined in the attack on the greatest of them, Strafford. But while he is known to have helped with the preliminaries of Strafford's impeachment, it is not certain what part he played in the later stages of the affair; there are grounds for believing that he was among those who would have been content to banish the fallen Minister from public life. It also seems likely that with the prosecution of Strafford, he began to feel apprehensive at the way things were going. Already, in March 1641, he had felt obliged to oppose the bill depriving the bishops of their vote in the House of Lords because he regarded it as unconstitutional. Hyde considered that Parliament's duty was to uphold, rather than tamper with, the constitution for which he had so high a regard. As a moderate and a true Parliamentarian, he can never have approved of Pym's use of mass-hysteria as a means of sending Strafford to his death; such methods could only disrupt the country and jeopardize everything that Parliament had achieved to date.

As it became increasingly apparent that Pym and his friends intended to carry their reforms beyond the bounds of constitutional propriety, and to use the methods of violent partisanship to force measures through Parliament which were in themselves highly disruptive, it was inevitable that Hyde should have broken with them. The rift, however, widened gradually. Thus, while totally disagreeing with the Parliamentary leaders over their church policy—opposing the Bishops' Bill in March and the far more radical Root and Branch Bill in May—he continued to work with them in the abolition of Prerogative rule, and in July served as chairman of a committee inquiring into the judges' conduct with regard to Ship Money.

In that very month, or at the beginning of August, Hyde had his first meeting with the King, who interviewed him and other leading opponents of the Root and Branch Bill in order to encourage them to continue their defence of the church. The meeting certainly affected Hyde's future, for the King, who rarely departed from a favourable first impression, took a liking to him. As to its more immediate significance, it may have given Hyde the idea of keeping in personal touch with Charles as a means of bringing about the reconciliation between King and Parliament which, as a constitutionalist, he so ardently desired.

At the end of the summer it must have seemed to Hyde that

there was every chance of such a reconciliation. Parliament's victory over Prerogative rule—for which he would have felt a sense of personal achievement—was by now complete. There was no need for any further legislation such as would continue to antagonize the King; the Commons could afford to be magnanimous. At the same time, the disbandment of the army following the conclusion of a peace treaty with the Scots in July had removed a major cause of tension. But when the House met after the summer recess, it was clear that Pym and his friends were in no mood for a settlement such as Hyde hoped for. They proceeded to dictate to the King whom he should and should not have as his councillors, which Hyde immediately condemned as unconstitutional. Then Pym, who with the outbreak of the Irish rebellion was once again able to exploit the popular fear of a standing army, as well as the Popish and Irish bogies, virtually pointed a pistol at the King with his so-called 'Additional Instruction'. Finally in November came Pym's fierce assault on the authority of the Crown known as the Grand Remonstrance, which enumerated all the King's alleged misdeeds to date. To Hyde, this seemed like sheer provocation, calculated to cause an irreparable split between King and Parliament, and in the nation as a whole. When the Remonstrance was debated in the Commons—a debate famous as one of the longest and most unruly in the history of the House—Hyde led the opposition to it. This was the real moment of truth between Hyde and Pym. The Remonstrance was passed, though only by a narrow majority. It was a poor victory for Pym; on the other hand, it was a crushing defeat for Hyde, who saw Parliament divided and an exacerbation of ill-feeling between the majority and the King.

All his hopes of achieving peace through the Commons had now been shattered, and he retired disconsolately to the back benches. There was still, however, the chance of a settlement through the House of Lords, which continued to be led by the moderates; in particular by the Earl of Bristol and his son, the talented but unreliable George, Lord Digby. George Digby had been a member of the reforming party in the Commons until, having fallen foul of the leaders he was, in the modern phrase, 'kicked upstairs', and Hyde now began to work with him. It was Digby who prevailed upon the King to make Falkland Secretary of State and Sir John Culpeper, another moderate reformer,

Chancellor of the Exchequer. One can detect Hyde's influence in this; and while he himself declined the post of Solicitor-General which was offered to him, he henceforth endeavoured to moderate Royal policy through his friends and various reforming members of the Privy Council.

A government headed by Falkland and Culpeper, advised by Hyde and with the backing of the Lords might easily have prevailed over Pym and the Commons, had not Digby almost immediately undone all his good work by inciting the King to attempt the arrest of the Five Members, which played into the hands of Pym. Once again, Hyde was thwarted in his policy of moderation by the extremists, this time on the Royalist side. The division of the country into Royalist and Parliamentarian can be dated from this time. Hyde, though separated from the majority in the Commons, was still a Parliamentarian. He had not changed sides like Digby, who from being a reformer was now entirely on the side of the court.

Hyde continued to work for a reconciliation between King and Parliament until well into the spring of 1642. 'Your greatest strength is in the hearts and affections of those persons who have been the severest assertors of the public liberties,' he told the King in March, when tactfully rebuking him for his 'quick and sharp treatment' of the deputation which presented him with Parliament's message intended to justify the Militia Ordinance. His real chance came at the end of February, when he was invited to draft all the King's future replies to Parliament. It is remarkable that Hyde was entrusted with this momentous task when he was actually attending on the King as a member of another Parliamentary deputation, to beg Charles not to move the eleven-year-old Prince of Wales from Richmond. That he should have been chosen as one of this deputation is still more remarkable, for he had been regarded as an out-and-out Royalist by Pym and the other Parliamentary leaders ever since the attempt on the Five Members, although he and Falkland had been kept completely in the dark over that affair, which they 'perfectly detested'.

As the author of numerous messages, replies and declarations issued in the name of the King, Hyde was in a better position to convince Parliament of Charles's sincerity than he had ever been, and he could no longer be torpedoed by Digby, who had fled abroad. But it was now too late. Pym was determined not to trust the King and would consider no settlement short of dictating terms to him from a position of strength.

Hyde was at first helped in his work by being able to observe the exact temper of the Parliamentary leaders, since, like Falkland and Culpeper, he occupied his seat in the Commons for as long as he could. By May it was clear that he would be arrested if he stayed in London any longer, so he slipped away and went to join the King at York. This can be said to mark his final change from Parliamentarian to Royalist. From then on, as spokesman for the King, his language became more stern. He was no longer trying to convince Parliament of the King's good faith, but appealing to the nation at large and counteracting the poison of Pym's propaganda.

Hyde's object was to force the Parliamentary leaders to see sense by the pressure of public opinion. This was more than he was able to achieve, though his appeals to the people won widespread support for the King's cause. In fact, it was Hyde's 'reasonableness', coupled with Pym's reign of terror, which was responsible for the rapid growth of the Royalist party, so that by the end of the summer the King was strong enough to resist the might of Parliament. He was able to expose the arbitrary and unconstitutional nature of Parliament's own actions, giving full rein to his lawyer's mind and his mastery of the English tongue. When Pym repeated the somewhat stale contention that the King showed no sign of giving up the tyranny of Prerogative rule, he turned the tables on him and accused him of setting up a far worse tyranny than Prerogative rule had ever been. As a defender of the rule of law against arbitrary government, it was no less consistent for Hyde to be with the King in 1642, than for him to have been with Parliament in 1640.

Throughout the war, Hyde drafted most of the King's proclamations, as well as many of his letters and speeches. The King used to complain good-humouredly that he could not recognize himself in his public utterances, the language was so elegant. Charles once bet Falkland that he could always recognize Hyde's writings from his style, but lost when he read and commented on a speech in a newspaper, which purported to be by the Roundhead Earl of Pembroke, without realizing that it had been written for the paper by Hyde.

Almost immediately after the outbreak of hostilities, the

Parliamentary leaders recognized Hyde's importance in the Royalist camp by including him among the 'delinquents' who were to be excepted from the general pardon which they offered in their peace proposals. But his position remained unofficial until early in 1643, when he became Chancellor of the Exchequer and a Privy Councillor, being knighted at the same time. Later that year, the King intended to make him Secretary of State in succession to Falkland; but then, through the Queen's influence, he appointed Digby. So Falkland's death in battle, as well as leaving a gap in Hyde's affections that could never be filled, meant that instead of working with his best friend, he now had a colleague who was treacherous and unreliable, who had bedevilled him at the time of the Five Members and was to charm the King into other fatal moves.

Unlike Falkland, Hyde never took up arms himself, though he was only thirty-three at the start of the war. On the whole, he disliked soldiers and did his best to prevent the King from being influenced by the military. As a result, Charles did not rely on his generals as much as he should have done. This was unfortunate from the point of view of winning the war in the conventional military sense; but Hyde had his own, essentially civilian, idea of how the war should be waged, namely, that the Royalists should build up their strength and remain on the defensive, avoiding the pitched battle on which the military men pinned all their hopes. In this way, he was certain that Parliament could be forced to come to terms. As a Parliamentarian, he understood his fellow-Members and he knew that most of them were desperately anxious for peace. Pym and the other leaders had never imagined that the King would put up an armed resistance to their show of force; the very fact that he had done so was a major defeat for their policy.

After Edgehill, Hyde was for halting the army at Oxford and waiting for Parliament to open peace negotiations, which he knew they intended to do. The King's march on London, which was too late and too slow to be successful, not only revealed his weakness, but gave the impression that he was out to crush Parliament rather than come to terms with it. Nevertheless, Parliament went on with its peace moves, and at the beginning of 1643 the Parliamentary Commissioners came to Oxford. Hyde played a leading part in the negotiations that followed, and even after they had broken down, he continued his efforts for peace. Regarding it as essential to his policy that the men at Westminster should be recognized as a lawful Parliament unlawfully coerced, rather than condemned as rebels, he succeeded in dissuading the King from proclaiming Parliament dissolved. This made it possible to put into effect Hyde's scheme for summoning those Members of Parliament who were free to come—and they included the great majority of the Lords and a third of the Commons—to meet at Oxford and provide a backing to the King in a new bid for peace. An early end to the war was imperative now that the Parliamentary leaders had taken the drastic step of calling in the Scots; there was the hope that the men at Westminster who, apart from the extremists, disliked the idea of a Scottish invasion just as much as the Royalists did, might listen to their fellow-Members at Oxford.

Westminster failed to respond to the peace overtures of the 'Oxford Parliament', even though Pym was now dead. The Scots army moved southwards, and the war entered a new and vicious stage. There was, however, one more attempt to make peace early in 1645, when delegates from both sides met at Uxbridge, in Roundhead territory; a sign of how far the King's position had weakened. Hyde led the Royalist Commissioners and afterwards declared that he was never so tired in all his life as during the twenty days of negotiations which were doomed from the start; for the Scots, though anxious for peace, insisted on the impossible condition that England should become Presbyterian, while the old Parliamentary peace party was now at the mercy of the Independents, who were far more militant than Pym had ever been.

For Hyde, the Civil War ended with a year of frustration in the West Country as one of the Council appointed to advise the fifteen-year-old Prince of Wales, when he did little else but contend with the vagaries of the army commander, Goring. After the collapse of the King's cause, Hyde and the other Councillors retreated to Jersey with the Prince, who then went to Paris at the behest of his mother. Hyde, who was strongly opposed to his going, refused to accompany him and remained in Jersey, where he spent the next two years at a loose end. To occupy himself, he wrote his *History of the Rebellion*, of which he had completed the first four books when, in 1648, he was summoned to the Continent by the Prince who, after becoming King, sent him on an embassy to Spain.

Hyde returned from his rather unsuccessful Spanish mission in 1651, and from then until the Restoration he followed the fortunes of the exiled Charles II, at times so poor that he and his family were barely able to procure the necessities of life. As well as being the young King's chief adviser, drafting his State papers for him as he had done for his father, he had to conduct a widespread intelligence service, keeping in touch with Royalists everywhere. Not the least of his labours was having to cope with the quarrels and jealousies of the exiled court.

His task was made no easier by the fact that he was far from popular. His rigid Anglicanism alienated the Catholics, led by the Queen, as well as the Presbyterians; he had enemies among the military men. The majority of Royalists, who thought in terms of plots and insurrections, disagreed with his policy of what, at a later date, might have been described as 'masterly inactivity'. In his own words, he 'believed that the King had nothing at this time to do but to be quiet, and that all his activity was to consist in careful avoiding to do anything that might do him hurt, and to expect some blessed conjuncture from the amity of Christian Princes, or some such revolution of affairs in England by their own discontents and divisions amongst themselves, as might make it seasonable for His Majesty again to show himself.' In advocating this policy, he had the support of Ormonde, the only one of the King's advisers who was anything like his equal. The 'blessed conjuncture from the amity of Christian Princes' never materialized; but in 1660 there came a 'revolution of affairs in England' and Charles II returned triumphantly to his kingdom, having promised, in the Declaration of Breda, religious freedom to all his subjects and pardon to the Roundheads, except for the regicides—those who had played a leading part in Charles I's trial and execution. Hyde, who had been made Lord Chancellor in name three years before, now became Lord Chancellor in fact. At the same time, he kept his office of Chancellor of the Exchequer; soon, he was a Chancellor three times over, for he became Chancellor of the University of Oxford. As Charles II's chief minister, he was easily the most powerful man in the kingdom next to the King.

Shortly after the Restoration, an unexpected circumstance made Hyde's position more than ever exalted; though for a time he feared it would bring him disgrace. This was the marriage of his daughter, Anne, to the King's younger brother, James, Duke of York, which had taken place secretly at Breda in the previous autumn. James kept the matter quiet until the court had returned to England, when Anne's pregnancy obliged him to make a clean breast of it to the King, who broke the news to Hyde. According to Hyde's own account, this was the first he ever knew of it—though one would have thought he would have suspected something, since his daughter was by then six months gone with child—and his fury and dismay on hearing the news immediately convinced the King that he was in no way guilty of the treasonable presumption of contriving to marry his daughter to the heir to the throne; in fact, that the very idea of such a marriage was utterly abhorrent to him. From what he tells us of his protestations to this effect, he appears in rather a mean light, as though ready to sacrifice his daughter to save his own position. He declared that he would 'much rather his daughter should be the Duke's whore than his wife', for, in that case, 'he would turn her out of his house, as a strumpet'. But as she was married to the Duke, he could only advise the King to throw her into the Tower and have an Act of Parliament passed for the cutting off of her head, 'to which he would not only give his consent, but would very willingly be the first man that should propose it'. As if in anticipation of this rigorous course of action, Hyde ordered his daughter to be confined to her room, where, however, the Duke managed to visit her clandestinely at night.

All ended happily, despite officious attempts by some of the Duke's entourage to give him grounds for repudiating Anne by blackening her character. Though the marriage was not what the King would have wished, he was prepared to make the best of it. Anne was publicly acknowledged as Duchess of York, and to set the seal of Royal approval on her family, Hyde became Earl of Clarendon, taking his title from an old Royal domain in Wiltshire which he had bought with the help of a £20,000 gift from the King, who also gave him the estate of Cornbury in Oxfordshire, not many miles from Great Tew.

Clarendon need not have worried about falling from Royal favour on account of his daughter's marriage, for at the time

Charles could not do without him. He was too fond of his pleasures to wish to be overburdened with the affairs of state, and he felt that they could be safely left in the hands of a minister of Clarendon's worth. On the whole, Clarendon well repaid Charles's trust. As the principal architect of the Restoration Settlement, he gave the country a system of government which did not need to be changed until 1689, and then only as a result of James II's conversion to Catholicism. Even now, when he had acquired an almost idolatrous regard for the House of Stuart, the old common lawyer in him made him endeavour to keep the Royal Prerogative within what he believed to be its constitutional limits. He moderated the Royalists in their flush of victory, and made sure that the promise of pardon to the former Roundheads in the Declaration of Breda—which, needless to say, he had himself drawn up—was faithfully carried out, forcing a somewhat reluctant Cavalier Parliament to pass the Acts of Oblivion and Indemnity. But such was his attachment to the Church of England that he failed to honour the other promise made at Breda, that of religious freedom; he did nothing to prevent the Anglican majority in Parliament from legislating against Catholics and Dissenters; in fact, the Corporation Act, the Five Mile Act and the other repressive measures of the early years of Charles II's reign came to be known collectively as the 'Clarendon Code'.

Clarendon's religious bigotry, while naturally alienating the Dissenters and Catholics, should at least have won him credit with the Anglicans. But there were reasons why they too came to dislike him, so that within a very few years of the Restoration he was the most unpopular man in England. There was his cold, haughty manner; he became irascible and autocratic, such as when he bullied Pepys and the Commissioners of the Admiralty into allowing him to keep the oaks in Clarendon Park which the King had reserved for the use of the navy. Then he was blamed for his land settlement, which provided no compensation for those hundreds of Cavaliers who had ruined themselves in the King's cause and had been obliged to sell their estates. He was said to have favoured 'old rebels' in preference to 'royal sufferers', because the former were rich and could pay for his services: 'My Lord Chancellor . . . never did, nor will do anything, but for money,' Evelyn told Pepys. As well as being accused of taking bribes in cash, he was alleged to have filled his houses with pictures and furniture which the 'old rebels' had plundered from the 'royal sufferers' during the war. One certainly wonders how Clarendon obtained some of the Van Dycks and Janssens of prominent Royalists and their ladies in his famous collection of portraits, which was still intact a century ago; for the sitters were neither related to him, nor his particular friends. One wonders, too, how he was able to build himself the largest private palace in London, facing down St James's Street from the north side of Piccadilly. He was rich, but not inordinately so; in his anxiety not to be thought rapacious, he had refused a much larger grant of Crown lands than he actually received. The perquisites of his office were handsome, but hardly sufficient for his semi-regal way of life. People believed that his great mansion was built with French gold, paid to him for having engineered the sale of Dunkirk to France; it consequently became known as Dunkirk House.

The loss of Dunkirk was only one of many national misfortunes for which Clarendon was blamed; he was even held responsible for the childlessness of Queen Catherine of Braganza, on the grounds that he had deliberately married the King to an infertile princess so as to ensure that the crown would go to his own descendants. This last accusation is patently absurd; though, as it turned out, his two grand-daughters, Mary and Anne, did in fact succeed to the throne. Apart from giving rise to accusations such as this, Clarendon's connection with the royal family served greatly to increase the jealousy aroused by his wealth, his honours and his power. He was seen, in fact, as a reincarnation of that medieval monster, the overmighty subject.

In 1667, the blow fell. The King gave way to the general clamour and dismissed him. His fall from power was followed by a move to impeach him for high treason; it was defeated by the Lords, but he nonetheless felt it prudent to retire to France, where, soon after his arrival, he narrowly escaped being murdered by some English sailors. From then until his death in 1674 he lived mostly at Montpellier; he was unable to return to England having been sentenced to perpetual banishment after his departure. Twice he wrote to the King, begging to be allowed to come home to die, but each time there was no answer.

His years in exile were lonely, for he was now a widower; but he kept himself occupied by writing his *Life* and completing his

History of the Rebellion, a work which has earned him a place among the immortals of English literature, and in the select company of those who, like Caesar and Churchill, have made history as well as writing it. As the most important contemporary account of the events in which he played a leading part, Clarendon's *History* is remarkably fair, though it naturally has a Royalist bias and tends to play down his earlier role as a Parliamentarian. While he does not attempt to conceal the mistakes of Charles I, his admiration for him is apparent on almost every page. As a Parliamentarian, Clarendon quarrelled with many of Charles's ideas of government; but as a devoted High Anglican, he regarded him as 'the best Christian in the world'.

7

George, Lord Goring

'The worst of the bad men who brought reproach on the name of Cavalier.' This is a typical nineteenth-century opinion of George, Lord Goring, perhaps the best cavalry commander on the Royalist side in the Civil War. One can understand why Goring did not appeal to the Victorians. Though brave, brilliant and charming, he was also frivolous and irresponsible. He was frequently drunk, which was taken as a sign of his moral degeneracy; though for most of his life he probably could not help drinking, being almost certainly an alcoholic. Then he suffers from having been given a particularly 'bad press' by Clarendon, who had been exasperated by his dealings with him in the West Country.

It is unfortunate for Goring's memory that later historians have tended to follow Clarendon's account rather than that of Sir Richard Bulstrode, who, as Goring's secretary during the western campaign, saw him at his worst, just as Clarendon did. Bulstrode's description of Goring makes no attempt to hide his faults; we are told quite frankly that 'he strangely loved the bottle, was much given to his pleasures and a great debauchee'. But it also gives his virtues their due. 'He was a person of extraordinary abilities, as well as courage, and was, without dispute, as good an officer as any that served the King, and the most dexterous in any sudden emergency, that I have ever seen... if his conscience and integrity had equalled his wit and courage, he had been one of the most eminent men of the age he lived in; but he could not resist temptations, and was a man without scruple, and loved no man so well, but he would cozen him, and afterwards laugh at him.'

This is not the rakish villain of popular legend, but a man in whom great gifts were combined with grave defects of character.

The worst that is said of him is that he would 'cozen', or deceive, when it suited his book. The fact that he needed to implies that he lacked some quality necessary for succeeding by straightforward means. He was so clear-headed that he was known to dictate admirably-phrased dispatches to several people at once; but 'his mind would not long be bent'. To be brilliant but prevented from doing great things by lesser men who work harder than oneself can produce a bitter sense of unfulfilment, which may have been the cause of Goring's unhappiness; for unhappy he surely was, though his contemporaries do not mention the fact in so many words. Almost everything they tell us of his character would, however, suggest this: his drinking, his perpetual need to be amused, his taste for danger. There is an air of restless discontent in his expression; it is particularly noticeable in contrast to the placid good-humour of his friend, the Earl of Newport, in Van Dyck's double portrait of the two of them together.

This, and other portraits, shows him not to have been of conventional good looks, but possessing a type of lean, interesting face somewhat reminiscent of an intelligent fox-terrier, which one not infrequently meets among the English aristocracy. It was a face which, since he was tall, certainly made people think of him as handsome, particularly as his movements were graceful and he had charm. That fatal charm was due not just to his wit and his beautiful manners, but to an ingenuous, boyish diffidence; Lady Fanshawe, a diplomat's wife, who met him when he was no longer young, noticed how 'he would blush like a girl'.

George Goring started life with advantages over and above his gifts of mind and body. He was heir to estates in Sussex, where his father's family had owned land since the Middle Ages. In 1628, when he was twenty, he also became heir to a peerage, for in that year his father, a courtier who had long enjoyed Royal favour, was made a baron.

On coming down from Cambridge, he quickly acquired the reputation of being one of the gayest young gallants of the court, a gambler and a spendthrift. Even after he had married the pretty, rose-cheeked Lady Lettice Boyle, daughter of the wealthy Earl of Cork, who had a dowry of £10,000, he was short of money. He was continually trying to borrow from his father-in-law, to whom he must have been a sore trial; though there is evidence that the shrewd, self-made millionaire had a soft corner for him. By 1633 he had got through most of his wife's marriage portion and Lord Cork refused to lend him any more. So, being in Ireland, he went to the Lord Deputy, Strafford, and asked for his help. Strafford was impressed by his 'frank and sweet, generous disposition' and recommended him for a military command in the Netherlands, as well as persuading Lord Cork to put up the necessary money for buying his commission.

Having entered the Dutch service as a Colonel in command of twenty-two companies of foot and a troop of horse, Goring immediately showed an unexpected military genius. At the Siege of Breda in 1637 he inspired the English troops by his gallantry and zeal, offering to reward at his own expense all those who volunteered to work with him in the advanced sap. More than twenty men were shot around him but still he stayed at his post, until his ankle was shattered by a musket-ball and he was carried unconscious from the field. In England, it was rumoured that he had been killed, and Davenant wrote a poem comparing him to Sir Philip Sidney. He eventually recovered the use of his leg, being left with a Byronic limp by which, as we are told, 'he appeared the more comely and prevailing'; but as a result of his wound he suffered pain and ill-health for the rest of his life, which may have been what drove him to drink.

Goring's wound put an end to his service abroad, so, through the influence of his father, he was appointed Governor of Portsmouth. The Scots Wars gave him a fresh chance of active service, and he fought in both of them, acquitting himself well enough to become something of a popular hero—'To Goring! To Goring! See him crown'd' sang the poet Lovelace—though neither campaign offered much scope for his talents and ambition. After the war of 1640 was over, he intrigued to be made Lieutenant-General in the north, so that he could have taken charge if there was a renewal of hostilities. He was, however, defeated in this object on account of the opposition of certain senior officers, and also because the Queen, who had a high opinion of him as a soldier, preferred him to remain at Portsmouth, which looked like being a place of great importance if the situation in England deteriorated further; both as a port for landing supplies from France and as a possible refuge for herself.

In the spring of 1641, a group of army officers conspired to force Parliament, by threatening military action, to moderate its legislation against the power of the King and the bishops, and to pay the arrears due to the army. Goring attended a meeting of the conspirators, at which he was made to swear an oath of secrecy. Having heard the officers' proposals, he argued that a mere threat of military action would not be enough; the army, he said, should march on London and seize the Tower on behalf of the King. This plan had the worthy object of releasing Strafford, who was then in the Tower and in the process of being impeached; Goring appears to have felt a genuine sense of gratitude to the former Lord Deputy for having procured him his commission in the Netherlands. But to the other conspirators it seemed a 'wild mad undertaking', typical of its author.

Soon afterwards Goring told his friend, Lord Newport, of the conspiracy. Through Newport the information reached the ears of Pym, who made the most of it to inflame public opinion against Strafford, playing on the popular fear regarding his alleged intention of bringing an Irish army into England. Some of the conspirators were eventually arrested, others fled the country.

Goring's reputation never really recovered from the betrayal of the so-called Army Plot. His motive for so discreditable an act has not been satisfactorily established. It was said to have been his vexation at not being promised a high command if the conspirators succeeded in gaining control of the army. Some believed that he intended all along to betray the plot. Most likely he joined the conspiracy in good faith, and then became convinced that it would fail, or be revealed through indiscretion, and so decided to save his own skin by turning informer.

After the flight of two of the conspirators, Goring was examined before the House of Commons, and so well did he convince the Parliamentary leaders of his good intentions that they actually believed him to be on their side. He was allowed to return to his post at Portsmouth and ordered to fortify the town on behalf of Parliament, which granted him £5,000 for this purpose. In the following year, he was appointed Lieutenant-General to the Earl of Essex. All the time, however, he was in correspondence with the Queen, assuring her of his loyalty;

and she, certain that his works at Portsmouth were really for her benefit, gave him an additional £3,000 towards them.

Most writers have regarded Goring's behaviour at this juncture as totally cynical; as though he were hoodwinking both court and Parliament before making up his mind which side to join. But there seems no reason to believe that he was not always a Royalist or that his pretence of supporting Parliament was anything worse than a somewhat underhand way of serving the King—or, at any rate, the Queen. Had he been of doubtful allegiance, a Lieutenant-General's command under Parliament would surely have presented a more attractive prospect than chancing his hand with the Royalists, many of whom had not forgiven him for betraying the Army Plot.

Then we are told that he frequently aroused the suspicions of the Portsmouth Roundheads by expressing Royalist sentiments when drunk. Adverse reports of his conduct reached London, but he managed to justify himself and in the summer of 1642 was ordered to take up his command in the Parliamentary army. For a time he managed to find excuses for not going, but by the beginning of August he felt that he could prevaricate no longer. He was thus forced to declare for the King sooner than he had intended, even before the Royal Standard had been raised at Nottingham. This meant that the Royalists were not yet ready to march to his assistance when, early in September, he was besieged by a Parliamentary force. His defences were too weak to sustain a siege of any length of time and so he surrendered on advantageous terms and sailed for Holland, where he joined the Queen.

The loss of Portsmouth was a great blow to Royalist morale, and Goring's reputation sank still lower. He was accused of having neglected the fortifications, of having attended to nothing but his own pleasures. According to Clarendon, after the Queen had gone abroad Portsmouth no longer seemed to him of much importance, for it would not after all be required as a stronghold for her. So he lost interest in defending it, regarding it as 'too low a sphere for him to move in'. He certainly can have spent little if any of the money which both Parliament and the Queen gave him for the town's defence, since he took most of it with him to Holland. There, he put it to good use; the Queen was desperate for money with which to buy arms for the King. He also served the Queen well in Holland by raising men, which he did most successfully.

Having finished his recruiting, Goring set sail with a party of officers and veteran soldiers and landed in the north of England, where he became General of Horse under the Earl of Newcastle. He scored his first success in the spring of 1643 at Seacroft Moor, near Leeds, when he was surprised by Fairfax with a much larger force; the Roundheads expected him to flee, instead of which he charged; so that they were taken off their guard and routed, suffering heavy losses. During the rest of that spring, Goring rode high; he spoke confidently of 'sweeping away the rubbish, crowded in two or three holes of this country'. Then, towards the end of May, just as he was about to have the honour of accompanying the Queen on her journey south in command of her troops, his luck turned. He was lying ill in bed with fever at Wakefield, of which he was then Governor, when the town was stormed by Fairfax. Showing both courage and presence of mind, he got up, mounted his horse and headed a charge; but he was nonetheless taken prisoner, and spent the next nine months in the Tower of London. In April 1644 he was exchanged and returned north with a regiment of horse, eventually joining Prince Rupert at Preston.

It is during this Lancashire campaign that we first hear of Goring's troops being accused of plundering and other obnoxious behaviour, an accusation which was to be repeated several times before the end of the war. But the Roundhead Major Edward Robinson, in reporting how they made themselves unpopular with the Lancastrians, can tell us nothing worse than that they lived on the country, forced people to winnow corn for their horses on the Sabbath, and 'carried along with them many strumpets, whom they termed "Leaguer Ladies". These they made use of in places where they lay, in a very uncivil and unbecoming way.'

At Marston Moor, Goring led the left wing of the Royalist cavalry in a devastating charge against Fairfax and the Roundhead right. Driving the enemy troops off the field, they pursued them for several miles with great slaughter. Goring has been blamed for pursuing the enemy too far—in other words, for making the mistake which Prince Rupert made at Edgehill and Naseby—but it seems that the lie of the land made a lengthy chase inevitable if Fairfax was to be prevented from rallying. It is doubtful too whether Goring, had he stayed on the field, could have done much good, in view of the havoc caused by Cromwell to the Royalist right at the very beginning of the battle. As it was, he was able to save most of his troops from the fate which overtook Rupert's. In the days following the battle, he scoured the country to bring in the rest of the scattered Royalist cavalry. When numbers counted for much, this was an invaluable service to the King's cause.

When the accounts of Marston Moor reached the court, Goring was acclaimed as the hero of the day. Admittedly, there was not much competition; Rupert had lost his reputation and Newcastle had left the country under a cloud. But to be the hero of a defeat was always something and it did wonders in making people forget the Army Plot, at any rate for the time being. A month after Marston Moor he was made General of the Horse, in place of Prince Rupert, who went up to being General-in-Chief.

He was ordered to the west of England, and arrived there in time to take part in the Royalist victory near Lostwithiel in Cornwall, when an army commanded by the King in person succeeded in cornering Essex's army on the Fowey peninsula. Essex himself made a getaway by boat, his infantry were obliged to surrender, and his cavalry escaped through the Royalist lines under cover of darkness. Goring has been generally blamed for the escape of the Roundhead horse; this is due to Clarendon's version of what happened, according to which they actually passed through his quarters and he had notice of their coming, but at the time 'was in one of his jovial exercises', so did nothing about it. It is certain, however, that the enemy horse did not pass through Goring's quarters; and we know that he heard nothing of their escape until seven next morning, when he received a note from the King, ordering him to pursue them. He immediately assembled his troops and went after the enemy 'with great diligence', but by now they had already gone so far that they could not be overtaken.

After Lostwithiel, the King planned to retire to his winter quarters at Oxford without taking on the combined armies of Manchester and Waller, which, together with the London trained-bands and Essex's fugitive horse, were approaching him from the direction of London. Passing through Hampshire, he was persuaded by Goring to interrupt his march in order to engage Waller, who had become separated from the rest of the Parliamentary host. With a troop of 200 gentlemen, Goring beat Waller out of Andover where he was quartered; his army fled before the Royalists in great confusion, and would have been destroyed if night had not fallen. Owing to this diversion, and further delays caused by the King's desire to relieve a couple of garrisons on the way, the Parliamentary army caught up with the Royalists before they could reach Oxford, and the second battle of Newbury was fought. In that ill-managed action, as indecisive as the first battle of Newbury, Goring distinguished himself by leading several gallant charges. Like Marston Moor, the second Newbury fight was his day; and when the memory of it was still green, he put forward a daring plan. This was that he should make a lightning march through the south of England and raise the King's standard in his own home county of Sussex, where he was certain the gentry were loyal and would rise for the King at the first opportunity.

The King agreed to Goring's plan and made him provisional Commander-in-Chief of Sussex and Hampshire. With this titular command, and the courtesy title of Lord Goring which he had recently acquired on account of his father's elevation to the Earldom of Norwich, he set out from Salisbury at the beginning of January 1645. Striking across Hampshire, he got as far as the town of Farnham in Surrey, putting the enemy forces in the neighbourhood to flight. He had hoped to pursue and engage them, but his officers did not share his enthusiasm for the enter-prise and insisted on halting for 'refreshment'. So at Farnham he made a stand, hoping that his presence on the borders of their county would encourage the Sussex gentry to rise. The rising did not materialize, so that after a few days, Goring was obliged to withdraw.

With the failure of his grand design, Goring began to go to pieces. His drinking grew worse, and he promoted his even more bibulous brother-in-law, George Porter, whom he described as 'the best company but the worst officer that ever served the King', to be his second-in-command. He could still, at times, be a brilliant commander: when Cromwell invaded the West Country in April 1645, he fell on him at Dorchester and drove him back to Salisbury. But his behaviour became increasingly erratic. A few weeks before he successfully tackled the might of Cromwell's army, he allowed the port of Weymouth, which had been recently captured by the Dorset Royalists, to be recaptured by an insignificant Parliamentary force. He failed to intercept a party of horse and foot sent to the relief of Taunton, which with Plymouth was one of the two remaining Roundhead strongholds of any importance in the now predominantly Royalist western counties.

It seemed to Clarendon and others that he deliberately allowed the relief of Taunton and what Digby spoke of as the 'wild misfortune' of Weymouth, in order to justify the presence of his troops in the west, where he hoped to become an independent Commander-in-Chief like Newcastle had been in the north, subject to nobody but the King; an object for which he intrigued incessantly. He found it particularly galling when, in March 1645, the conduct of the war in the west was put into the hands of a Council composed of soldiers and civilians—including Hyde—appointed to advise the fourteen-year-old Prince of Wales who became the nominal Commander-in-Chief. Henceforth, the Royalist cause in the western counties was constantly bedevilled by disputes between Goring and the Prince's Council.

Even more unfortunate was the coolness which arose between Goring and Prince Rupert, despite the admiration which Rupert had for Goring as a soldier. It was caused primarily by Goring's intrigues for an independent command, which Rupert saw as a threat to his own authority. Yet the fault seems also to a certain degree to have rested with Rupert himself.

When, in the spring of 1645, the armies of Rupert and the King were about to come together near Oxford in preparation for the march northwards that was to end with Naseby, Goring was ordered to draw off Cromwell who threatened to attack the King's army before it could join with Rupert's. He did so with great success, charging some of Cromwell's troops as they were about to cross the Isis, killing many of them and taking others prisoner; a victory which 'made him exceedingly welcome' when he rode into the King's camp next day. His presence, however, was not so welcome to Rupert, who feared that Goring's eloquence would all too easily prevail with the King. And according to Sir Edward Walker, Rupert was jealous of Goring's 'master wit' and the reputation he had gained from having driven Cromwell out of the West Country and beaten his troops near Oxford.

Whatever his motive, Rupert wished to send Goring back to the west, whereas some of the other Royal advisers were for taking him and his troops with them on the march northwards. According to the King's confidant, Sir Philip Warwick, Goring himself favoured the latter course; having heard through his intelligence that Cromwell and the New Model Army had resolved to engage the King in a major battle which they hoped would be decisive. Had Goring and his 2,500 good cavalry fought for the King at Naseby, the outcome of the battle, and consequently of the war, might well have been different. But Rupert had his way and Goring, with the best cavalry the King possessed, returned to the West Country, ostensibly so as to prevent the relief of Taunton, which the Royalists were once again besieging. His powers were increased so that he became to all intents and purposes the Commander-in-Chief of the western army, nominally subject to the Prince of Wales but independent of the Council.

After he had marched for a couple of weeks, the King, as so often happened, changed his mind, and wrote ordering Goring to join him immediately. Goring replied that he would come as soon as Taunton had been reduced, begging the King in the meantime to avoid any engagement and to take up a defensive position on the Trent. Goring is alleged to have had no intention of leaving the west and to have used the siege as a pretext; yet there was some sense in his not wishing to leave it before it had been brought to a conclusion, knowing that if the King took his advice—which was also the advice of Rupert—and retired across the Trent, he could postpone giving battle indefinitely. Unfortunately Goring's letter was intercepted by Fairfax, causing him to engage the King without delay.

On hearing the news of Naseby, Goring lost heart altogether, and so neglected his operations against Taunton that the town had still not been reduced when, at the beginning of July, Fairfax entered Somerset. Goring was obliged to raise the siege and give battle with him at Langport, where he suffered the only major defeat of his career. He was outnumbered by two to one, but as at Taunton there was an element of carelessness, though not so much on Goring's part as on the part of the egregious Porter, who was drinking with some other officers when the enemy approached. They could be seen a mile off but nobody bothered to give the alarm, so that some of the Royalist soldiers were asleep, and others were swimming in the river or walking in the fields, when the Roundheads fell upon them.

Goring arrived on the scene to find his cavalry in full flight, and Porter fleeing with the rest. Declaring that his brother-in-law ought to be shot for cowardice, he succeeded in rallying what remained of his horse after the enemy had wrought havoc among them, and withdrew to a strong position between the river and a bog, where the rest of the army was stationed. When, on the following day, the enemy returned to the attack, he fought bravely with his own bodyguard to hold the passage across the bog; but was eventually forced back by weight of numbers and there was a general rout. Now it was Goring's turn to be careless, for he left the field and retreated to the town of Bridgwater without finding out what had become of his infantry and his cannon. He was certain they were lost, and so distraught about it that his secretary, Bulstrode, stayed with him all that night in his room; but next morning, to his joy, they turned up, having been brought away safely by two of his commanders.

After Langport, Goring retired to Exeter, where he remained until October when the town rose against him, obliging him to make a further retreat into Cornwall. During those months, though he still had four thousand horse, he remained almost totally inactive; while Bristol, Bridgwater, Sherborne and other major towns of the West Country fell to the enemy. Yet he remained as jealous as always of the dignity of his command, and in his proclamations gave himself the grandiloquent but improper title of 'General of the West'. And while neglecting the Roundheads, he waged constant warfare with the Prince of Wales's Council, complaining ceaselessly of want of pay, powder and provisions. Hyde, on behalf of the Council, assured him repeatedly that they were doing their best to keep him supplied, but this was never enough to prevent his troops from plundering. At first when the local inhabitants complained about the misdeeds of his troops, he endeavoured to placate them, and such was his charm that he usually succeeded. Then, he ceased to bother; and when people came to him with complaints, he merely laughed.

The only excuse which can be made for Goring's behaviour during the latter part of 1645 is that he was ill, for towards the end of the year he begged leave of the Prince of Wales to go to France for the sake of his health. He did not wait for an answer, but took ship at Dartmouth and spent some time in France and Holland seeking employment. Eventually, he became a Lieutenant-General in the Spanish service, which seems to have brought him more honour than pay, for during the few years that remained of his life he was chronically short of money. It may, of course, have been that his income did not match his extravagance, for according to Lady Fanshawe, who met him in Madrid in 1650, he still kept to his raffish ways. But though constantly in need, he showed a stoical resolve not to be a burden to his family or friends; adversity seems to have made him less selfish. 'I say not this to give your Lordship any thoughts of providing for me,' he assured his father when writing to him from the siege of Barcelona in 1652, having spoken at length of his poverty as well as of his ague and gout, which made it almost impossible for him to stand though he could still sit on a horse. Old Lord Norwich had troubles of his own, and was now in exile in France having narrowly escaped a death sentence after leading one of the Royalist risings of 1648; his estates had been released from sequestration, but the revenues from them were being pocketed by dishonest agents.

Goring died in Madrid in 1657 at the early age of forty-nine. There is a legend that he ended his days as a Dominican, having lost his wife some years before; but this is disproved by a letter from Henry Bennet, Charles II's envoy at the Spanish court, who saw him a month before he died and reported him to be 'in miserable want' and anxious to serve the King in whatever capacity he could. It is possible, however, that he became a Dominican Tertiary, a lay member of the Order not living in community and only wearing the habit on certain occasions. This was then a not uncommon practice among Catholic gentlemen; Milton alludes to it in *Paradise Lost* with the words: 'Dying, put on the weeds of Dominic.' We know that Goring died a Catholic; Lady Fanshawe, who heard of his conversion after his death, assumed it to have been merely an 'artifice' to get money out of the Spaniards. But it is possible that his unquiet spirit, reputedly godless for most of his life, may at last have found fulfilment in religion.

8

'Stone Walls do not a Prison Make': The Cavalier Poets

Suffolk House at Charing Cross, its four corner towers and cupolas rising high above the roofs of the lesser dwellings which huddled up to the walls of its riverside gardens, was, in January 1641, the scene of great festivities for the marriage of the Earl of Suffolk's daughter, Lady Margaret Howard, to Lord Broghill, a son of the wealthy Earl of Cork. Among the brilliant crowd which filled the hall was Sir John Suckling, a sandy-haired young man of slight build, with large, intelligent eyes, a classical nose that was red through too much high living, and a curling moustache and tuft which gave him a 'brisk and graceful look'. He was very much a man of fashion, as gorgeously dressed as any man present, for clothes were one of his weaknesses; he was a courtier, a Member of Parliament, a soldier, a wit and something of a rake. He was also, as one would have expected, a poet, but more talented than most of the courtier-poets of his time. That day at Suffolk House, the curvaceous beauty of the bride and her bashful tenderness inspired him to write verses which were to become immortal:

Her feet beneath her petticoat,
Like little mice, stole in and out,
   As if they fear'd the light:
But O she dances such a way!
No sun upon an Easter-day
   Is half so fine a sight.

Three years hence, that wedding party must have seemed like a dream. The bridegroom was fighting a grim campaign against the

Irish rebels; his brother-in-law, George Goring, was a prisoner of war in the Tower. The bride's sister, the lively Kate, Lady Aubigny, whose husband had fallen at Edgehill, was in prison for having taken part in a plot to overthrow Parliament. And the poet himself, after being implicated in an earlier plot against Parliament, had gone into exile, where he had died in poverty, by his own hand.

It is fitting that Suckling's best-known poem should tell of a celebration on the eve of a cataclysm, for there is a sense of eat-drink-and-be-merry about him, just as there is about the other Cavalier Poets. They were, more than anybody else, the Sacrificed Generation of the Civil War; though since the Cavalier Poets—as distinct from Cavaliers who happened to write poetry—were only four in number, they could hardly be called a generation, and in any case, two out of the four lived to see Charles II restored. But while they themselves may have survived, their Muse did not flourish in the changed world of Restoration England, being essentially a flowering of that court which vanished for ever when Charles I and Henrietta Maria left London in 1642.

So much does one associate the Cavalier Poets with the court that it does not seem right to include in their number the country parson Herrick and the Cambridge academics Crashaw and Cleveland, though all three of them were Royalists who suffered for their opinions. Nor should one include Thomas Carew, who though a courtier and a rake and a friend of Suckling, died in 1639 and thus did not live to see the conflict between King and Parliament. So as the true Cavalier Poets, we are left with Suckling and three others—William Davenant, Richard Lovelace and Edmund Waller. The four of them were friends and they were of an age, except for Lovelace who was ten years younger; and except for Davenant, they were men of substance. Suckling was the son of a former Secretary of State and a nephew, on his mother's side, of James I's financial wizard, Lionel Cranfield, Earl of Middlesex. Lovelace owned an estate in Kent, where his family had been gentry since the time of Edward III. Waller, who also came of an old Kentish family, had an estate in Buckinghamshire; he was richer than either Suckling or Lovelace, for as well as inheriting a large fortune from his father, he had married the daughter of a wealthy alderman.

Davenant was of humbler background, being the son of a

vintner and inn-keeper at Oxford. He came to court as page to the Duchess of Richmond and to Sir Philip Sidney's friend, Fulke Greville, Lord Brooke, and quickly made a name for himself as the 'Sweet Swan of Isis', writing plays as well as poetry and producing masques. In 1638 he succeeded Ben Jonson as Poet Laureate, thus confounding Suckling's good-natured prophecy in *A Session of the Poets* that he would be turned down for this office because his nose was eaten away by the pox:

> Will Davenant, ashamed of a foolish mischance,
> That he had got lately travelling in France,
> Modestly hoped the handsomeness of his muse
> Might any deformity about him excuse.
> And surely the company would have been content,
> If they could have found any precedent;
> But in all their records either in verse or prose,
> There was not one Laureate without a nose.

According to Aubrey and Anthony Wood, it was not France but 'lying with a handsome black girl in Axe Yard in Westminster' which occasioned this misfortune, the subject of many a cruel jest.

Women were also Suckling's downfall, but in his case it was his pocket rather than his health which suffered. He lavished his money on the reigning beauties of the day, giving sumptuous entertainments for them, at one of which his fair guests were served with silk stockings and garters as the last course of their banquet; his unsuccessful courtship of a certain lady cost him thousands of pounds. These extravagances were sometimes supported by his winnings at bowling and cards, for he loved gambling as much as he loved women; but even though he was one of the best bowlers and card-players in the country—he is said to have invented the game of cribbage, and he is also said to have cheated, by using marked cards—he lost as often as he won, so that no shopkeeper would give him so much as sixpence credit.

Lovelace did not need to squander his fortune on women, for they found his rather disdainful good looks irresistible. He made his first conquest as an Oxford undergraduate during the Royal visit to Archbishop Laud's library, when a great lady in attendance on the Queen was so struck by his beauty and charm that she used her influence to get him his Master's degree, to which he was not yet entitled; and after that, his social success was assured. Court life gave him a taste for entertaining in grand style and dressing in cloth of silver and gold, but it never made him a rake; he was altogether a more virtuous character than either Suckling or Davenant, though not quite as clever.

Waller managed to be clever and worldly as well as leading a virtuous life, but his character was not exactly heroic. There is something slightly treacherous about his thin, sensitive, intelligent face, but it is easy to believe that he was good company. He was, moreover, disarmingly frank about himself, declaring that his principle was to look first to his safety and then to his honour. He was popular at court with both sexes, but the ladies thought of him as a cosy and amusing companion rather than as a lover. His wit was more rarified than that of Suckling, whose particular talent seems to have been for repartee, so that Davenant described him as 'the bull that was baited'.

One is left with the impression that all the Cavalier Poets sang for their supper; if not literally, as in the case of the professional writer, Davenant, at any rate in order to maintain their position in the fashionable world. Their poetry was part of their stock-in-trade as courtiers, like their looks and their wit. This is where they differed from the true amateurs, the great nobles for whom poetry was simply one of the accomplishments of the Complete Man, something to which they turned their hand occasionally for their own delectation. Though Suckling, Lovelace and Waller were all gentlemen of means, they were not quite the social equals of the nobility; we know that Suckling, at any rate, had his fair share of snubs, so that he would sometimes complain that lords were 'damnably proud and arrogant', remarking on how the French, whom he knew well, 'would say that my Lord d'Angleterre looked comme un mastiff-dog'. He was beaten up over a love-affair by a bully of the Digby clan, and then scoffed at by the ladies for having wisely refrained from fighting a duel with him, knowing him to be a much better swordsman than he was.

But though their poetry was more to them than a mere diversion, the Cavalier Poets, with the exception of Davenant, were men of action and men of affairs before they were poets. They all took part in politics, Waller, like Suckling, being a Member of Parliament. Even Davenant was closely involved in the affairs of his time, and when the first Scots War broke out, he followed the call to arms. Suckling and Lovelace were also soldiers at various stages of their careers. Suckling fought under Gustavus Adolphus in Germany, and afterwards, like Lovelace and Davenant, he took part in the first campaign against the Scots, spending £12,000 of his own money on raising and equipping a troop of horse which he clothed in white doublets with scarlet breeches and coats. Lovelace thirsted for military glory more than any of the other Cavalier Poets, being addressed as Captain and painted in armour. This portrait shows him to have been clean shaven, but for a mere suggestion of a moustache. With his lofty brow and sensitive lips, he appears as the ideal of poetic chivalry; in short, as the reincarnation of Sir Philip Sidney.

Not just Lovelace, but all the Cavalier Poets lived under the spell of the hero of Zutphen. Davenant's early patron, Fulke Greville, had been his friend. Waller's 'Sacharissa', the seventeen-year-old Lady Dorothy Sidney for whom, as a young widower, he conceived a romantic but hopeless passion, was without doubt enhanced in his eyes by the fact that she was the hero's great-niece; that among the groves surrounding the grey battlemented walls of Penshurst, her ancestral home, was Sir Philip Sidney's oak. Apart from the Sidney legend, the Cavalier Poets were very much influenced by the literary giants of the Elizabethan age. Suckling and Davenant were both friends of Ben Jonson. Davenant as a child had known Shakespeare, who used to stay at his father's inn while travelling between London and Stratford; in fact, he was reputed to be Shakespeare's godson, and in his more expansive moments would claim to be his son.

To a certain extent, the Cavalier Poets followed the Elizabethan lyrical tradition; but they were also influenced by the so-called Metaphysicals, notably Donne, whom Suckling may have known personally since he was a friend of his financier uncle, Lionel Cranfield. Like the Metaphysicals, they expressed deeper feelings than the Elizabethans did, and they used more colloquial language. A leavening of everyday words and phrases makes their poetry appear to have been written casually, so that as poets they are Cavalier in both senses of the word.

This easy-going, amateur carelessness is found to the greatest degree in the works of Suckling. Lovelace and Waller are amateurish in the opposite way of taking too much trouble. But if Lovelace's poems are less spontaneous than Suckling's, they always give the impression of having been written from the heart; whereas Waller all too often seems to have forgotten his heart in his effort to achieve the 'smoothness' which, according to Aubrey, was his avowed object: a suitable ambition for one who was himself, in present-day parlance, smooth. Even the love poems which he wrote to Sacharissa seem mostly to have been written for an audience rather than for the loved one herself. One suspects that, having found that she in no way responded to his advances, and that her parents, the Earl and Countess of Leicester, though they liked him as a friend, did not regard him as a suitable match for her, he allowed his passion to cool; but kept it going as an agreeable literary exercise. Yet his love for Sacharissa inspired him to write a lyric which, in its freshness and simplicity, is very different from some of his other verse, and which has earned him a place among the great English poets:

> Go, lovely Rose,
> Tell her that wastes her time and me,
> That now she knows,
> When I resemble her to thee,
> How sweet and fair she seems to be.

In the case of Davenant, a sure professional touch takes the place of both Suckling's 'careless ease' and Waller's laboured smoothness. But although his contemporaries would have regarded him as the greatest poet of the four, he is the only one who has left no immortal verse behind him. Perhaps this is because much of his poetry was meant to be set to music and sung by people in exotic costumes, like the song written for a masque performed before the Queen in 1636, in which that fashionable and talented pair, Endymion and Olivia Porter, took part:

> The Lark now leaves his wat'ry Nest
> And climbing, shakes his dewy Wings;
> He takes this Window for the East;
> And to implore your Light, he Sings,
> Awake, awake, the Morn will never rise,
> Till she can dress her Beauty at your Eyes.

While the Cavalier Poets aped Sir Philip Sidney as the perfect
Renaissance gentleman, they did not share his attitude to love.
Whereas the Elizabethans in their love poems made women into
unapproachable goddesses, the Cavaliers treated them as flesh-
and-blood human beings who could be loved physically as well
as spiritually. In his poem about the wedding of Lady Margaret
Howard, Suckling does not omit to mention the obvious sequel:

> At length the candle's out, and now
> All that they had not done they do.
>   What that is, who can tell?

This is just an elegantly suggestive hint, but in some of his other
poems he speaks much more openly of sex, even of its most
sordid aspects, as in *The Deformed Mistress* and *Upon Thomas Carew
having the Pox*. And he treats of love with an imagery that would
have made the Arcadians gasp:

> Love is the fart
> Of every heart;
> It pains a man when 'tis kept close
> And others doth offend when 'tis let loose.

Lovelace was too chivalrous and Waller too fastidious to write of
sex with Suckling's Rabelaisian frankness, yet they both touched
on the sensual side of love. Waller dwelt on the joys of Sacharissa's
'slender waist' in *Lines on a Girdle*; Lovelace became unashamedly
erotic in *To Amarantha, That she would dishevel her hair*:

> Here we'll strip and cool our fire . . .

Amarantha is another name for Lovelace's 'Lucasta', who,
though her identity remains a mystery—it is possible that she was
called Lucy Sacheverell, but that is not certain—seems much more
like a real girl than the unattainable half-goddess Sacharissa. The
poems which Lovelace addressed to Lucasta cover the whole
spectrum of his feelings during a long love-affair; ranging from
noble sentiments in *To Lucasta, Going beyond the Seas*, and sweet
fantasies in *To Lucasta, the Rose*, to contemplation of more

mundane aspects of the beloved's life in *Lucasta, taking the Waters at Tunbridge*. In the latter poem he is as frank as Suckling, but not at all Rabelaisian; seen with the eyes of love, the grosser bodily functions are ennobled:

Ye happy floods! That now must pass
The sacred conduits of her womb . . .

If the Cavalier Poets were cavalier in their approach to the poetic conventions, they also took a cavalier attitude to life. Religion only features incidentally in their poems, though they lived in a profoundly religious age. This can be taken as a sign that they lacked the religious fervour of most of their contemporaries; though, at any rate, three of them, Suckling, Davenant and Waller, must have been able to hold their own in a theological discussion, for they used to go and stay with Falkland at Great Tew. In fact, Suckling once retired with Davenant to Bath in order to write a religious treatise; but theology for him seems to have been no more than one of the many branches of learning with which he was familiar, like cosmography and chorography. Both his and Davenant's inclinations were towards Catholicism; Davenant subsequently became a Catholic, while appearing to be ecumenical in his views.

Whatever their feelings towards other forms of Christianity, the Cavalier Poets would certainly have found the bigotry and earnestness of Puritanism not at all to their taste. This alone was enough to make them Royalists in the Civil War—even Waller, who was a first cousin of John Hampden—but there was also their love of the splendours and gaieties of the court, and of the theatre, to which the Roundheads were so unrelentingly hostile. For Lovelace, however, these reasons would have been of small consequence compared with his loyalty to the King.

Suckling's service to the Royalist cause was brief and disastrous. He became implicated in the so-called Army Plot, and when the plot was discovered he fled to Paris, where a few months later, having come to the end of his money, he committed suicide by taking poison. After his death, the Roundheads went to extraordinary lengths to blacken his memory, while the Cavaliers thought wistfully of him as a spirit from a happier age.

Davenant was also on the fringes of the Army Plot. He

attempted to flee the country, but was captured on his way to the coast and imprisoned in London. Two months later he successfully escaped and joined the Queen in Holland, from where he crossed to the north of England with military stores for the Earl of Newcastle, who appointed him Lieutenant-General of Ordnance. We do not know what sort of Lieutenant-General of Ordnance Davenant made; but in a letter which he wrote to Prince Rupert before Marston Moor he showed a certain grasp of strategy, even mentioning the importance of the coal, lead and alum mines in Durham. In the previous year, the King had knighted him near Gloucester, which can be taken as implying that he did not acquit himself too badly. After the King's defeat he went to Paris; but towards the end of 1646 the Queen sent him back to England to try and persuade the King to save his throne by taking the Covenant. The mission was not a success, and when Davenant was rash enough to speak slightingly to Charles of the Church of England, 'His Majesty was transported with so much passion and indignation that he gave him more reproachful terms, and a sharper reprehension, than he did ever towards any other man; and forbade him to presume to come again into his presence.' Poor Davenant, who had meant well, returned to Paris 'dejected and afflicted', and consoled himself by writing *Gondibert*, a romance in verse. One of the characters in this long heroic poem was said to have been based on the girl who gave him the 'terrible clap' which cost him his nose.

In 1650, Charles II appointed Davenant Governor of Maryland and he set sail, taking with him a number of weavers recruited from the French gaols, who were to be established as a colony in the New World. While in the Channel, his ship was captured by a Commonwealth man-of-war, and he was taken as a prisoner to England, to be tried for his life. Eventually, however, the proceedings against him were dropped, thanks to the intercession of Milton—for whom Davenant was himself to intercede when his life was in danger at the Restoration. It was also said that Davenant owed his life to the republican, Henry Marten, who repeated the remark of Falkland's which had saved Marten's own life ten years earlier: 'In sacrifices they always offered pure and without blemish: now ye talk of making a sacrifice of an old rotten rascal.'

Waller also narrowly escaped being executed by the Roundheads, but at the cost of betraying his friends. After the outbreak of war he returned, with the King's approval, to London where he was allowed to live unmolested, though he made no attempt to conceal his Royalist sympathies. The Parliamentary leaders even let him express his opinions quite openly in the House of Commons, feeling that this would show how tolerant they were, without in any way being a danger to them since they were so secure in their majority.

In 1643 he became involved in a plot to organize the other Royalists who were still in London into an armed force, which was to arrest various Members of Parliament including Pym, and seize the Tower and other places of strength. It was then hoped that the King's forces would be able to surprise the capital. For their authority, the plotters had the King's commission, brought to them from Oxford in a box attached to the thigh of Lady Aubigny, the sister of the bride in Suckling's wedding poem. The plot was discovered; Lady Aubigny was imprisoned; Waller faced almost certain death. He saved himself by confessing all and disclosing the names of the other conspirators, including that of his brother-in-law, Nathaniel Tomkins, who, together with one Richard Chaloner, was hanged. Waller also made an eloquent and abject speech to Parliament: 'I have already confessed enough to make me appear worthy, not only to be put out of this House, but out of the world too.'

After being imprisoned for a year, he was allowed to go into exile abroad, on paying a fine of £10,000. According to Clarendon, he also 'distributed great sums' to various influential Puritan ministers 'for their prayers and ghostly counsel', having impressed them with his penitence and tears when they visited him in prison. Whether or not this is true, one imagines that his escape was partly due to his cousin, the Roundhead general Sir William Waller, and to Cromwell, a connection of his by marriage. Certainly it was through their influence that he was allowed to return to England in 1654, to put what was left of his estate into order, and he showed his gratitude to Cromwell by writing a Panegyric on him.

One wonders if, when he was back in England, Waller did anything to help his fellow-poet, Lovelace, whose loyalty to the King had by now reduced him to extreme poverty. Though so ardent a Cavalier, Lovelace was prevented from drawing his sword on the King's behalf until the war was almost over, because he had been foolhardy enough to lead the deputation which, in 1642, presented the House of Commons with the Kentish petition for restoring the King to his rights. The Commons promptly ordered him to be thrown into the Gatehouse prison; and though he was released after a couple of months, he was unable to leave London because his friends had been obliged to put down £10,000 as surety for his good behaviour.

But while he was himself prevented from fighting for the King, he gave money to those of his brothers who were able to do so, and also helped the cause by providing arms and horses at his own expense for anybody willing to join the Royalist army. These lavish disbursements, and his generosity to 'ingenious men in want, whether scholars, musicians or soldiers', soon got him into financial difficulties, and he was obliged to sell part of his family estate in 1643. At last, towards the end of 1645, he was able to leave London and join the King at Oxford; by then it was clear that the friends who had stood bail for him would not get their money back anyhow.

During his imprisonment in the Gatehouse, Lovelace had written one of the two poems which have done most to keep alive the memory of the Cavalier Poets:

Stone Walls do not a Prison make,
    Nor Iron bars a Cage;
Minds innocent and quiet take
    That for an Hermitage;
If I have freedom in my Love,
    And in my soul am free;
Angels alone that soar above
    Enjoy such Liberty.

The other, *To Lucasta, Going to the Wars*, he wrote before setting off to join the King:

Yet this inconstancy is such,
    As you too shall adore;
I could not love thee (Dear) so much,
    Lov'd I not Honour more.

Here is Lovelace at his very best. To excel as a poet, he needed to be a 'lover militant under the banner of Lucasta', or a soldier fighting for the honour of the King; and in this poem, with a wonderful economy of words, he was able to weave these two great themes into one.

Whether the tail-end of the war afforded Lovelace any scope for the military glory he so craved is a matter of speculation, for there is no record of his career during those months. After the King's defeat, he entered the service of the King of France, and fought under the great Condé at the capture of Dunkirk, where he was severely wounded. Having recovered from his wounds, he returned to England as a colonel, and took part in the rising of the Kentish Royalists in 1648, which landed him once again in prison. By now he was in a sorry plight; he had spent everything he had, so that in the following year he was obliged to sell what was left of his estate, as well as his family portraits, to pay his debts. As though that were not enough, he had returned to England to find Lucasta married to someone else, for she had heard a false report that he had died of his wounds at Dunkirk. A poem written during this second imprisonment expresses his disillusionment and despair for the future; all he had left was his loyalty:

What then remains, but th' only spring
Of all our loves and joys, the KING.

He was released from prison in 1649 and spent the few remaining years of his life in London, in 'obscure and dirty places, more befitting the worst of beggars'. He published his *Lucasta* poems which brought him a certain renown and the friendship of the Roundhead poet, Andrew Marvell; but presumably little in the way of money, for in his last years he was ragged and lived on the charity of his friends, who would get up small collections to save him from utter want. While continuing to write, he became very melancholy and fell into a decline, dying at the early age of forty in 1658, in 'a mean lodging in Gunpowder Alley, between Shoe Lane and Fetter Lane'. Perhaps he was fortunate to have died when he did. Had he lived until after the Restoration, he would most likely have suffered the final disillusionment of being let down by the son of the King for whom he had sacrificed all; for having sold, rather than forfeited, his estate, he would not have been entitled to any compensation.

While Lovelace lay dying in his 'mean lodging' in Gunpowder Alley, Davenant was putting on highly successful stage performances in Drury Lane, only a couple of streets away. He got round the Puritans' ban on the theatre by producing his plays in *recitativo*, so that they counted as operas. After the Restoration, he opened the Duke of York's Theatre, where his productions achieved a standard of luxury and polish hitherto unknown on the English stage, with elaborate painted scenery, which he had first introduced into England in 1656. The Sweet Swan of Isis became the elderly and prosperous impresario; and when he died, aged sixty-two, in 1668, he was buried in Westminster Abbey.

Waller, though the same age as Davenant, survived him for nearly twenty years. It may have been because he drank nothing but water; though this was once nearly the death of him when somebody made him 'damnable drunk' as a joke, with the result that he had a nasty fall down the steps of Somerset House. At the Restoration, he made his peace with Charles II by presenting him with a poem *Upon His Majesty's Happy Return*: when the King remarked that it was not as good as his Panegyric on Cromwell, he replied: 'Sir, we poets never succeed so well in writing truth as fiction.' Such was his wit and his charm that he quickly lived down his shameful past and became once again a popular figure in society; and though his lyrics were no longer fashionable, he never lacked a public for his ponderous heroic couplets on national events. He remained on friendly terms with Sacharissa, now the widowed Countess of Sunderland, and would visit her often. But when she playfully asked him when he intended to write some more verses for her, as he used to do in the old days, he ungallantly replied, being in a bad humour: 'When you are as young again, Madam, and as handsome as you were then.'

9

Ormonde

The situation in Ireland during the Civil War was extremely confused. The country was torn between three or more warring factions; leaders frequently changed sides. One figure, however, stands out in his consistent and steadfast loyalty to the King, and that is James Butler, known to history as the Great Duke of Ormonde. Ormonde's loyalty was based on the feudal concept of service; he served the King just as he himself expected to be served by his own people. He was, in fact, the last of the great feudal lords, something of an anachronism even in his time. Nobles as powerful as the Earls of Ormonde had been virtually unknown in England since the Wars of the Roses; and in Ireland there had been none comparable to them since the downfall of their traditional rivals, the Geraldines, Earls of Desmond, in the reign of Elizabeth. Unlike the Desmonds, the Ormondes had always been staunch supporters of the English Crown. It was, however, his character as much as his family tradition which made Ormonde so loyal. He was upright, straightforward and conscientious, very much an officer and a gentleman; to have acted like the mighty lords of old and taken advantage of his vast territorial powers to embarrass the King would have seemed to him like not playing the game.

In appearance, Ormonde was a typical tall, fair-haired cavalry officer, vigorous and alert, of splendid physique, clean-shaven but for a slight moustache. His face—intensely aristocratic, with the sensitive, disdainful nostrils of a thoroughbred horse—was neither intellectual nor particularly clever, but intelligent, commanding and, above all, trustworthy; he looked at people straight in the eye. He had other characteristics of the officer of the old school, though many of these are also, of course, the traits of the aristocrat. He loved outdoor sports; he was meticulous in matters of dress, whether it was dressing correctly at court, or putting on a waistcoat of the right thickness for the prevailing wind when going out with his hawks or hounds. He had an orderly mind and lived according to an invariable routine: rising almost every day of his life before six, having his meals at exactly the same times. His sense of humour was simple—a mock-heroic poem about people throwing food at each other made him laugh uncontrollably—and so were his tastes: his favourite dish was a boiled leg of mutton. On the other hand, he always lived in semi-regal state, whether at his ancestral castle dominating the town of Kilkenny, or at his more homely manor house at Carrick by the reed-fringed waters of the River Suir.

As well as having simple tastes in food, Ormonde drank sparingly, apart from indulging now and then in a convivial evening with a few men friends—one might say, a regimental dinner. He was even more virtuous as regards women, his only recorded lapse being a youthful affair with the beautiful and rather too passionate Lady Isabella Rich, who bore him a son. The lapse occurred when Isabella was helping him in his courtship of his cousin, whom he wished to marry because she was heiress of half the Ormonde estates, which had passed to her branch of the family through the machinations of James I. Having married his cousin for dynastic reasons, Ormonde was strictly faithful to her, and the marriage was extremely happy.

Ormonde pursued and married his cousin during his years as a young man at court. Much of his earlier youth was also spent in England, in the household of the Archbishop of Canterbury, where he was placed by order of James I, having been declared a royal ward after losing his father in a shipwreck when he was nine years old. The Archbishop neglected his education, so that he lacked the classical learning which in those days was regarded as one of the attributes of a finished nobleman; though he was fond of books and studied Latin after he was married. The King's object in sending him to be brought up by the Archbishop was not so much to educate him as to make a Protestant of him. So successfully was this achieved that, for the rest of his life, Ormonde was as pious an Anglican as his grandfather—known to the Irish as 'Walter of the Rosary Beads'—had been a Catholic.

In spite of his Protestantism, his English upbringing and the English blood which came to him from his mother, Ormonde belonged first and foremost to Ireland, where his family, of Norman descent, had lived since the twelfth century. When in 1634 he first attended the Irish Parliament, it made him furious to hear the Lord Deputy, Strafford, speak of Ireland as 'a conquered nation'; and he was bold enough to warn Strafford never to use that slighting expression again. A couple of days later he braved the Lord Deputy's wrath for a second time; on this occasion, it was his own honour, rather than that of Ireland, which he was defending. Strafford had issued an edict forbidding noblemen to wear swords in Parliament. 'If you have my sword it shall be in your guts!' Ormonde told the official who tried to take his from him. But instead of punishing the insolent young Earl, Strafford decided to win his friendship. He knew how useful it would be to his government to have the support of the richest and most influential nobleman in Ireland; he had also been impressed by Ormonde's forceful personality, prophesying that he 'would make the greatest man of his family'.

And so, at the age of only twenty-four, Ormonde became Strafford's right-hand man, learning the art of government from him, repaying his friendship with characteristic loyalty. When Strafford was summoned to London in 1640, he left Ormonde in command of his troops; later, shortly before his trial, he urged the King to make him Lord Deputy in his place. But Charles preferred to entrust the government of Ireland to the tactless and unpopular Lords Justices, Sir John Borlase and Sir William Parsons. Within a few months came the Irish rebellion, which had a disastrous effect on the King's fortunes. Not only was Pym able to make the most of the tales of horror coming out of Ireland to recover his hold on Parliament and the public; but the need to raise an army to fight the rebels led to the controversy as to whether it should be controlled by Parliament or the King, which, more than anything else, sparked off the Civil War.

Had Ormonde been ruling Ireland at the time, it is possible that the rebellion of 1641 might never have taken place. With his knowledge and understanding of the Irish he would not have provoked them in the way that the Lords Justices did, and the Irish, for their part, would have been slower to rebel against the head of the much-revered House of Butler than against a government which they regarded as alien. At any rate, the rebellion would have been confined to the 'Old' or Celtic Irish. The

Catholics of Norman-Irish stock who subsequently joined the rebels would have remained loyal to a government headed by Ormonde, for he was one of them. The fact tht he was a Protestant mattered less than that he was a Butler, for, contrary to the popular belief, religious loyalties have never counted for so much in Ireland as ties of kindred and race.

Ormonde, however, was too much of a Protestant and an upholder of law and order to have any great sympathy for the Confederates, as the rebels came to be called, even though they included many of his own family; indeed, one of their leaders was a Catholic Butler, Lord Mountgarret. As Commander-in-Chief of the King's forces, he marched speedily against them, and in April 1642 he routed Mountgarret's army in a bloody battle at Kilrush, near the town of Kildare; a victory for which the English Parliament sent him its thanks, together with a jewel worth £500. A year later at Old Ross in County Wexford, Ormonde defeated the chief Confederate commander, General Thomas Preston, whose army was more than twice the size of his own. During this action, he showed both courage and toughness, spending the night on the ground, for he liked to share the hardships of his men.

The King acknowledged Ormonde's services by creating him a Marquess; but after the Civil War had been raging for a few months, he ordered him to negotiate with the Confederates, who had maintained from the start that they were not in rebellion against their Sovereign but only against Parliament, the Anglo-Irish Protestant settlers and the Dublin government. Charles hoped that if there could be peace in Ireland, the Confederate army as well as that of Ormonde could be brought over to England to fight for him. Ormonde was reluctant to make peace with the Confederates; had he not been so loyal, he might have continued to fight them under the banner of Parliament, which was in fact what many of the Irish Protestants eventually did. But, never wavering in his loyalty to the King, he managed to arrange a truce or 'Cessation' at the end of 1643. Soon afterwards, he sent a force of 2,600 Irish over to England in the King's service, but no sooner had they landed than they were routed by Fairfax.

When it came to negotiating a more permanent peace, Charles was torn between having to grant concessions to the Confederates and not wishing to antagonize the Irish Protestants. He entrusted

Ormonde, who was appointed Lord-Lieutenant in January 1644 and thus became the official ruler of Ireland, with the task of thrashing out a settlement acceptable to both parties. It was a daunting task. Ireland was not simply divided between the Catholic Confederates and the Protestants. There were, within the Confederate camp, the Old Irish and the Norman-Irish, the latter more amicably disposed towards Ormonde than the former. The Protestants were divided between the Presbyterian Ulster Scots, who were inclined to support Parliament and their Covenanting brethren in Scotland, and the Anglo-Irish Protestants in the south, some of whom remained loyal to the King and others, like Lord Broghill, a son of the wealthy Earl of Cork, who eventually declared for Parliament in order to be able to continue fighting the Confederates. To make matters still more complicated, there was a Scots army in Ulster under General Robert Munroe which had been sent over early in 1642 to deal with the rebellion; Ormonde was saddled with the additional problem of finding a means of keeping Munroe occupied in Ireland, to prevent him from returning with his troops to fight on the side of Parliament. Finally, there was that irresponsible courtier, the Marquess of Antrim, chief of a clan of Catholic Macdonnells with a footing on both sides of the narrow seas between Ulster and south-west Scotland, who intrigued with the King and the Confederates in the hope of supplanting Ormonde as Lord-Lieutenant.

As though Ormonde did not have enough to deal with inside Ireland, he also had to contend with interference from without. There were Parliamentary Commissioners over from England, bent on sabotaging his work. Then the King, impatient for the peace that was to bring ten thousand Irish troops to his assistance, and always ready to listen to plausible men who had his ear, sent an English Catholic, the Earl of Glamorgan, son of the Marquess of Worcester, over to Ireland to negotiate secretly with the Confederates behind Ormonde's back. Glamorgan, a many-sided genius with a claim to have invented the steam engine, but lacking in political judgement, managed to conclude his secret treaty; but before he could return to England, a copy of it fell into Ormonde's hands and he found himself a prisoner in Dublin Castle, up before the Lord-Lieutenant and Council for interrogation. The affair did no good to the King, who was seen to be guilty of duplicity, but Ormonde loyally pretended to believe that Glamorgan's commission to negotiate on Charles's behalf was not genuine.

A visitor to Ireland more difficult to dispose of than Glamorgan was Archbishop Giovanni Battista Rinuccini, who arrived at the end of 1645 as the Pope's Nuncio to the Confederates, bringing arms and money. His object was to prevent the Confederates from agreeing to any peace terms which did not restore the Irish Catholic Church to its rightful position. Any idea of a compromise such as Ormonde envisaged was therefore anathema to him, and he conceived a dislike for Ormonde personally. Ormonde wryly referred to him as 'Ireland's unbidden guest'; the Nuncio was also his own unbidden guest, having established himself in the Castle at Kilkenny, which had become the Confederate capital.

Fortunately Rinuccini was not always at Kilkenny, and during one of his absences, in March 1646, the Confederates, who were dominated by the more moderate Norman-Irish, signed a peace with Ormonde. The terms which he granted were not ungenerous and went a long way towards relieving the disabilities which the Catholics had suffered, though they fell far short of what the Nuncio expected. Ormonde was able to return home to Kilkenny, from which he had been exiled ever since the Confederates first made it their headquarters. The streets of grey stone houses leading up to the Castle were festooned in his honour; there were triumphal arches and inscriptions proclaiming his own and his ancestors' brave deeds. Ormonde's firmness and integrity during the tortuous intrigues of the past few months won him praise from an unexpected quarter. The devious George, Lord Digby, who as Secretary of State was over in Ireland for the negotiations, wrote back to his colleague, Hyde: 'The Marquess of Ormonde is not only the wisest young man, but the most steady, generous and virtuous person that I have ever known.'

The peace, however, came too late to be of service to the King, who had already lost the war; an Irish army could now do little to help him, and in any case could not be landed in England since all the ports were in the hands of Parliament. And in Ireland, the peace proved illusory. Only a fortnight after Ormonde's triumphal entry into Kilkenny, the town was threatened by an army of Old Irish from Ulster, led by Owen Roe O'Neill who was continuing the war with the Nuncio's backing; while at the same time the peace was repudiated by the Norman-

Irish General Preston. The decorations put up in honour of Ormonde were hastily taken down, and Ormonde himself retreated to Dublin. He was reluctant to leave Kilkenny, feeling that his presence there would keep the majority of Confederates from falling under the influence of the extremists; but he had no choice, if he was not going to be cut off by O'Neill's army which greatly outnumbered his own troops. Rinuccini returned to Kilkenny with a triumph even greater than Ormonde's in the previous month, and O'Neill and his Ulstermen marched on Dublin. The city was in no state to stand a siege, but Ormonde had just enough time to put the defences in order; Lady Ormonde herself carried baskets of earth to repair the fortifications, having organized a band of high-born women to help with the work.

While he thus managed to prevent an immediate attack on the city, Ormonde realized that his position was hopeless. O'Neill's army was growing in strength; he himself had his back to the sea, with no possibility of help from Roundhead England. Faced with the inevitability of surrendering Dublin to the Confederates and the Nuncio, he preferred to hand over the city to the English Parliament. He felt, as he told Digby, 'an incredible aversion . . . to shifting after this manner', but it seemed the only hope of saving the Irish Protestants from what he was certain would be a Catholic tyranny. It was also in accordance with the wishes of the King, who sent a message to Ormonde telling him that he would rather Dublin were surrendered to the English than to the Irish. Ormonde's negotiations with the Parliamentary Commissioners at first broke down because he asked for assurances that all Irish Catholics, except for the original rebels of 1641, would be allowed to keep their estates. But after holding Dublin against the Confederates for a few months longer—even though he was fortunate in that the weather was exceptionally wet, so that O'Neill's army was flooded out—he felt obliged to accept the terms offered by Parliament, unsatisfactory though they were.

At the end of July 1647, Ormonde embarked for Bristol. He had failed, and was virtually penniless, having lost most of his revenues early in the war and having spent what money he had left on the defence of Dublin. But he still had his honour and the approval of the King. On arriving in England, he made his way to Hampton Court, where Charles was now living as a prisoner, and was received by him most graciously; when he tried to surrender the Commission for the Lieutenancy, the King refused it, saying 'that either the Marquess himself, or nobody should ever use it with better success'. In order to be near his Royal master, Ormonde took lodgings at Kingston, and for the next few weeks was constantly in Charles's presence. Hitherto, he had only met the King on formal occasions, and at times during the past five years—particularly at the time of the Glamorgan episode—he must have found him exasperating to work for. But now that he got to know Charles in his misfortune, he fell entirely under his spell.

When Ormonde was frequenting Hampton Court, Cromwell and Ireton were negotiating for the King's restoration according to the terms which they had drawn up known as the Heads of Proposals. Ormonde doubted the sincerity of the army leaders, but if he influenced Charles against their terms, this was, for the time being, of no more than academic importance, since the Heads of Proposals were rejected by Parliament. He did more serious harm to the King by acting as his agent in the negotiations with the Scots, which led to the Scots invasion in the following year; but here he was merely acting as the dutiful royal servant.

By February 1648, it was no longer safe for Ormonde to remain in England, so he slipped away to France. In Paris, at the Queen's court, he found he was not the only person who had played a leading part in the affairs of Ireland. Glamorgan was there, as well as Lady Glamorgan who blamed Ormonde for her husband's misfortunes and cut him. Ormonde, who before his marriage had been one of her suitors, got his own back by saying, for all the assembled company to hear: 'Really, Madam, this would have troubled me eighteen years ago.' More important than the Glamorgans were the representatives of the Confederates, who were now begging the Queen for arms and money to help them in their struggle against the Roundheads. Since Ormonde's departure from Ireland, the situation there had changed. The Norman-Irish Confederates had finally broken with Owen Roe O'Neill and the Nuncio was largely discredited. The Roundheads and their Anglo-Irish Protestant allies were waging war fiercely and efficiently against the Catholics; Preston's army had been cut to pieces with the slaughter of five thousand Irishmen.

The Irish now longed for Ormonde's return, and the Queen commissioned him to go back to Ireland and resume charge of affairs there. He left Paris in August 1648 and, after being ship-wrecked on the way, landed at Cork where he was welcomed by Lord Inchiquin, the Protestant chieftain of the O'Briens, who had been fighting on the side of Parliament—so ferociously as to earn for himself the nickname of Morrogh of the Burnings—but who had now come over to the King, together with his largely Anglo-Irish and Protestant army.

Once again, Ormonde went home to Kilkenny, his reception being even more enthusiastic than on the previous occasion. Here he concluded what is known as the Second Ormonde Peace with the Confederates. Soon afterwards, he heard the welcome news that Rinuccini had taken ship at Galway and left Ireland for good. Then came the news of the execution of the King, which left Ormonde even more horror-struck than most of the Cavaliers.

With the proclamation of Charles II, Ireland became the rallying-ground of the young King's supporters. Large numbers of English Cavaliers flocked to Ormonde's army. Ormonde made a rapid march into the country north of Dublin with eighteen thousand men and captured the important towns of Drogheda and Dundalk which had been held by the Roundheads; he then besieged the Roundhead garrison of Dublin, establishing his camp at Rathmines, to the south of the city. By now, in the words of the regicide, Edmund Ludlow, 'nine parts out of ten of Ireland held for the King'. Even Owen Roe O'Neill and his Ulstermen showed signs of coming over to Ormonde.

But Ormonde's army was, in his own words, 'meanly pro-vided', whereas the Roundheads in Dublin were able to receive supplies from England. And now Cromwell was on his way. Ormonde tried to reduce Dublin before he arrived, but did not attack until the garrison had been reinforced by an advance contingent of English troops. Then he made the mistake of sending part of his army south, in the belief that Cromwell would approach from that direction. An attempt to fortify a ruined tower close to the city was mishandled; the garrison was roused and sallied out sooner than expected, taking the Royalists by surprise. In the ensuing battle, Ormonde suffered a crushing defeat and lost his reputation as a soldier; though he was fighting against fearful odds, for while he outnumbered the Roundheads, they were far better equipped than he was, and though he himself fought bravely, leading several charges and only escaping death thanks to the excellence of his armour.

The defeat at Rathmines was followed by the loss of Drogheda, which Cromwell took by storm, massacring the garrison and the inhabitants. Ormonde had been assured by the commander of the ill-fated garrison, which included some of his best English troops, that the town could hold out indefinitely, so he had remained too far away to be of any assistance. After Drogheda, Ormonde was powerless to stem the tide of the Cromwellian advance, though he soldiered on valiantly; a year later, after Cromwell had himself returned to England, leaving Ireton to finish the campaign, he still held out beyond the Shannon, in County Clare. Then came the news that Charles II, in order to appease the Scots, had taken the Covenant, repudiated the Second Ormonde Peace, and pledged himself to abolish Catholicism in his realms. This discredited Ormonde with the Irish Catholics; he had already been deserted in favour of Cromwell by most of the Protestants, so that he felt, as he put it, 'shut out everywhere . . . like a straggling freebooter'. His only consolation was that the King, having let him down, wrote to say that he had the highest regard for him and did not wish him to expose himself to the hazards of Ireland any longer than was necessary. The Duke of York sent a frigate to fetch him away; on a December night in 1650, Ormonde sailed out of the shelter of the Clare coast and into the mountainous seas of a midwinter Atlantic gale. He left an Ireland that was a desert after the long years of war, and was now suffering a fearful visitation of the plague.

From then until the Restoration, Ormonde spent most of his time in attendance on Charles II. Like most of the exiled Cavaliers, he was in dire poverty; in Paris, he and Hyde, who became his close friend, lived *en pension* with 'a poor English woman' at a pistole a week each for their food. Lady Ormonde returned to England to try and recover part of the family estates which had been her own inheritance; but though Cromwell treated her with courtesy and consideration and she was eventually given an income of £2,000 a year, she was not allowed to send any of it to her husband. Ormonde's noble altruism with regard to money did not help: 'in matters of interest you are so very a goose,' Digby once told him good-naturedly.

During those years of exile, Ormonde performed many useful services for the King, who relied on him as much as on Hyde. He negotiated with European princes; he fetched away the King's young brother, the Duke of Gloucester, from the Queen who was trying to make him into a Catholic—pawning his Garter to pay the expenses of the journey. He escorted the Princess Royal to Cologne, where he achieved his celebrated feat of swimming the Rhine.

According to Clarendon, Ormonde was at one with him in urging a policy of what might be called 'masterly inactivity' on the King. On the other hand, he was involved in plots to assassinate Cromwell, and expressed his willingness to go to England at any time in support of a Royalist coup; or as he put it, 'to try for a hanging, whenever the King pleased'. Early in 1658 the English Royalists seemed about to rise, and it was necessary to have someone of authority on the spot to direct them. Ormonde volunteered for this dangerous mission and the King, reluctantly, allowed him to go.

He crossed over to a little harbour near Colchester, and in the guise of a pedlar—he is said to have used the same disguise as a young man, when courting his future wife—made his way to London, where he stayed for six weeks, contacting various Royalists who gave him to understand that the time was not yet ripe for a rising. During those weeks, he moved from one lodging to another, and had several narrow escapes; in order to improve his disguise, he attempted to dye his fair hair black, but the dye, which was made up for him by a well-meaning friend, contained too much aquafortis, so that it turned his hair a variety of colours and scorched his pate. In fact, he could all too easily be recognized, and the authorities knew that he was in London; but either out of regard for him or gratitude for his and Lady Ormonde's many acts of kindness to the Irish Protestants, Cromwell warned him that his whereabouts were known.

Ormonde took Cromwell's hint and returned to the Continent. He did not set foot again in England until two years later, when he stepped ashore at Dover behind the newly-restored Charles II. The Restoration brought Ormonde a greater degree of prosperity than it did to any other leading Cavalier. Not only did he recover all his lands, but he was given large grants to reimburse him for his losses during the war; though it is said that even after being so handsomely compensated, he was out of pocket to the tune of a million sterling. Honours were heaped on him as well as riches; he was made a Duke, a Privy Councillor, Lord Steward of the Household. Last but not least, the King presented him with a magnificent service of gold plate.

When he returned to Ireland as Lord-Lieutenant in 1662, he was given as tumultuous a welcome as England had given the King on his Restoration. Bells rang, bands played, wine flowed in the streets of Dublin; there were bonfires, cheering crowds and adulatory poems in Irish:

> To this country his coming is sevenfold better
> As protection from ignorant tyrants
> Than Conn of the hundred fights . . .

Certainly, of all the men who might have ruled Ireland on behalf of Charles II, none could have protected the Irish 'from ignorant tyrants' better than Ormonde. He protected Irish trade by doing his utmost to resist the discriminatory legislation of the English Parliament. He protected the Irish Catholics, and the Presbyterians of Ulster, against the Act of Uniformity—which, as in England, made Anglicanism the only officially recognized form of religion in the country—by seeing to it that the recusancy laws were not enforced. More than that, he could not do, for Protestant opinion, in England as well as in Ireland, would never have allowed the laws to be repealed altogether. In the same way, Ormonde went as far as he could to make the Restoration land settlement less unfair than it might otherwise have been. To have forced all the 'Cromwellian settlers' to give up the Irish land which they had been granted during the Commonwealth and Protectorate would have rendered Charles II too unpopular, but Ormonde persuaded them to relinquish part of their original grant, so that at any rate some of the dispossessed Irish could recover their estates.

Ormonde's achievement as Viceroy was not only to rebuild a country utterly devastated by civil war, but to make it more prosperous than it was at any other time in the seventeenth century; British government in Ireland was probably never so successful as under his rule. Nor was it ever so magnificent. He had a retinue of twenty gentlemen; he travelled in Vice-regal splendour with half-a-dozen coaches-and-six, escorted by forty mounted servants as well as his horse guards in their uniforms of grey, faced with scarlet and silver.

In the years immediately following the Restoration, Ormonde was, next to Clarendon, the most powerful man in the King's dominions. But unlike Clarendon, he did not let prosperity turn his head; he kept his natural modesty and simplicity, always treating his inferiors with the utmost consideration. 'He never let any man wait, lose his time, and dance attendance for an audience, and no one ever came uneasy to his presence, so assured were all beforehand of an obliging reception.' Inevitably, though, his great position aroused envy. In particular, he incurred the enmity of a powerful clique led by the Duke of Buckingham and his cousin, the King's mistress, Barbara Villiers. In 1669 this faction prevailed on the King to dismiss Ormonde from being Viceroy, and for the next eight years he was in the wilderness, cold-shouldered by the court and even by Charles himself. But all through those years he never showed the least sign of disloyalty or bitterness towards his Royal master. 'He will be loyal in spite of my teeth,' said Charles, as he watched Ormonde walk in lonely dignity along the gallery at Whitehall, his Lord Steward's staff in his hand. Such loyalty was not wasted on the King. In 1677, Ormonde suddenly found himself back in favour, and appointed Lord-Lieutenant of Ireland once again.

He held the office until 1685, three years before his death at the age of seventy-eight. Having known an Ireland that was still in the Middle Ages, he lived to be the ruler of a country that could in many ways be recognized as the Ireland of today. Thus, we hear of him going racing at the Curragh; he laid out Phoenix Park; he built the Royal Hospital at Kilmainham, which most people would regard as one of the monuments of Georgian Dublin, though it anticipated the Georges by more than thirty years. Nowhere was this change from the medieval to the modern more striking than at Ormonde's own ancestral castle of Kilkenny, which he transformed into something rather like the schloss or château of a contemporary European princeling, with high-pitched roofs and cupolas on the old round towers and terraced gardens instead of outworks.

Before he died, Ormonde suffered great personal sorrow. He lost his wife, and also his beloved eldest son, 'The Gallant

Osssry'. But by dying in the summer of 1688, he did not live to see the overthrow of James II later that year, which, as the last of the Cavaliers, he would have regarded as the greatest sorrow of all.

10

The Ladies

One of several instances where the Cavaliers were in advance of the Roundheads was in their attitude towards women. Puritanism taught that women should be submissive, a view which, in the middle of the seventeenth century, was almost universally accepted. But at court and among the smarter aristocracy, women were more emancipated than in the rest of society, so that it is not surprising that the heroines of the Civil War were mostly, if not all, on the Royalist side. Certainly, at the top level, there was no Roundhead equivalent of Queen Henrietta Maria. The Roundheads felt the same about women in high places as did John Knox when he blew his metaphorical trumpet blast against the Monstrous Regiment; they regarded the Queen as an evil influence not just because she was a Catholic and a foreigner, but also because she was a woman.

Whatever one may feel about Henrietta Maria's influence on Royalist policy, one cannot but admire her for the energetic and courageous way in which she worked for her husband's cause during the Civil War. The pleasure-loving little Queen, who had looked like an exquisite doll as she danced in the masques and revels of Whitehall, had in her nature a fibre of steel which bore her up throughout the troubles and anxieties of those years. Having gone to Holland in February 1642, she set about raising money with which to buy arms and ammunition for the King, by selling or pawning the jewels which she had brought with her. It was a particular wrench for her to have to part with her 'little chain' and with Charles's pearl buttons. 'You cannot imagine how handsome the buttons were,' she told the King wistfully, 'when they were taken out of the gold and strung into a chain.'

By the summer of 1642 she had raised enough to buy arms

and ammunition for four thousand men. She sent some of these munitions over to the King, but only a small part of them actually reached him, for the ships carrying them were mostly intercepted by the English navy, which was on the side of Parliament. As well as the difficulties and frustrations of her task, the Queen suffered the anguish of being parted from her husband and her children, often without hearing from them for weeks and with all kinds of disturbing rumours coming out of England. The letters she wrote to Charles during her year in Holland are mostly matter-of-fact—having addressed him as 'My dear heart', she gets down to business—but every now and then she blurts out her true feelings: 'If I do not turn mad, I shall be a great miracle; but, provided it be in your service, I shall be content—only if it be when I am with you, for I can no longer live as I am without you.'

By the end of the year, the situation in the north of England had improved sufficiently for it to be safe for her to cross to Newcastle, the only major port on the east coast which remained in Royalist hands. Early in February 1643, she set sail with a fleet of eleven warships, which carried some soldiers and what was left of her munitions, as well as herself and her retinue of two hundred. No sooner had they put to sea than they ran into the worst storm in living memory. For nine days the ships were tossed and buffeted; two of them foundered. During those days, the Queen lay lashed to her cot, surrounded by her ladies, who were likewise tied down, in a cabin that was crowded with officers, chaplains and friars. Everyone was convinced that the next moment would be their last; the Catholics were in such a hurry to confess themselves that they forgot to lower their voices, shouting their sins for all to hear. Having made up her mind that she was going to die, the Queen recovered her spirits enough to be able to laugh at the thought of these embarrassing revelations; she was also able to eat and drink. But it must have been extremely unpleasant for her to be tied to her cot for so long. When at last the ship managed to put back into a Dutch port and she went ashore, her clothes were in such a state that the stench was unbearable.

By the time the Queen and her companions were ready to face the sea once again, two Parliamentary warships were lying in wait off the Dutch coast. They threatened to sink her ammunition ship if it showed itself outside the harbour, so there was a further delay. Then the Dutch authorities refused to let the ship sail because it had no licence. Having dealt with this piece of bureaucracy, the Queen determined to run the gauntlet of the Parliamentary vessels, and though her ammunition ship was fired at, it escaped being hit. This time, the sea was calm, but when the Queen's ships were a few hours from Newcastle the wind changed, blowing them south, so they put into Bridlington Bay, between Scarborough and Hull, and anchored off a small fishing village. Here the Queen landed, and spent her first couple of nights ashore in a cottage on the waterfront. She was awakened at dawn on the third day by the boom of cannon and the whistling of cannon-balls. Four Parliamentary ships were now in the bay and bombarding the village; one of them was actually aiming at her cottage, the captain having landed and found out where she was lodging. Throwing on a dress, she hurried barefoot to the shelter of a high bank some distance from the village, accompanied only by the other women of the party, for the men stayed behind to defend the munitions. As she dashed along the village street, the cannon-balls singing around her, a sergeant was killed only twenty yards away. Then, half way along the street, she insisted on going back to rescue her dog, an 'ugly bitch' called Mitte, who slept in her bed and had somehow been forgotten. Having at last reached the shelter of the bank, the Queen and her companions crouched beneath it for two hours, while the cannon-balls passed over their heads or struck the ground near them, spattering them with mud. At last, the falling tide obliged the enemy ships to retire, and the barrage ceased.

The Earl of Newcastle came with his army to escort the Queen to York, where she held court for the next three months. As the weeks passed, she came to regard the Yorkshire campaign as her own special war, and was reluctant to go south to join the King until the Royalists had captured Leeds. She immersed herself in strategy and parted with most of her munitions to Newcastle; though she managed to send a much-needed supply of gunpowder to the King at Oxford, taking advantage of a truce which she obtained by pretending to respond favourably to a Parliamentary peace move. And when, at the beginning of June, she finally did set out to join her husband, she was able to take him not only munitions but a small well-equipped army: three thousand foot, two thousand cavalry and six cannon. This force was under the command of her favourite courtier, Harry Jermyn, but Henrietta Maria herself was, in her own words, 'She-Majesty Generalissima over all'.

She was in high spirits as she rode southwards at the head of her troops. She spurned her coach, preferring to be on horseback; *sans nulle délicatesse de femme*', as a lady of the French court remarked. She lived with her officers, eating with them in the open air with none of the ceremony due to her as Queen, treating them all as brothers. 'Very diligent am I, with one hundred and fifty waggons of baggage to govern, in case of battle,' she told Charles when writing to him from Newark.

On 13 July, the Queen was reunited with the King and her two elder sons, who rode out from Oxford to meet her. During the months which she spent with the King at Oxford, she continued to take a close personal interest in the conduct of the war, but she was prevented from further active service by her pregnancy in the following year, and the grave illness which accompanied it. Oxford was thought to be too near the front line for her confinement, so having said goodbye to her husband for what proved to be the last time, she set out on a long and painful journey to Exeter, where her child, her youngest daughter, Minette, was born. The birth of her child did nothing to alleviate her sufferings; in fact, her illness grew worse, with a form of paralysis as well as agonizing pain, and she was not expected to live. When, to add to her troubles, Exeter was threatened by a Roundhead army under the Earl of Essex, she decided to escape to France, where she knew she would get a warm welcome from her sister-in-law, the Queen Regent Anne of Austria, who had sent her a *sage-femme* and a handsome sum of money—which she promptly sent on to Charles. In her last letter to the King before sailing from Falmouth, she wrote: 'If I die, believe that you will lose a person who has never been other than entirely yours.'

Even when Henrietta Maria was aboard ship and out of the harbour, her troubles were not yet over. There were Parliamentary men-of-war in the offing, which opened fire; though not so much in order to do damage as to keep her fleet at a safe distance. Fearing that she was about to fall into the hands of the

Roundheads, the Queen, who had taken shelter in the hold of the vessel, summoned the Captain and ordered him to set fire to the magazine if there appeared to be no chance of escape. At this her ladies and servants broke into piteous cries; but she sat awaiting her end in stoic silence. Then, realizing that it would not be a very Christian end, she repented of her decision, but continued to hesitate between her pride and her conscience until her ship was safely at anchor off the Breton coast.

After a few months in France she recovered her health, and for the next sixteen years she held court in Paris to the exiled British Royalists, working indefatigably for her husband's and her son's cause. She returned to England after the Restoration, but spent much of the time that was left to her on long visits to France, where she died in 1669, owing to the carelessness of her doctor, who allowed her to take too large a sleeping-draught. Her death inspired a couplet in French about the way in which her father, her husband and herself had met their end:

Tous les trois sont tués par assassin:
Ravaillac, Cromwell et médecin.

Not long before the Queen set out on her march from York, a Parliamentary force appeared before the towering, silvery-grey walls of Wardour Castle, which stood in Arcadian surroundings on the borders of Wiltshire and Dorset; a castle built towards the end of the Middle Ages for chivalry rather than for war, and given Renaissance touches in the reign of Elizabeth I. The owner of the castle, the Catholic nobleman, Lord Arundell of Wardour, was away fighting for the King; but his wife Blanche was at home, together with his daughter-in-law and three grandchildren. When the Roundhead commander, Sir Edward Hungerford, summoned the castle to surrender, he was told that 'Lady Arundell had a command from her Lord to keep it, which order she would obey'.

To defend her home against thirteen hundred Roundheads, Lady Arundell had a household of about fifty, of whom only half were fighting men. She was no longer young; a posthumous portrait shows her to have been a woman of somewhat frail elegance. Yet there is a look of determination in her delicate, aristocratic face. The blood of the Plantagenets flowed in her veins; she was a sister of the Marquess of Worcester, one of the greatest of the Catholic nobility and a staunch Cavalier.

The Roundheads brought their cannon close to the walls and bombarded the castle for six days and six nights. During that period, the defenders kept up a continuous musket fire, which meant that they had to be either shooting or watching the whole time. After a mine had been sprung in a vault beneath the outbuildings, shaking the castle to its foundations, Hungerford offered quarter to the women, though not to the men. But Lady Arundell and her daughter-in-law, 'both infinitely scorning to sacrifice the lives of their friends and servants' to save their own, declared that they would sooner die with them. By the sixth day, however, the defenders were worn out for want of sleep. They were so tired that they would let food fall out of their hands instead of putting it into their mouths. And having got to the point where they could no longer remember whether they had put the bullet or the powder in first when loading their muskets, it became necessary for the maidservants to load their weapons for them.

When the Roundheads prepared to let off a much larger mine, which would have endangered the whole fabric of the castle, Lady Arundell realized the hopelessness of her position, and surrendered on terms. Quarter was to be given to the men as well as to the women; she and her family and six servants were to be afforded safe conduct to wherever they chose to go; and the castle and its contents were to be preserved. Though the Roundheads stood by their promise of quarter, they failed to observe the other terms. While Lady Arundell and her daughter-in-law were still in the castle, the rooms were invaded by frenzied Puritan soldiers, who tore up the valuable collection of pictures, and with pole-axes smashed the carvings on a magnificent chimneypiece valued at £2,000. And instead of being allowed to go where they wished, the ladies were taken as prisoners to Shaftesbury, where they were regaled with the sight of cartloads of plundered furniture and tapestries from Wardour trundling through the town.

At the same time as Lady Arundell was being besieged, another lady was defending her castle against the Roundheads only a few miles away to the south. She was Mary, Lady Bankes, wife of an eminent lawyer, Sir John Bankes, Chief Justice of the Common Pleas. Unlike Lady Arundell, she seems, from her portrait, to have been a woman of powerful build, with a prominent nose and a small and very determined mouth. She also differed from Lady Arundell in being a Protestant; indeed, her husband inclined towards Puritanism, though this in no way affected his loyalty to the King.

Lady Bankes's castle, Corfe, was no Arcadian castle like Wardour, but a grim Norman fortress with a bloodstained history crowning a hilltop in the middle of the so-called Isle of Purbeck, that eastern protuberance of the Dorset coast which encloses Poole Harbour. From the days when it had been used by medieval kings as a palace and a prison, it was renowned as one of the most impregnable strongholds in the kingdom; and while it no longer served any military purpose, having been sold by Queen Elizabeth I and eventually bought by Sir John Bankes, it was still a place of great strategic importance. As such—and also because Bankes had incurred the particular displeasure of Parliament, having formerly been in its good books—it was a natural target for the Dorset Roundheads, who, under the leadership of Sir Walter Erle and Sir Thomas Trenchard, were very active during the early summer of 1643, capturing Poole, Wareham and other towns in the neighbourhood.

Knowing that Lady Bankes was alone at home with her children, her husband being away at Salisbury Assizes, Erle and his troops planned to surprise the castle when the tenants and menservants were taking part in the annual May Day staghunt. Someone, however, got wind of their plan; the hunt was called off, and when the Parliamentary troops arrived at Corfe they found the gates shut against them. The troops withdrew, and their leaders now pretended to have no hostile intentions; but they asked Lady Bankes to give up her 'four small pieces' of cannon. Lady Bankes begged to be allowed to keep them, and it was agreed that she could, on condition she took them off their carriages. A few days later, however, a party of forty seamen arrived from Poole to remove the cannon by force. Although Lady Bankes only had five men and her maidservants with her in the castle, she put the sailors to flight by having one of her guns remounted and fired.

Lady Bankes now summoned her tenants and friends to her

defence, by beat of drum. The Roundheads retaliated by threatening to burn the houses of anyone who responded to her call, so out of humanity she had to dispense with all outside help, relying on her household alone. Her enemies also kept a strict watch on the castle, to prevent messengers from going in and out; while tradesmen at local markets were browbeaten into refusing to supply her with provisions. Faced with starvation, Lady Bankes agreed to hand over her cannon provided she was left in peace. The Roundheads, confident that they could now take the castle whenever they wished, relaxed their vigilance. This was Lady Bankes's opportunity, and she hastened to get in provisions and gunpowder, as well as sending an appeal for help to Prince Maurice and the Marquess of Hertford who were advancing from the direction of Blandford with a Royalist army. The Royalists sent her a detachment of eighty men under Captain Lawrence, which was not enough to deter the Roundheads, who, soon after Lawrence's arrival, laid siege to the castle with a force of five or six hundred.

Though superior in numbers, the Roundheads fell far short of Lady Bankes's little garrison in courage. Some of their soldiers were felons from the gaols, others were undisciplined yokels. The defenders were much amused to hear a party of Roundheads calling 'Shoot, Anthony!' to a comrade who was sheltering in a house, and who despite this encouragement did not dare go near the window: 'Shoot, Anthony!' became the taunt with which they would greet the enemy. When the Roundheads brought up two miniature Trojan Horses, one of them was abandoned by its crew as it came under fire. Sir Walter Erle himself was not exactly heroic: having been shot through the coat, without being hurt, he put on a bear's skin and crept away on all fours until he was out of danger.

Six weeks passed and still the castle held out, though it was bombarded from all sides and there were attempts to bribe Lady Bankes's servants and Lawrence's men to open the gates. Finally, having been reinforced with a hundred and fifty sailors, Erle attempted to take the castle by storm. His offer of £20 to the first man who scaled the walls brought no response; but after he had made his troops drunk, they attacked furiously in two places at once. In one place, they were driven off by Lawrence and his men; in the other, by Lady Bankes, her daughters, her

women and five soldiers. With their own hands, the ladies
heaved stones and red-hot embers over the battlements which
prevented the assailants from climbing the scaling-ladders. Then
came news that the Royalist army was approaching, and the
Roundheads fled. They had lost a hundred men killed and
wounded; the defenders, only two.

In the early months of 1646, Lady Bankes, who was now a
widow, stood a second siege which lasted as long as the first.
In the end, she was obliged to surrender owing to the treachery
of one of her officers. After she had left the castle, it was, by
Cromwell's orders, blown up.

The most famous of the ladies who defended castles during the
Civil War, Charlotte de la Tremouille, Countess of Derby, was
a Junoesque figure like Lady Bankes. In one of her portraits
she appears as a bounteous Britannia, wearing a helmet and
holding a spear, though there is something unmistakably French
about her plump and placid face and humorous eyes. It is,
however, the face of a comfortable *bourgeoise* rather than of the
daughter of a Duke and Peer of France, who on her mother's
side had Bourbon blood and was the grand-daughter of William
the Silent. Like her cousin Prince Rupert, she came from the
rarefied world of the Calvinist royalty and high nobility of
Europe; but though a Calvinist, she had no love for the Puritans
who, by May 1643, were in control of most of her husband's
county of Lancashire. She regarded them not just as rebels
against the King, but as rebels against her husband's family,
who, in Lancashire, occupied the position of local royalty:
'God save the Earl of Derby and the King!' was the loyal Lan-
castrian's toast. And indeed, the Lancashire Roundheads were
revolting against Lord Derby's domination even more than
against Charles I's Prerogative rule; for had not the somewhat
high-handed Earl made himself unpopular with certain sections
of the community, they would never have gained the support
they did in a county predominantly Catholic and Royalist.

In May 1643, while her husband was campaigning ineffectually
on the borders of the county, Lady Derby was summoned to
surrender the principal family seat, Lathom House, a few miles
north-west of the strongly Puritan town of Manchester. Lathom

was not so much a castle as a fortified palace, dating from the reign of Henry VII who is said to have modelled his own palace of Richmond on it. A battlemented quadrangle with seven towers and numerous turrets, enclosing a rabbit-warren of buildings in half-timber, was itself surrounded by a walled enclosure with yet more towers, outside which was a moat, for the house stood in a marshy hollow, closely hemmed in by steep wooded hills. It was thus in a situation of great military strength: difficult to storm because of the moat, and no less difficult to bombard, since guns could not be trained on it except at such close quarters as to be under fire from the house itself. To defend her secluded fastness, Lady Derby had a small garrison, under the command of a Scottish professional soldier, in addition to her army of retainers. One is not surprised, therefore, that having replied to the Roundheads' summons with an indignant refusal, she was left unmolested at Lathom for the next few months, particularly as she agreed to hand over the revenues of the Derby estates.

During those months, she was virtually a prisoner within her own walls; but she was nevertheless able to lay in supplies for a siege, and to raise men from the surrounding country, so that her garrison eventually numbered over three hundred. Having lost her revenues, it was difficult for her to pay for her stores; the Roundheads accused her of seizing them by force, or, worse, of obtaining money by sending her soldiers to kidnap local Parliamentarians and holding them to ransom. According to a Royalist account, she never obtained anything by violence, but either paid for it out of such money as she had, or was given it by her friends. The same writer tells us that, far from encouraging her soldiers to acts of terrorism, she restrained them, so as not to provoke the enemy. One can believe this, for otherwise she would not have been left undisturbed for as long as she was.

In February 1644, the local Roundheads decided that it was high time to put an end to this nest of Cavaliers in their midst. Lady Derby was denounced from the pulpit, one Puritan minister proving her to be the Scarlet Whore of Babylon, another comparing the seven towers of Lathom to the Seven Hills of Rome, regardless of her Calvinism; though this may have been in allusion to the many Catholic refugees who found shelter in the house. Lathom was surrounded by a Roundhead force of between two and three thousand. Before the house was attacked, however, there were attempts to shift Lady Derby by peaceful persuasion. Various terms were offered to her; the Roundhead general, Sir Thomas Fairfax, who was then in Lancashire, invited her to come and meet him for talks. She replied that it would be 'more knightly that Sir Thomas Fairfax should wait upon her, than she upon him'. Fairfax came to see her, and in order to ensure that the house would not be surprised during his visit, as well as to impress him with her strength, she lined her soldiers up on either side of the courtyard, from the entrance gate to the door of the Great Hall, with others manning the walls and towers. The meeting achieved nothing, except that Fairfax came away feeling that it would be 'ignoble and unmanly to assault a lady of her high birth and quality in her own house'. So he advised the local Roundhead commander, Colonel Alexander Rigby, not to storm the house but to besiege it, in the hope that she would eventually surrender.

Rigby, a virulent Puritan and a bitter enemy of the Derby family, followed Fairfax's advice; though not so much out of chivalry as for the reason that he had heard from one of his officers, who had spoken to Lady Derby's chaplain during Fairfax's visit, that her supplies would not last for more than two weeks. He only realized that the chaplain had fooled him when, at the end of two weeks, he summoned Lady Derby and found her as defiant as ever, having in fact enough supplies for a siege of several months.

The first shot was fired against the house on 12 March. The defenders were ready for it, Lady Derby having organized them into an efficient force, appointing six gentlemen who were with her as captains under the Scottish veteran, who became her major; she herself was very much the commander of the garrison, and took all the important decisions. The gamekeepers and fowlers, who were known to be the best marksmen, stood on top of the towers and 'shrewdly galled the enemy'. Only a day after the firing commenced, the defenders made a most successful sally, killing thirty and taking some prisoners at no loss to themselves; following it up with other sallies, while the enemy slowly constructed their earthworks. It was three weeks before they were able to start cannonading, and because of the lie of the land their shots went too high to do much damage.

Then the Roundheads opened fire with a new and terrible weapon which had been brought specially from London, a huge 'mortar piece' which rained 'grenadoes' or bombs and eighty-pound boulders on to the house. This, unlike the cannon, really did menace the lives of the defenders. One bomb exploded close to the room where Lady Derby, her two young daughters and her officers were at dinner; another fell into the courtyard and blew down some of the frail half-timbered buildings. A boulder fell through the window of Lady Derby's bedroom. The mortar was also capable of hurling fireballs, so that a fire-fighting party with wet hides had always to be in readiness. But though bombs and boulders were liable to come crashing through the roof at all hours of the day and night, the routine of the household went on as usual. Four times a day Lady Derby, attended by 'the two little Ladies'—who were as calm as their mother in the face of danger—joined the soldiers and retainers for prayers.

At the end of April, Rigby resolved to intensify his bombing and to use fireballs. Before doing so, he sent Lady Derby a note, ordering her for the last time to yield up the house. Lady Derby received Rigby's messenger in the presence of her soldiers, and having read his note, she tore it up contemptuously. 'Tell that insolent rebel', she said, in a voice for all to hear, 'that he shall neither have persons, goods, nor house; when our strength and provision is spent, we shall find a fire more merciful than Rigby, and then if the providence of God prevent it not, my goods and house shall burn in his sight; myself, children and soldiers, rather than fall into his hands, will seal our loyalty in the same flame.' At this, her soldiers burst into thunderous applause, and cried out with one voice: 'We'll die for His Majesty and Your Honour. God save the King!'

These were brave words, and as soon as the messenger had departed, Lady Derby and her officers planned to follow them up with an even more daring action: nothing less than the capture of the 'mortar piece' which was making their life so unpleasant. Next morning at dawn the soldiers sallied out, and with much slaughter drove the enemy away from the earthworks where the mortar was planted. Then a party of Lady Derby's servants, led by her faithful steward and cheered on by Lady Derby herself, who had come outside the gate to encourage her men, levelled the ditch and with ropes lifted the formidable piece of ordnance on to a trolley which they had brought with them. In triumph they dragged the hated mortar back into the house, where everybody shouted and rejoiced to see the weapon 'which had frighted them from their meat and sleep', lying harmlessly among them 'like a dead lion'.

Deprived of his mortar, Rigby could do little else but starve the garrison out. Lady Derby had provisions for another two months, but her powder was running low; everything depended on how soon Prince Rupert would come to her relief. Lord Derby was now with Rupert's army, and to encourage the soldiers to march quicker, he distributed £3,000 among them, having raised the money on his wife's jewels which she had smuggled out of Lathom during a sally. On 27 May, hearing that Rupert was approaching, Rigby and his troops fled. The siege was over; it had lasted three months, and during that time, only six of the defenders had been killed.

After inflicting a fearful punishment on the besiegers at Bolton, where they had taken refuge, Rupert presented their colours to Lady Derby, who hung them up as trophies in her hall. They were not there for long. Marston Moor spelt the ruin of the Royalist cause in Lancashire; Lathom was again besieged, captured and then razed to the ground. Lord and Lady Derby did not witness the destruction of their home, having retired before the second siege to the Isle of Man, where he had sovereign rights. After her husband's execution in 1651, Lady Derby continued to rule his island kingdom until she was betrayed by her deputy. She and her children then suffered imprisonment, followed by extreme poverty; and while her circumstances naturally improved with the Restoration, she was still poor compared with what she had been before the Civil War. From then until her death in 1663, she lived very quietly, a figure far removed from the world of the Restoration court, though as a young woman she had shone brightly at the court of Henrietta Maria. In her old-fashioned widow's weeds, she looked like a Mother Superior; a little severe and sombre, but still with a twinkle in her eye.

11

Montrose

Early seventeenth-century Scotland was wild and dour, a country of unruly lairds and fanatical ministers. Yet it produced James Graham, Earl and Marquis of Montrose, who of all the leading Cavaliers came closest to the Renaissance ideal of the Complete Man: the gentleman who is at once a soldier, a scholar and a poet, a gay gallant and a pattern of Christian chivalry. As a soldier, Montrose carried all before him in a manner reminiscent of his special hero, Alexander the Great. As a poet, he won a place among the immortals with the lines that were his own *leitmotiv*:

He either fears his fate too much,
　Or his deserts are small,
That dares not put it to the touch,
　To win or lose it all.

He was a fine horseman and excelled in every sport; he loved the classics and was sensitive to beauty; he was chivalrous and pious. He had romantic good looks and a splendid figure. His chestnut hair curled naturally; there was something elfin about his arched eyebrows. His grey eyes sparkled and were 'full of life', but also a little haunted—as if he had a premonition of his terrible fate, but did not fear it enough to prevent him from enjoying life to the full.

He also had an attractive personality. 'Of speech slow, but witty and full of sense; a presence graceful, courtly and so winning upon the beholder, that it seemed to claim reverence without serving for it, for he was so affable, so courteous, so benign, that he seemed verily to scorn ostentation and the keeping of state.' It is significant, however, that the writer of these words was one

of Montrose's followers, Patrick Gordon of Ruthven. Montrose
was always at his best with his inferiors, whether they were his
officers, his servants or his humbler kinsmen. With his superiors
or equals, apart from a few close friends, he certainly did not
scorn 'the keeping of state', but was very much the great noble.
He had little use for anyone who disagreed with his point of
view, for he suffered from the egoism which goes with a strong
belief in one's own destiny. Having set out purposely to be a
hero, he tended to live 'in a romance'; so that he was never
enough of a realist to succeed in politics.

Montrose's dreams of glory were doubtless coloured by the
vanity which seems to have been his worst fault, though it was
not so much vanity as a self-confident swagger: when thinking
out code-names, he called himself 'Venture Fair'. And it would
be unreasonable to expect so gallant and gilded a youth not to
have been a little conceited; indeed, it is to his credit that he was
neither arrogant nor spoilt. He was only fourteen when, in 1626,
he succeeded his father as Earl of Montrose, and thus became one
of the greatest of the Scots nobility. For centuries, the Grahams
had been the chief marcher lords of what has been called Scotland's northern border, that fertile strip separating the hills along
the northern shore of the Forth from the Highlands. Here, with a
chain of castles and estates stretching from the seaport of Montrose in the east to Loch Lomond in the west, they had served the
Crown by keeping the clansmen at bay.

For the first few years after leaving the University of St
Andrews, Montrose led a pleasant and carefree life, hunting,
shooting, playing golf; writing poetry, acting as patron to the
poet and traveller, William Lithgow; paying visits to the castles
of neighbouring lairds, with music and dancing during the long
winter evenings. In 1633, accompanied by a small retinue, he set
out for France and Italy to acquire something of the polish which
only foreign travel could give. Passing through London on his
return journey in 1636, he went to Whitehall to kiss the King's
hand, which he had not yet done. Among the courtiers he found
many expatriate Scots who had come south to bask in Royal
favour; the most influential of them being James, Marquis of
Hamilton, a stupid and treacherous intriguer of boundless
ambition. Seeing Montrose as a possible rival at court, Hamilton
made mischief between him and the King, who consequently

received him coldly, giving him his hand to kiss and then turning away without speaking a word.

This snub cannot have made Montrose any more favourably inclined towards Charles's attempt to force the Anglican Prayer Book on the Presbyterian Scots which caused an uproar in Scotland a few months later, starting with the famous riot in St Giles's Cathedral, Edinburgh, when the congregation threw their folding stools at the Bishop and Dean. As a devout though not at all bigoted Presbyterian, he had no hesitation in becoming the right-hand man of the Earl of Rothes, who organized the opposition to the King's religious policy. This would not have seemed to him in any way inconsistent with his family's tradition of loyalty to the Crown; for he and Rothes and their followers were not rebelling against the King, but merely opposing the Prayer Book.

When, early in 1638, the King's will regarding the Prayer Book was proclaimed with trumpets from the Mercat Cross in Edinburgh, the opposition leaders harangued the crowd from a platform erected alongside. Montrose, in order to be better heard and seen, climbed up on to a barrel which had been left conveniently on the platform, occasioning a good-humoured but prophetic reproach from Rothes: 'James, you will never be at rest till you are lifted above the rest in three fathoms of a rope.' The protest at Mercat Cross was followed by the signing of the Covenant, a nationwide pledge to defend the Kirk against all innovations not sanctioned by the Scots Parliament and the General Assembly. Rothes and Montrose were among the first of the thousands who put their names to the parchment spread out on a tombstone in Greyfriars churchyard.

In the following year when the King declared war on the Covenanters and the Scots took up arms against him, Montrose was appointed second-in-command to the Covenanting General, Alexander Leslie; though unlike Leslie and the other Scottish soldiers of fortune who had hurried home from foreign wars to fight for the Kirk, he was totally lacking in military experience. Before facing the English, the Covenanting army had to secure its rear by occupying Aberdeen in the country of the Gordons, who, being largely Catholic, had declared for the King. Montrose and his men, all wearing the blue ribbons which he had given them, entered Aberdeen without opposition, and he succeeded in persuading the Gordon chief, the Marquis of Huntly, to remain neutral for the rest of the war. But Leslie and the other Covenanting commanders sent Huntly and his son as prisoners to Edinburgh, even though Montrose had promised them somewhat rashly that they would be safe. For the first time, but not the last, Montrose saw his fellow-Covenanters fall short of his own high standards of honour.

Before Montrose could head south for the real business of the war, the King had made peace. So when eventually he did cross the Border, it was not with his army but with a deputation of Covenanting lords to meet the King at Berwick. Montrose's enemies were afterwards to allege that at this meeting the King induced him to change sides, which is unlikely, for by all accounts Charles gave him and the other Covenanting peers a cool reception; at the most, his chivalrous loyalty may have been awakened by the sight of his Sovereign in distress. In any case, Montrose never really did change sides. He continued to stand where he had always stood, true to the Covenant and in favour of the abolition of the Scottish bishops; but, like Falkland and Hyde in England a couple of years later, he grew disillusioned with his former friends as their policies and methods became more violent. His views as to the clergy's place in society were, like those of Falkland, in advance of his time; he held that they should confine themselves to their spiritual duties. Since the signing of the Covenant, however, the more extreme Presbyterian ministers had been using religion as a means of political intimidation. It seemed to Montrose that their object, and that of an increasingly large section of the Covenanting party, was not so much to defend the Kirk against royal tyranny as to set up a tyranny of their own.

By now, the party was dominated by the Earl of Argyll, a man of very different stamp from either the jolly, Pickwickian Rothes or the young gallant, Montrose. Small, lean, red-haired, pallid, with a squint, a pendulous nose and tight, bloodless lips, Argyll looked the fanatic he was. His Calvinist zeal, however, was not his only motive; there was also his ambition, both for himself and for his clan, for he was chief of the aggressive, expansionist Campbells. As the greatest Highland chief next to Huntly, and with the advantage of having his territory near the Lowlands, Argyll was well placed to become the most powerful man in Scotland, particularly as he was a wily politician.

When the Scots Parliament met after the peace, the extremists, led by Argyll and the able but neurotic lawyer, Archibald Johnston of Warriston, introduced legislation to deprive the King of his time-honoured means of influencing Parliament through the Committee of Estates. Montrose opposed this legislation, not only because he regarded it as an unwarranted encroachment on royal authority, but because he knew that without the restraining hand of the King, Parliament would be exploited by factions. Or, more precisely, by one faction; that of Argyll, which, having duly succeeded in abolishing the royal control, held Parliament in its grip.

In an attempt to check the growing power of 'King Campbell' —Scotsmen were already calling Argyll this, and it was more than just a nickname like King Pym, for there seemed a real possibility that he might end by usurping the Scots throne—Montrose and some of his friends bound themselves to resist 'the particular and indirect practising of a few'. The Covenanters were splitting into two parties, the Argyll faction and the moderates under Montrose; but all such dissensions were shelved on the outbreak of the 1640 war, in which Montrose led the van of the Scots army across the Tweed, fording the swollen river twice to encourage his men to follow him. After the speedy defeat of the English, the contest between Montrose and Argyll was resumed; and Montrose showed his political *naïveté* by making some tactical blunders which enabled Argyll to have him imprisoned in Edinburgh Castle, charged with plotting against the Covenant.

He was thus conveniently out of the way when the King visited Scotland in the late summer of 1641 and agreed to the Covenanters' demands. Had he been at liberty, he might, as leader of the moderates, have gained an ascendancy over the King. To make doubly sure that this could not happen, Argyll joined with the King's favourite, Hamilton, in a complicated plot to discredit Montrose still further. Argyll thus had the field to himself, and the King, who was in desperate need of Scottish troops to help him to put down the Irish rebellion which had just broken out, had no alternative but to conciliate him. When King Charles returned to England, King Campbell was stronger than ever, and so sure of his position that he allowed Montrose to be released.

Montrose spent the next year quietly at his principal seat, Kincardine Castle, under the shadow of the Ochil Hills not far from the town of Perth. It was the last time he was ever at home with his wife and children. During that time, he collected his thoughts about politics, writing them down in a letter to a friend. His recent experiences had convinced him of the need for an unquestioned centre of authority, as a safeguard against 'the oppression and tyranny of subjects, the most fierce, insatiable and insufferable tyranny in the world'—in other words, the tyranny of Argyll backed by the ministers, the middle classes and the Edinburgh mob. The obvious centre of authority was the King; the King's power should be limited by law, but only limited to a certain extent; even a tyrannical King was better than sectarian conflict and the tyranny of factions. He expressed his political convictions in simpler terms in the celebrated love song which seems to date from about this time, and which contains the lines beginning 'He either fears his fate too much'. The 'mistress' to whom the song is addressed is thought by some writers to be Scotland, rather than his wife or any other woman; in which case the sentiments in it are meant even more to be taken at their face value.

> My dear and only love, I pray
>   That little world of thee
> Be governed by no other sway
>   Than purest monarchy;
> For if confusion have a part,
>   Which virtuous souls abhor,
> And hold a Synod in thine heart,
>   I'll never love thee more.

If Scotland's only hope lay in a strong monarchy, the prospects for monarchy did not look so good at the beginning of 1643. There were signs even then that the Scots were planning to intervene in the English Civil War on the side of Parliament. But Hamilton, who was in Edinburgh, reported glibly to his Royal master that they would never enter the war. Montrose felt that the King should be warned as to the true state of affairs, so he went to meet the Queen when she was at York. Henrietta Maria at first listened to him with sympathy. Then the showy and plausible Hamilton arrived from Edinburgh with a completely different story. The Queen forwarded both reports to the King, who chose to follow that of Hamilton.

Montrose went back to Scotland, where shortly after his arrival he was approached by some of his old Covenanting friends and offered a high command in the army which was about to invade England in support of Parliament. He knew that to refuse this offer would be to show his hand and risk incurring the vengeance of Argyll, so he played for time and disappeared from Scotland once again. He went to Oxford, where at first he had the frustration of finding that the King still preferred to listen to Hamilton's sanguine assurances rather than to his own more realistic advice. Then, in January 1644, the Scots army crossed the Border and Montrose was proved right. Hamilton, who had recently been made a Duke for his services, was discredited and put under arrest.

Montrose was now the man of the moment, and he had no difficulty in getting the King to agree to a plan whereby he would invade Scotland with as many English troops as could be spared at the same time as ten thousand Irish Macdonnells crossed over from Ulster to Galloway. This, he hoped, would frighten Argyll into recalling the Scots army from England. The assistance of the Macdonnells was promised by their chief, the Marquess of Antrim, a rather foolish gallant of the court. If they materialized, they would be useful allies, for they were of the same stock as those brave warriors, the Macdonalds. And like their Scottish kinsmen, they were blood enemies of the Campbells, who had driven them out of their lands in Kintyre a generation earlier.

Armed with the King's commission as Lieutenant-Governor and Captain-General of Scotland—and also with the noble Prince Henry's sword which Charles, as a knightly gesture, had given him—Montrose set out northwards on his 'venture fair'. Truly, he was putting all 'to the touch'; with such troops as he could beg from Newcastle, and the uncertain Macdonnells, he hoped to raise Scotland for the King and take on the hitherto invincible army of the Covenant. On reaching York, he suffered his first set-back: Newcastle, who was hard pressed by the Scots, could only spare him a hundred horse. He was, however, allowed to recruit his own troops in Cumberland, where in less than a month he succeeded in raising an army of two thousand, with which he crossed the Border. On entering Scotland, he issued a manifesto, which showed him to be still very much in the Covenanting spirit. He would not, he declared, have taken up arms for the King had he not been certain of Charles's intention to defend the religion and rights of his subjects. 'Did I but see the least appearance of His Majesty's change from these resolutions,' he added, 'I should never continue longer my faithful endeavour.'

The town of Dumfries opened its gates to Montrose, and, on hearing the news of his first success, the King made him a Marquis. There was no sign of the Macdonnells, however, and Argyll was advancing towards him with a strong force. Montrose hoped to make a dash for his own home country, north of Stirling, but his English troops mutinied at the prospect of going so far into Scotland. There was nothing for it but to return to Carlisle, and await the arrival of the Macdonnells there. While he was waiting, the Royalists were defeated at Marston Moor, and he was obliged to give up most of his troops to help make up Prince Rupert's losses. He was now left with only his original hundred horse; the Macdonnells continued to be silent. It looked as though his grand design had come to nothing.

But still he would not give up. He took a crazy gamble: disguised as a groom, he made his way to his home country without any troops at all, hoping to be able to achieve something there. After he had spent six days and nights hidden in the woods and heather near the house of one of his kinsmen, on the fringe of the Highlands not far from Perth, news came that the Macdonnells were on their way. When word got around that these Irish warriors were coming, two of the clans in Atholl, just north of where Montrose was hiding, took up arms to resist them. The Highlanders and Ulstermen met and were just about to join battle when Montrose appeared, on foot and in Highland dress, alone but for his kinsman. As he walked between the two armies, the Highlanders, realizing who he was, broke into shouts of welcome; then word reached the Ulstermen that Montrose had come and they threw their caps into the air and fired a salute. Such was the magic of his presence that Ulstermen and Highlanders forgot their differences and all agreed to fight for the King under his banner. Two days later, the Royal Standard, which Montrose had brought with him folded in the lining of his saddle, was unfurled on a grassy knoll above the River Till.

It was a brave sight, but Montrose had little cause for optimism. The Macdonnells were not the ten thousand promised by Antrim, but little more than a thousand. The Highlanders numbered about the same, and were armed only with dirks and swords. A few miles away, defending the Lowland town of Perth, was a well-equipped Covenanting army of six thousand. Montrose met the Covenanters to the west of Perth, at Tippermuir. It was a Sunday, so he asked for a truce in order that the Sabbath might not be profaned. The Covenanting General, Lord Elcho, replied that he had 'made choice of the Lord's day for doing the Lord's will'. Elcho's choice of day had the approval of the ministers, who, earlier that morning, had been in full voice, exhorting the men: 'If ever God spoke certain truth out of my mouth,' one of them had declared, 'in His name I promise you today a certain victory.' Montrose's musketeers fired and under cover of the smoke the Highlanders charged. The shock was too much for the Covenanting army and it crumpled; soon there was a general rout in which nearly two thousand died. That night, Montrose entered Perth in triumph.

During the next twelve months, Montrose roved about Scotland with his army of Highlanders, winning battle after battle. Such was his magnetism as a leader and his ability to handle men that he managed to do what had, up to now, been regarded as impossible: to make an army out of many different clans, each under its own chief. It was an army of varying strength, for clans joined him as he marched, and then, after a time, returned home; the Gordons were always coming and going at the behest of their unreliable chief, Huntly; though Huntly's son, the young Lord Gordon, stayed constantly with Montrose until he was killed in action. As well as keeping his clans together, Montrose managed to prevent them from fighting among themselves, even though some of them were Catholic, like the Macdonnells, and others Presbyterian. It was a remarkable feat; yet not entirely due to Montrose's personal qualities for the clans were all united in their hatred of the Campbells.

Montrose's plan was to make lightning raids on important enemy garrisons within striking distance of the Highlands, and then to draw Argyll's Lowland troops into the mountains where the Highlanders could fight them on their own ground. After Tippermuir, he attacked Aberdeen, where he made the mistake of

James Butler, Duke of Ormonde

Queen Henrietta Maria,
by van Dyck

(*Left*) The Earl and
Countess of Derby,
by van Dyck

(*Right*) James Graham,
Earl of Montrose,
after Honthorst

Sir Hugh Cholmley,
by Janssen

John Cleveland,
attributed to Dobson

Dr. Gilbert Sheldon, studio of Lely

Dr. Richard Sterne, from his
effigy in York Minster

Dr. John Fell

Dr. Richard Dolben, from his
effigy in York Minster

(*Above*) Sir Charles Lucas, by Dobson

(*Right*) George, Lord Digby, (*left*), and his brother-in-law William, Lord Russell, by van Dyck

Prince Rupert (*left*), with two cavalier officers, by Dobson

allowing his men to sack the town, so that over a hundred citizens were slaughtered, including women; while other women had their lives spared only to be carried off as spoil by the Macdonnells. Aberdeen provided the Covenanters with a useful fund of atrocity tales, and taught Montrose a lesson. From now on, he enforced the strictest discipline. During the rest of his campaign there was looting and burning but no more murder or outrage. He also treated prisoners with courtesy and humanity, adhering rigidly to the code of military honour. 'If the meanest corporal in my army had given quarter to their general,' he once said, 'I would abide by it.' His behaviour was in sharp contrast to that of his enemies, who killed prisoners, hanged messengers sent to them under a flag of truce, and imprisoned Montrose's friends and relatives. When his eldest son, whom he took with him for safety, died, his second son, though only twelve, was kidnapped and confined in Edinburgh Castle.

Montrose was even able to enforce his orders against indiscriminate killing when, early in the winter, he invaded the country of the Campbells, an exploit very dear to the hearts of his men. The Campbells were completely taken by surprise, for their territory, around the sea-lochs of Argyll, was separated from the rest of the Highlands by mountains which they believed no enemy could cross. But somehow Montrose's troops managed to cross them, and in deep snow; and they swooped down to the very gates of Argyll's castle of Inverary on Loch Fyne. Argyll, when he heard they were coming, escaped by boat; his clansmen likewise made themselves scarce, leaving Montrose's men to burn their houses and drive away their cattle and feast themselves in the rich seaport town of Inverary.

A month later, the Campbells nearly had their revenge when Montrose was trapped between them and their allies, the Mackenzies, as he was retreating northwards along the Great Glen, but he escaped by doubling back over the high hills around Ben Nevis. It was an epic march through snow and ice, an incredible feat of endurance; particularly as Montrose's army included a troop of cavalry; the horses most probably had to be carried for much of the way by the men. Having crossed those fearful icy mountains, Montrose was able to fall on to the Campbells at Inverlochy from the side they least expected. Fifteen hundred of them were slain, almost as many as Montrose's entire army; the power of the Campbells as a fighting force was broken for ever.

Argyll still had his Lowland army under the command of a professional soldier, General William Baillie, but in the following June Montrose lured Baillie's forces into the Highlands west of Aberdeen and routed them at Alford on Donside. Baillie and his surviving cavalry escaped, forming the nucleus of a new army which was hurriedly raised in the Lowlands during the month of July, and which went northwards to meet Montrose in August. Montrose was now so strong that he felt equal to taking on the Covenanting army in the Lowlands. The two armies met at Kilsyth, near Glasgow; and Montrose's men, fighting in their shirts, for it was sweltering hot, were once again victorious.

The Covenanters now had no forces left except for the army which was away in England fighting for Parliament. Argyll fled across the Border to the Scots garrison at Berwick. Montrose was, for the time being, the undisputed master of all Scotland. He planned to raise a properly equipped army in the Lowlands which he could take south to help the King. To provide money for the enterprise, Charles commissioned him to call a Parliament and preside over it in his name. But long before Montrose could put these plans into effect, the Scots army in England, commanded by General David Leslie, hurried home to reconquer Scotland for the Covenant. To fight Leslie with any hope of beating him, Montrose would have had to resort to his old tactics of drawing him into the Highlands. But the King, who was in desperate straits after Naseby, was so impatient for Montrose to come to his help that he ordered him to attack Leslie without delay.

Montrose agreed, even though he now had only a comparatively small army at his disposal, the Gordons having left him and most of the Macdonnells having gone to drive the Campbells out of Kintyre. He was, however, promised help by two great Border lords, Roxburghe and Home; but when he had already marched to join his Border allies within striking distance of the enemy, he heard that they had been surprised by the Covenanters and, in order to save themselves, had gone over to them. Montrose retreated as quickly as he could in the direction of Glasgow, but Leslie was too quick for him and surprised and utterly routed his small force at Philiphaugh, in Selkirk. Montrose refused to abandon his infantry and would have died fighting, but his friends took his bridle and forcibly led him away. The infantry surrendered to Leslie, who promised them their lives; but he was overruled by the ministers and they were all put to the sword, together with all the camp-followers, the cooks and horse-boys, the Irishwomen and their children. 'Mr John, have you not once gotten your fill of blood?' Leslie, sick of the slaughter, asked one of his chaplains.

Montrose himself was still at liberty, but Philiphaugh had broken his spell. And even without this disaster, one wonders how much longer his luck would have held. Truly during the past months he had been living 'in a romance'; or rather in a dream, from which he was bound to be awoken sooner or later. He had worked a miracle by keeping an army of Highlanders together for a year; but this was not to say that he could do so indefinitely.

Still Montrose refused to accept defeat and he retreated to the far north where he set about raising the clans once again. Then he heard that the King had surrendered to the Scots army in England. In an attempt to win the support of Argyll, Charles repudiated Montrose, who eventually escaped to Norway disguised as a servant.

In exile, Montrose found that his fame had gone before him. He was honoured by many of the princes and great men of Europe; Mazarin offered him the rank of Marshal of France if he would enter the French service. But he had no intention of selling his sword to a foreign prince, his one object being to win back Scotland for his King. He could not, however, do much without the King's approval; and Charles was now once again under the influence of Hamilton. In 1648, 'Captain Luckless', as Montrose nicknamed the resplendent but futile Duke, invaded England with part of the Scots army, only to be defeated by Cromwell at Preston and later executed.

Hamilton died a month after the King. When Montrose heard the news of Charles's execution, he fell down in a dead faint. Then, having revived, he locked himself in his room for two days and nights and during that time swore 'to avenge the martyred sire and raise the son to his father's throne'; putting his vow on paper in the form of a poem:

I'll sing thine obsequies with trumpet sounds,
And write thine epitaph in blood and wounds.

This was the Montrose who, less than five years earlier, had coolly
announced that he would not have been fighting for the King had
he not been convinced of his good intentions. Since then, he and
Charles had never met, so unlike Ormonde, Hyde and many
others, he did not have a chance of falling under the King's spell
through being close to him. Far from seeing Charles at his best,
he had been the victim of his deplorable tendency to sacrifice his
friends in order to placate his enemies. But having heard that the
King for whom he had endured so much had been put to death,
Montrose now lived for nothing but to serve his memory and
his son, with the blind devotion of a paladin.

Meeting Montrose at The Hague, the young Charles II
immediately agreed to his plan for an invasion of Scotland. Then
Argyll and his party, who had been deeply offended by the
execution of their King, even though they had been at war with
him for most of the past ten years, proclaimed the younger
Charles in Edinburgh and invited him to return to Scotland on
terms. Charles, showing signs of having inherited his father's
fatal propensity for playing several games at once, negotiated
with the government in Edinburgh, which entailed giving it some
degree of recognition, while at the same time ordering Montrose
to go ahead with his invasion plans. He felt that if Montrose were
successful, he would be able to negotiate from a position of
strength, but by recognizing the Argyll régime, he cut the ground
from under Montrose's feet. The ruling junta were able to offer a
£30,000 reward for his capture, in the King's name.

'I can make no other acknowledgement but with the more
alacrity to abandon my life for your interests,' was Montrose's
reply to the King's letter, telling him what he had done. Montrose
meant what he said; he knew that in going to Scotland now he
was almost certainly going to his death. Yet when he sailed from
Gothenburg in March 1650, his mood was certainly not one of
gloomy fatalism. There was always a chance that he might
succeed; he would put it to the touch. And if he won, there
might have been another prize as well as the satisfaction of having
avenged 'the martyred sire' and given the son his rightful kingdom. While at The Hague, he had seen a great deal of Charles I's

sister Elizabeth, the Winter Queen, and her lively and talented twenty-seven-year-old daughter, Princess Louise. He had been a widower since 1648; according to Louise's younger sister, Sophia, he had hopes that if he could restore the King to his throne, Charles would show his gratitude by bestowing on him the hand of his cousin. If that had happened, the House of Graham might one day have ascended the throne of Great Britain instead of the House of Hanover.

After a stormy voyage, Montrose landed in the Orkneys, where he raised troops; then, in April, he crossed to the Scottish mainland. He marched south into Sutherland, where some of the clans were by way of joining him; but before they appeared, he was surprised and routed by a party of Leslie's cavalry. Montrose galloped away, then turned his horse loose and took to the hills on foot. Four days later, weak from hunger and exposure, he fell in with one of the McLeods who handed him over to his enemies.

He began his journey southwards in a cart, bound hand and foot, for he was too ill to ride; then, though he was still feverish, he was mounted on a pony and led in procession through the towns and villages in order to make him an object of scorn. But such was his dignity and 'countenance high' that most of the people, instead of reviling him, treated him with kindness and respect. When he reached Edinburgh, in the third week of May, his enemies had him driven slowly along the crowded Canongate, tied to a high seat on a hangman's cart, certain that at least the Edinburgh mob would not let them down. But on seeing him pass, even the women who had been paid to pelt him with filth and stones were so moved by his dignity that, in the words of his chaplain and first biographer, George Wishart, 'their insults and curses melted into tears and prayers'.

In Lord Moray's house, Argyll and others of the ruling clique were assembled to witness his degradation. But such was the temper of the crowd that they only dared peer at him through half-closed shutters. Nevertheless, Montrose caught a glimpse of Argyll and for a moment their eyes met. Then the shutters were slammed to and an English soldier in the crowd cried out: 'They durst not look him in the face these seven years bygone.'

At the Mercat Cross, Montrose saw the thirty-foot gibbet which had been put up to receive him, for he was to die by hanging like a common criminal. It was on the very spot where Rothes had prophesied that he would be 'lifted up above the rest in three fathoms of a rope'. Before being put to death he spent two days in prison, constantly tormented by ministers and laymen who tried in vain to make him admit his guilt. On the morning of the day when he was to die, they found him combing his long hair. One of them reproached him for his vanity, to which Montrose replied: 'My head is still my own. Tonight, when it will be yours, treat it as you please.' He was determined to die in style; his nephew's wife had sent him some elegant clothes, so that he went to the scaffold in a scarlet coat laid over with silver lace, an embroidered shirt and ribboned shoes. 'There goes the finest gallant in the realm!' exclaimed the bystanders. He was only thirty-seven. On the scaffold, he said: 'I leave my soul to God, my service to my prince, my goodwill to my friends, my love and charity to you all.' His last words were: 'God have mercy on this afflicted land!' The hangman was in tears as he pushed him off the ladder.

After hanging for three hours, Montrose's body was dismembered. The head was fixed to the side of the Tolbooth, the arms and legs were sent to be exposed in four other towns of Scotland. Two months later, when Charles II landed at Aberdeen on his way to take the Covenant and court Montrose's enemies, he saw one of the shrivelled limbs over the town gate: a grisly reproach to him in the most shameful episode of his career.

12

Sir Hugh Cholmley and his Wife

The seafaring town of Whitby, with its houses growing out of the rock of the north Yorkshire coast, was still a small place in 1639, but the ruin of Whitby Abbey on the bare, windswept hill above the town would have been even mightier then than it is now, after the gales of three hundred more winters have taken their toll of transept and nave and tower. Close to the great roofless church stood the house of the local magnate, Sir Hugh Cholmley, whose ancestor, a Cholmley from Cheshire, was granted the abbey and its lands at the Dissolution. During the past few years, Cholmley had carried out great improvements to the house, which was tumbledown and 'all unhandsome' when he inherited it from his father in 1631; he had put in piped water and heightened the courtyard walls, to get a little more shelter from the wind. Indoors, his wife Elizabeth had worked wonders, for she had a flair for decoration and furnishing, something which, as her admiring husband afterwards remarked, 'many cannot do, though they have stuff'.

She had inherited this talent from her mother, who grew up at the Elizabethan court, a world far removed from the coast of North Yorkshire; and indeed, Elizabeth Cholmley had herself grown up in a country very different from that bare hill overlooking the North Sea, being the daughter of a wealthy baronet of Kent. All her inclinations were towards the warmer and more civilized south; but she was content to live at Whitby out of love for her husband who, for his part, adored her. In his memoirs, written towards the end of his life for the benefit of his sons, he speaks tenderly of her beauty, which she kept until her death at the age of fifty-three: her dark eyes 'full of loveliness and sweetness', her finely drawn eyebrows, her well-shaped mouth, her chestnut hair. Yet her beauty was, in his view, exceeded by 'the inward endowment and perfections of her mind'. She was virtuous, compassionate and always ready to help others; she was well-read, particularly in history, and had a sense of humour. All this more than made up for her quick temper, and her tendency to become over-upset when things went wrong, which her husband attributed to her being 'of a timorous nature' and 'spun of a fine thread'.

Cholmley's marriage was only one of the many blessings with which he was then endowed, though he certainly counted it as the greatest of them. He had sons and daughters and an estate which, thanks to his good management, brought him an income of nearly £3,000 a year—something like £100,000 in today's money—enabling him to live as a grandee, with a household of thirty or forty, including a chaplain who said prayers in the morning and before dinner and supper. There were always three or four unexpected guests at his table, and twice a week the poor came to his gate where they were served with 'bread and good pottage made of beef'. At the age of thirty-nine he was a highly respected county figure, a Deputy Lieutenant, a Justice of the Peace, appearing at public meetings 'in a very gentlemanly equipage'. His present well-being contrasted with his earlier life. He had been a weakly child, supposedly because of the poor quality of his nurse's milk, and had suffered from every sort of illness, including smallpox and a fever which he gave to his mother, who, to his great grief, died of it. And he was, as a child, singularly accident-prone; he fell out of a window, he was nearly trampled on by a horse, he was savaged by an angry sow. Having somehow reached manhood, though without the height and stamina of his forebears, he narrowly escaped becoming a drunkard at Cambridge and took to gaming at Gray's Inn. It was only after his marriage that he mended his ways, which was just as well, for his father was heavily in debt and it took several years of hard work and frugal living to put the family estate to rights.

Though everything seemed well for Cholmley himself in 1639, the country was growing restive as the King embroiled himself in the first Scots War. Cholmley made his own protest against Prerogative rule by refusing to pay Ship Money, and every taxpayer in the Liberty of Whitby Strand followed his example. It was clearly a matter of principle rather than because he objected to the tax in itself. He did not even have the flimsy excuse of people living inland that the fleet was no concern of theirs; and in any case, it was just as much their concern as the breakwater of Whitby harbour, for the rebuilding of which he had himself raised a contribution throughout England in 1632, with Strafford's permission. And he had surely learnt the lesson of sea power during the Spanish War, when the ship carrying all his and Elizabeth's belongings from London to Whitby was captured by an enemy vessel.

In the Short Parliament of April 1640, Cholmley sat as Member for Scarborough. As a veteran of the previous Parliament, and of the two before it, one would have expected him to gravitate towards the old Parliamentary hands who were more active in airing grievances than the newcomers unversed in procedure. And he was drawn still closer to the malcontents on account of his defiance over Ship Money, which not only made him something of a hero in their sight, but caused Strafford to pass him by 'with some scorn' when he called to pay his respects. Cholmley found this particularly hard to bear, since he was related to Strafford's first wife and had hitherto been on good terms with him. Strafford also deprived him of his commissions, and put him to the annoyance of being summoned before the Council every day for a month. After such treatment, it is not surprising that he should have helped to get up the two great petitions of the Yorkshire gentry complaining of the Royal Prerogative, which so angered the King that he sent for Cholmley and three others and threatened to hang them if they 'meddled' any more. Cholmley protested that having no acquaintances at court, they had no means of redress but by petitioning; whereupon the King was mollified, and said: 'Whenever you have any cause of complaint, come to me, and I will hear it.'

The calling of the Long Parliament found Cholmley back at Westminster, and held in high esteem by the Parliamentary leaders, who in May 1642 sent him as one of their Commissioners to meet the King at York. Ostensibly the Commissioners were to convince Charles of Parliament's sincerity, but Pym also instructed them to muster the trained-bands against him, which Cholmley refused to do, saying that he had no intention of starting the war. But finding the King in an uncompromising mood, he was 'infinitely troubled', and prayed for guidance.

Opening his Prayer Book at random, his eye lit on the verses, 'My soul hath long dwelt with him that hateth peace' and 'I am for peace, but when I speak, they are for war', which gave him heart, and he set to work raising troops for Parliament with an easy conscience.

This turning for guidance to the psalms is one of several indications that Cholmley verged towards Puritanism; a seventeenth-century writer tells us that while not actually a Puritan himself, he was 'kind and friendly to the Puritans'. Unlike the High Anglicans among the Parliament men, he remained in Pym's party even after it had attacked Episcopacy. He was on friendly terms with Mr Remmington, the Puritan incumbent of St Mary's, the parish church of Whitby just outside the Abbey precincts. In his memoirs, he has the Puritan habit of attributing material prosperity to Divine favour; he also disapproves of swearing. But while making it clear that he is something of a reformed character, and advising his sons not to let their children get a taste for hunting, hawking or horse racing because he himself has been unable to put these sports out of his mind, though he now sees the vanity of them, there is no hint of his having undergone a sudden spiritual regeneration. And to keep him from straying too far out of the Anglican fold, there was his beloved wife, Elizabeth, whom he describes as 'a true daughter of the Church of England'.

On the eve of the Civil War, he seems to have been less alarmed by the growing determination of Parliament to overthrow the English Church, than by the hardening of its attitude towards the King. Nevertheless, he agreed to put a Parliamentary garrison into Scarborough, the seaport town some twenty miles south of Whitby for which he was Member, still hoping that these military preparations would end in a treaty; and when, instead, the country went to war, he continued to hold Scarborough for Parliament. With its harbour guarded by a vast medieval castle on a headland jutting out into the sea, the place was deemed to be of great strategic importance; the Royalists at York 'had a special eye towards it' as a port for bringing in supplies and reinforcements.

As the months passed, Cholmley suffered increasingly from heart-searchings and doubts. 'I am forced to draw my sword not only against my countrymen but many near friends and allies

some of which I know both to be well-affected in religion and
lovers of their liberties,' he wrote, after making a successful
sortie against the Royalists. Many others found themselves in
this predicament, but it was especially hard for Cholmley, whose
Yorkshire neighbours were very much divided in allegiance—
among his own cousins there were extreme Puritans as well as
the Catholic Cholmleys of Brandsby. He also found his Parliamentary masters increasingly difficult to serve under. They
criticized him for not being more active against the Royalists,
though this would have meant leaving Scarborough unprotected;
they failed to give him proper instructions, or to send him
adequate supplies.

When, early in 1643, the Queen came to York, Cholmley
made up his mind. He entered into correspondence with her
and on 20 March rode out from Scarborough alone but for a
servant, telling one of his officers that he was going to confer
with the Parliamentary governor of Hull. Instead he went to
York, where he was admitted in disguise into the Queen's
presence, kissed her hand and was commissioned by her to hold
Scarborough for the King. 'Alas, poor Hugh Cholmley, that
could turn traitor and sell his honour, for the kiss of a lady's
hand!' a Parliamentarian afterwards lamented. 'See what a toy
took the man in the head, the love of a little court-idolatry put
him quite out of his wits, and religion too!' But whilst Cholmley
may well have felt chivalrous towards the gallant little Queen
who had braved stormy seas and a hostile fleet in her husband's
cause—her lively dark eyes may well have reminded him of
Elizabeth, whom he had left behind in London—it is hard to
believe that he was won over by her. All the indications are that
he had already decided to turn Royalist when he set out from
Scarborough; according to one of his officers, he had for some
time before that made various remarks which sounded like
Royalist propaganda.

One would be more justified in thinking that he changed
sides because of the way Parliament was treating him, or because
the King appeared to be winning. Yet his own explanation of
why he acted as he did seems both valid and sincere: 'I did not
forsake the Parliament till they did fail in performing those
particulars they made the grounds of the war when I was first
engaged, viz, the preservation of religion, protection of the

King's person, and liberties of the subject.' As proof of his sincerity, we know that he did not surrender to the Queen unconditionally, but only after she had agreed not to deter the King from observing the laws passed by Parliament to which he had already given his consent, nor to prevent him from making a peace. In other words, he still stood for what the Long Parliament had achieved before the Grand Remonstrance. The only significant change in his attitude is that he was now concerned with 'the preservation of religion'. Perhaps not having the lawyer's mind of a Hyde, he had failed to grasp the full implications of the attack on Episcopacy, but they had been brought home to him in a practical way by nine months of Puritan dictatorship.

When Cholmley returned to Scarborough and declared for the King, most of his garrison seems to have been willing to change sides with him. There were, however, some Parliamentary diehards, notably a 'worthy captain', a kinsman of his, who was only deterred from assassinating him by the thought of how, by 'taking him away in his sin', he would 'send him in all probability to Hell'. Instead, he planned to make Cholmley prisoner with the help of soldiers 'cordial to the Cause'; but in the event it was the 'worthy captain' who was made prisoner by Cholmley, before being allowed to leave for Hull with his wife, children and goods. After a brief interlude when another Parliamentary officer managed to get control of the Castle during Cholmley's absence by means of a midnight ruse and a distribution of beer and tobacco to the troops, Scarborough was firmly settled as a Royalist stronghold.

On hearing of Cholmley's defection, the Commons resolved that he should no longer be a member of the House, and that he should be impeached for high treason. They also deprived Elizabeth Cholmley of her coach horses, and 'used her coarsely'. She had, up to now, been 'very earnest' for Parliament; her habit of obstinately refusing to change her mind once it had been made up, which Cholmley mentions as one of her 'frailties', may explain how, as a devoted Anglican, she could continue to support a party bent on destroying Anglicanism. But this ill-treatment, added to some persuasion on the part of her husband, now made her into as staunch a Royalist as he had himself become. She and her two young daughters sailed from

London to Whitby and so joined Cholmley at Scarborough. During the year of comparative quiet that followed, they lived at the castle in a style befitting his position as Governor, though he received no pay.

The defeat of the Royalists at Marston Moor in July 1644 left Cholmley 'in a very sad condition'. Those of his officers who were drawn from the Yorkshire gentry mostly went home or to join Prince Rupert, which discouraged the soldiers, many of whom ran away. A Parliamentary army under Fairfax advanced to within five miles of Scarborough. The town, though walled, was untenable on account of its position; the Castle was very much dilapidated and was short of living quarters, as well as of ammunition and provisions. But by pretending to treat with Fairfax, Cholmley gained time in which to put the town and castle into a better state of defence, and to get in corn as it was harvested. He equipped some armed vessels and sent them out of the harbour to intercept any ships that were carrying coal; he had a pinnace constantly employed bringing in supplies; but the Parliamentary fleet soon blockaded Scarborough by sea, just as it was invested by land.

Early in the following February, the besiegers, who were now commanded by Sir John Meldrum, a Scottish soldier of fortune, tightened their grip. Elizabeth refused to leave her husband, but they sent their two young daughters to Holland for safety in the care of Mr Remmington, the former incumbent of Whitby, and his wife. For all his Puritanism, Remmington must have been a Royalist; unless, of course, he merely accompanied the two girls abroad out of Christian charity. After three weeks of fierce fighting, when several of the townspeople were killed by the besiegers' cannon fire, the town fell; Meldrum being rewarded for his success with a present of £1,000 from Parliament. Cholmley and a garrison of 200 retired into the castle, which the Parliamentarians proceeded to invest, bombarding it from the north and south. They also had a battery firing through the east window of the nearby parish church, but this was silenced, and the chancel of the church wrecked, by vigorous and well-directed fire from the castle. Cholmley had planned to escape in a pinnace which he called his 'running horse', since he did not imagine that the castle could hold out for any length of time; but the enemy cut off this last line of retreat. It must have given the beleaguered garrison some satisfaction to learn at the end of March that Meldrum, while reconnoitring from a rock, had been blown down by a violent wind and bruised.

March became April, and April May, and still the Royalists in Scarborough Castle held out, though they suffered increasingly from sickness and fatigue. Elizabeth Cholmley, who normally became both melancholy and ill in the face of adversity, showed the greatest courage throughout the siege, and endured much hardship. After the destruction of the Governor's lodgings, she had to sleep 'in a little cabin on the ground level', the damp of which left her with a 'defluction of rheum upon one of her eyes' which bothered her for the rest of her life; she was also afflicted with scurvy. But ignoring her own troubles, she nursed the sick and wounded with such devotion that, as her husband afterwards recalled, 'her maids were so overwrought and toiled with it that one of them, in the night, stole away, thinking to get into the town; but the enemy's guards, taking her for a spy, caused her to return, which was acceptable to her lady.' When, in May, Meldrum threatened to give no quarter, Elizabeth begged her husband not to accept terms dishonourable to himself or prejudicial to the King's affairs out of consideration for her.

Cholmley duly ignored Meldrum's threats, and the castle was stormed. The besiegers penetrated as far as the foot of the keep, where they met with a desperate resistance, and were repelled with stones and other missiles. Meldrum was mortally wounded, and four of his officers and fifty of his men were killed; whereas Cholmley lost only one officer and four men. By now, however, the defences of the castle had been reduced to ruins by incessant battering; stores were running out, scurvy was rampant and the soldiers were broken-spirited. So on 22 July, 1645, after a siege of almost a year, Cholmley surrendered and was granted honourable terms. 'Many of Sir Hugh's officers and soldiers belonging to the castle were in such a weak condition that some of them were brought forth in sheets,' an eye-witness recorded.

Cholmley himself was in as pitiable a state as his men—though this did not prevent the women of Scarborough from trying to stone him, blaming him as they did for the heavy damage suffered by the town. Feeling that if he attempted to join the King at Raglan he would most probably die on the way, so broken was he in health, he took ship for Holland, leaving Elizabeth to return by herself to the house at Whitby. According to an article in the terms of surrender, the Parliamentary garrison which had occupied the house was to hand it over to her; however, the captain in charge of the garrison liked the place so much that he refused to move out. Winter came, and he was still there; but then one of his servants died of the plague, and he left in a hurry. Before he dared to return, Elizabeth made an adventurous dash across the snow-covered moors and took possession, regardless of the germs. She found the house in a sad state, having been plundered. Gone were all her beautiful furnishings; she had to make do with a bed 'so hard she would complain she could not be warm, nor able to lie in it'. She could only afford one maidservant and a man, having no money other than what she could borrow. All Cholmley was able to give her when he left England was £10; he had been sent £200 by his brother, but had distributed most of it among his officers and men in an attempt to relieve their sufferings.

He himself kept just enough to pay for his passage, with £5 to spare. For a time after arriving in Holland he was in great distress, being lonely as well as poor since he had sent his two daughters back to Elizabeth in England. But then, 'by God's Providence', he obtained £600, which enabled him to live comfortably. After seeing the sights of The Hague and Amsterdam, he went to Paris, narrowly escaping being captured by a party of Spanish horse on the way. Finally he settled at Rouen, where he was joined by his two grown-up sons, one of whom had been so short of money that he had thought of enlisting as a pikeman in Catalonia. Elizabeth's brother and nephew were also here, and in the spring of 1647 Elizabeth herself and the two girls came over, so that the family was reunited. They lived 'handsomely and plentifully' at Rouen until the beginning of 1649, when they moved to Gaillon on account of the plague; arriving there just as news came of the King's execution, which so infuriated the populace that they were nearly stoned because they were English, only just saving themselves by explaining that they were Royalists.

When, later in 1649, Parliament allowed Royalists to compound for their estates, Cholmley and his family returned to England. Apart from being imprisoned for eight weeks in 1651 during the scare over Charles II's invasion, he was able to live peacefully enough during the Commonwealth and the Protectorate; though not 'retiredly' as was his intention, for there were seldom less than thirty people in his house at Whitby, what with family, servants and guests. He could soon well afford to maintain them, having started an alum works which helped him to recoup his losses during the war. Elizabeth set to work refurnishing the house, though her efforts in this respect were now 'more for necessity than ornament'. She and her maids did, however, make a set of needlework hangings of flowers on a green ground which her husband particularly prized, enjoining his sons to preserve them 'with an extraordinary care'.

She did not have time to make any more, for she died while on a visit to London in 1655, attended at her deathbed by the exiled Archbishop of Armagh, the venerable and scholarly James Ussher, having refused to see a Presbyterian minister. After her death, Cholmley could no longer bear to live in the house at Whitby, and 'endure the sight of those rooms and places in which I had used to enjoy her company'. So he went to live with his brother-in-law in Kent, devoting the last two years of his life to writing his memoirs. He died at the end of 1657, when Cromwell was still Protector and the Restoration for which he would so earnestly have hoped was not yet in sight.

13

The Cavaliers of
Oxford and Cambridge

In these days of radical dons and rioting undergraduates it is easy to forget that, on the eve of the Civil War, the Universities of Oxford and Cambridge were pillars of the established order. Subversive and anti-Royalist teachings could never be tolerated at these seats of learning, for their chief purpose was to educate the clergy of the Church of England; and with the pulpit as almost the sole channel of communication throughout the country, it was essential for the King's government to have a clergy whose loyalty could always be counted upon. The Early Stuarts took a personal interest in the Universities rather similar to that which later monarchs took in the armed forces. James I frequently held court at Trinity College, Cambridge; the marriage contract between Charles I and Henrietta Maria is believed to have been signed in the Long Gallery of the neighbouring college, St John's. When the other St John's College, at Oxford, opened its new Library in 1636, the King and Queen and all the court were present at the celebrations.

The new Library at St John's, Oxford, was the gift of Archbishop Laud, whose influence was felt throughout the University of which he was Chancellor. But if Oxford was thus a stronghold of Arminianism, so was Cambridge, despite its situation in the Puritan Eastern Counties. In fact, with the exception of Laud himself and his disciple, Juxon, all the great figures of the so-called Laudian Revival, including Laud's mentor, Lancelot Andrewes, were Cambridge men; High Anglicanism in the early seventeenth century was essentially a Cambridge movement, just as it was an Oxford movement in the nineteenth. The movement reached its mystical climax at the Cambridge college of

Peterhouse, where the Master, Dr John Cosin, and his predecessor, Matthew Wren, built and furnished a chapel specially designed for High Church worship with a glittering display of candlesticks and a Heavenly Host of carved angels. Among the Fellows of this college was the young scholar-poet Richard Crashaw, who, in the words of a contemporary, 'made his nest' in the adjoining Little St Mary's Church, praying 'like a primitive saint' and writing his spiritual poems, *Steps to the Temple*, at all hours of the night. Crashaw was a frequent visitor to Little Gidding, where, in Cromwell's home county of Huntingdon, there was another flowering of High Anglicanism deriving from Cambridge: a religious community of married couples, founded in 1626 by Nicholas Ferrar of Clare and enjoying the friendly support of both Laud and the King.

The Arminians were not alone among the Fellows of Oxford and Cambridge in being Royalists. As members of Universities where so many of the colleges were Royal foundations, most Fellows felt a special allegiance to the King, rather similar to that which court officials felt towards him. Most Fellows, too, being clergymen of the Church of England, had a particular reverence for the King as Supreme Governor of the Church; and as Church of England clergymen, they supported Episcopacy—if not, perhaps, without hope of becoming bishops themselves.

When the great majority of the dons were Royalists, it was natural that the undergraduates should have been Royalists too. Seventeenth-century youth followed, rather than reacted against, its mentors; and in any case the undergraduates then would have been easier to influence than those of today, being younger—indeed, no older than public schoolboys. The fact that the townspeople of both Oxford and Cambridge were predominantly Roundhead made the undergraduates more Royalist than ever; it was yet another fight between Town and Gown.

Gown joined issue with Town at Cambridge in 1640, when the townspeople—influenced by the local Puritan gentry—elected Oliver Cromwell as one of their two Members of Parliament. Active in opposing Cromwell's election was a popular and influential young don, John Cleveland, a poet like Crashaw but a much more worldly figure, renowned as a satirist and also as an orator—the Latin speech which he had made before the King had been much admired. He was a Fellow of the large and important college of St John's, which, under the Mastership of Laud's friend, Dr William Beale, was as Arminian as any college in Cambridge and second to none in loyalty. It was the college of Strafford and Newcastle, and also, in a manner of speaking, of Falkland; who, though he does not appear to have actually come into residence, was admitted to it and would afterwards claim to be a St John's man.

As Member for Cambridge, Cromwell quickly mobilized the town and the surrounding country on behalf of Parliament. When, in 1642, many of the colleges were about to send plate to the King, he and his men entered the town and stopped it from being sent. However, according to a Royalist account, the colleges had already managed to smuggle out one consignment. Cromwell and 'a disorderly band of peasants' were lying in wait for it between Cambridge and Huntingdon, but the University sent the plate along side roads, accompanied by a small party of horse, so that it eventually arrived safely at the King's headquarters. The expedition was commanded by a distinguished Fellow of Clare, Barnaby Oley, 'a man of great prudence, and very well acquainted with all the by-ways'.

Most of the Oxford colleges also sent plate to the King, the most generous being Magdalen and All Souls—of which the Warden was Falkland's friend, the eminent Laudian divine, Gilbert Sheldon. As at Cambridge, the local Roundheads made an attempt to stop the plate on its way, but were unsuccessful. Though Oxford was in a much less Puritan part of the country than Cambridge, there was, nevertheless, a powerful Parliamentary faction in the neighbourhood led by Lord Saye and Sele, an extreme Puritan and one of Pym's chief supporters. At first, however, Saye and his friends were fairly inactive, and the University was able to make preparations to resist them. Dr Robert Pincke, the acting Vice-Chancellor and Warden of New College, mustered the 'Scholars and the privileged men of the University', who collected what arms they could find in their various colleges and drilled under his eye in New College Quad. They were also 'put into battle array and skirmished together in a very decent manner'. According to Anthony Wood, who was a boy in Oxford at the time, the Scholars were 'so besotted with the training and activity and gaiety therein . . . that they could never be brought to their books again.' While the Scholars drilled and skirmished, trenches were dug near Wadham, Magdalen Bridge was barricaded with logs to keep out horsemen and stones were carried up to the top of Magdalen Tower, ready to be flung down upon the enemy.

These brave efforts did not prevent Saye and his Roundheads from occupying Oxford in September 1642. Dr Pincke was sent to London as a prisoner; but Saye, who was High Steward of Oxford and claimed to be a Fellow of New College by hereditary right, on the whole treated the University with forbearance, apart from relieving the dons of Christ Church and University College of their plate, which they had attempted to conceal, and ordering 'the combustion of divers Popish books and pictures'. When he cast a jaundiced eye at the paintings on the screen in Trinity chapel, the President, Dr Ralph Kettell, a tall and terrifying though kind-hearted octogenarian, fended him off by saying: 'Truly, my Lord, we regard them no more than a dirty dishcloth.'

Saye's occupation did not last long. At the end of October after the battle of Edgehill, the King and his army entered Oxford where they were given a rapturous welcome by the University. From then until 1646, Oxford was the headquarters of the court and the Royalist seat of government, as well as a military camp with continual troop movements. Christ Church was turned into a palace for the King, who lived there when he was not on campaign; Merton became the Queen's palace during the months when she was at Oxford, the two colleges being connected by a private way made through the gardens. Other colleges housed lords and ladies, courtiers, judges, officials and Privy Councillors; others again were arsenals or barracks. The tower and cloisters of New College were turned into a magazine for powder; wheat was stored in the Guildhall, oats and corn in the Law and Logic Schools. As one would expect, the life of the University was totally disrupted. Few if any lectures were given, many of the younger Fellows and older undergraduates went off to fight in the King's army. Others, while remaining at Oxford, put on 'buff and bandolier' and formed part of the local garrison, helping to guard the town on the occasions when it was threatened by the Roundheads.

Until the summer of 1644, there were no such alarms, and the gentlemen of the court idled away their time hunting and hawking, fighting duels and taking part in the gaieties of wartime Oxford, which reached a climax in July 1643 after the arrival of the Queen. All was song and music, poetry and wit, flirting by the bank of the river. The youth and beauty which had formerly graced Whitehall was here in force. In the grove of Trinity, which was 'the Daphne for the ladies and their gallants to walk in', Lady Isabella Thynne—who as Lady Isabella Rich had led the virtuous Ormonde astray—would make her appearance with a theorbo or lute played before her, watched by adoring undergraduates. The seductive Isabella and her friend, Margaret Fanshawe, used to attend Trinity chapel in the mornings 'half dressed, like angels'; and one day, for 'a frolic', they called on the President, Dr Kettell, intending to make fun of him. But the redoubtable old Doctor guessed the purpose of their visit, and said to Margaret, who was a future Ambassadress: 'Madam, your husband and father I bred up here, and I knew your grandfather; I know you to be a gentlewoman, I will not say you are a whore; but get you gone for a very woman.'

Kettell did not long survive his verbal triumph; though he was in excellent health, the war proved too much for him. Not only was he teased by women, but he was 'affronted and disrespected by rude soldiers'. The billeting of soldiers on the College was a perpetual source of annoyance to the Fellows, as well as a severe financial strain. Like the epidemics caused by overcrowding, it was part of the price which the University had to pay for the honour of having the King and court as its guests.

The good times at Oxford ended with Naseby. The King left secretly to join the Scots in April 1646. A few days later the town was besieged by Fairfax. This was not the first time that Oxford had been in range of Roundhead guns; there had been a fortnight's siege just before Naseby, and in the summer of 1644 the armies of Essex and Waller had closed on the town. But the siege of 1646 lasted for nearly two months, at the end of which the garrison surrendered. Out went Prince Rupert and Prince Maurice, followed by three hundred people of quality; in came the Parliamentary forces and their chaplains, including the much-hated Hugh Peters, who immediately 'thrust themselves into the pulpits'. Even the ordinary soldiers attempted to preach; and not content with that, they invaded the schools and started lecturing. Many a Fellow must have felt the same as the aged William

Finmore of St John's, who, as his epitaph tells us, 'in the year of our Lord God one thousand six hundred and forty-six, when Loyalty and the Church fainted, lay down and died'.

Then, in 1648, came the serious business of ejecting Fellows and Scholars who refused to submit to Parliament. In at least half of the eighteen Oxford colleges, the majority of dons preferred to lose their Fellowships than to submit. Some of these colleges were so overwhelmingly Royalist that the Parliamentary Visitors made virtually a clean sweep: at Corpus Christi, even the college servants were ejected. The Bursar of the rich and strongly Royalist Magdalen was imprisoned for withholding his keys, while at the no less loyal All Souls the Warden himself, Dr Sheldon, refused to hand over his keys to the Visitors and was sent away under guard; people blessed him as he passed along the street. Another Oxford worthy who was put into custody was Dr Samuel Fell, Dean of Christ Church. His wife, and some ladies who were with her, refused to leave the Deanery, so were forcibly carried out and dumped in the Quad.

The Visitors did not have to look far for candidates to fill the vacant places, for Oxford was full of 'seekers', noted for their close-cropped hair, their 'mortified countenances' and their unfailing attendances at sermons, who had come here in anticipation of the pickings. Some Oxonians called them 'the scum of Cambridge', which shows not only that the proverbial rivalry between the two Universities existed then as it did later, but also that the long-standing myth that Cambridge was Roundhead goes back as far as 1648 at least. The most likely origin of this myth, the fact that Cromwell was a Cambridge man—though he does appear to have felt a certain obligation to protect his *alma mater* against the worst violence of his soldiers—did not make him any more lenient towards the Cambridge Royalists. In August 1642, he descended on Cambridge at the head of a troop of 'factious citizens' and arrested the three Heads of Colleges who had been most active in the attempt to send plate to the King: Dr Beale of St John's, Dr Richard Sterne of Jesus and Dr Edward Martin of Queen's.

The three doctors were taken up to London and led captive through the crowds gathered for St Bartholomew's Fair; according to a Royalist account, this was 'on purpose that they might be hooted at, or stoned by the rabble-rout', but it seems more likely that they just happened to arrive on the day when the Fair was in full swing. For the next few years, Beale, Sterne and Martin were moved from one prison to another, starting with the Tower; for ten days they were confined below hatches in a ship lying at Wapping, with eighty other 'prisoners of quality', unable to stand upright and with neither benches to sit on, nor straw on which to lie. They were not the only Cambridge dons imprisoned in London. The Vice-Chancellor, Dr Richard Holdsworth, Master of the traditionally Puritan college of Emmanuel, was sent to the Tower for printing the King's proclamations. The Parliamentary committee before which he appeared charged him with licensing them, to which he retorted that 'he would not be so saucy as to license anything which the King commanded to be printed'.

Cromwell turned Cambridge into an armed camp and Parliamentary troops were quartered on the colleges. The Fellows were thus put to the same expense and annoyance as the Oxford Fellows, with the difference that whereas the soldiers at Oxford were by way of being friends, those at Cambridge were enemies. According to an admittedly biased account, the Roundheads made the colleges into 'mere spittles and bawdy-houses for sick and debauched soldiers, being filled with queans, drabs, fiddlers and revels night and day'. Eighty soldiers were turned into Pembroke, then one of the smallest colleges, and told by their officers to shift for themselves, so 'without any more ado' they 'broke open the Fellows' and Scholars' chambers, and took their beds from under them'. The fact that Pembroke was almost entirely Royalist, the Master, Dr Benjamin Lany, being a Laudian and a Chaplain to the King, though he came from the Puritan town of Ipswich, cannot have made the soldiers any less inconsiderate.

As might be expected, the Roundhead troops did not stop at using the colleges as billets, but noisily set about imposing their own religious views on the University. They tore up the prayer books in Great St Mary's, and when the Lady Margaret Preacher, William Power of Christ's, was on his way to the church to give his sermon, they chased him 'furiously' across Market Hill, with shouts of 'A Pope, a Pope!' On the pretext of searching for arms or for hidden Papists, they entered the rooms of Fellows and Scholars, many of whom were seized and held in captivity for three or four months without any charge being brought against them. To accommodate these and other offending members of the University, the Old Court of St John's was turned into a gaol. Here, in 1643, some of the Heads of Colleges were imprisoned after refusing to vote a loan of £6,000 to Parliament. They and their colleagues were sitting in Consistory, when they were surrounded by a party of Roundhead troops and told by the officer in charge that they would not be permitted to leave until they had voted the money. The weather was cold—it was, in fact, Good Friday, which made the affair seem even more shocking to pious Royalists—the room they sat in was unheated and they had no food; but the Doctors were prepared to sit there all night rather than be bullied into voting as the Roundheads wished, and they passed a unanimous resolution that it was 'against true religion and good conscience for any to contribute to the Parliament in the war'. At midnight, some of them were allowed to go, but others were imprisoned, including the elderly Dr Samuel Ward, Master of Sidney Sussex, Cromwell's college, who died soon after his release.

In the wake of the soldiers came William Dowsing, one of the more fanatical of the Suffolk gentry, who was appointed by Parliament to 'purify' the college chapels. His first target was the chapel at Peterhouse, so richly and lovingly adorned by Dr Cosin, where he pulled down 'two mighty great angels with wings, and divers other angels, and the four Evangelists, and Peter with his Keys over the chapel door, and about a hundred cherubims [sic] and angels'. Other chapels fared no better: 120 'superstitions of saints and angels' were destroyed at Jesus, and 'eighty superstitious pictures' at Pembroke, together with 'ten cherubims'. Dowsing planned to crown his iconoclastic labours by smashing the stained glass windows at King's, then for some reason desisted; perhaps the Fellows paid him the fee which he was entitled to claim for his work of 'purification', and persuaded him to leave the windows alone.

Towards the end of 1643, the local Roundhead grandee, the Earl of Manchester, arrived in Cambridge with his two Puritan chaplains and set about purging the University of 'malignant members'. Everyone who refused to take the Covenant was ejected; the numerous Fellows and undergraduates who were absent, having gone to serve in the King's army or been driven away by the persecutions of the Roundhead troops, were ordered to return to Cambridge within ten days, after which they were declared to have forfeited their places. Among those who left before Manchester's visitation were the poets, Crashaw and Cleveland; the former having retired to the Continent, heart-broken at the desecration of Peterhouse chapel, the latter having gone to join the King at Oxford.

By the spring of 1644, over two hundred of the most learned men in the University had been ejected. They included almost all the Heads of Colleges, the first to go being Cosin, who had incurred the displeasure of Parliament as far back as 1641. One college, Queens', lost all its Fellows as well as its entire complement of Scholars; for the junior members of the University were also required to take the Covenant, and they did not fall short of the dons in refusing to do so. The vacant Fellowships were filled with good Roundheads, including a number of men who were described as 'obstreperous American lay-lecturers'.

Although Manchester succeeded in getting rid of the High Anglicans, there were still plenty of Royalists left in Cambridge after he had finished his work. Chief among them was Dr Ralph Brownrigge, Master of Catherine's Hall, who succeeded Holdsworth as Vice-Chancellor. Although Bishop of Exeter, he was a strict Calvanist and opposed to the policies of Laud, which, presumably, was why he was allowed to stay. A year later, however, he preached a Royalist sermon before the University on the anniversary of the King's accession, and was promptly deprived of his Mastership and forced to leave Cambridge. It was through Brownrigge's influence that the young William Sancroft, afterwards famous as the Archbishop of Canterbury whose loyalty to James II led to his being deposed as a non-juror, was allowed to retain his Fellowship at Emmanuel until 1651. As late as 1647 the University was still so Royalist that the soldiers were reluctant to bring the King as a captive through the streets of Cambridge on his way from Holmby House to Newmarket, for fear that there would be a demonstration in his favour. So they avoided the town, but allowed Charles to pause for three days at Childerley Hall, a secluded country house in the neighbourhood where 'many Masters, Fellows, Graduates and Scholars repaired, to most of whom the King was graciously pleased to give his hand to kiss'.

The survivors of Manchester's purge were drastically reduced in number in 1654, when members of the University were required to swear allegiance to the Commonwealth as it was then established, 'without a King or House of Lords'. This, the 'Engagement', was refused by many of those who had been prepared to take the Covenant. What with the exodus at the beginning of the Civil War, and the ejections resulting from the Covenant and Engagement, six or seven out of the sixteen colleges had, by the end of 1654, lost the vast majority of their former members. These included, in addition to Queens' which suffered a clean sweep, Peterhouse, where twenty-one out of the twenty-two Fellows were ejected; Pembroke and the two largest colleges, Trinity and St John's.

Of the Royalists who were ejected from Fellowships at Oxford and Cambridge, we are told that the majority 'betook themselves to the painful profession of schoolmaster'. This is something of an exaggeration, for while it is true that they were obliged to earn their living teaching the young, they tended to do so more congenially as tutors in Royalist families; it was through their influence that the rising generation of the English gentry— the generation which reached manhood in time to sit in Charles II's Cavalier Parliament—was so staunchly Arminian and loyal. A few ejected Fellows stayed in the shadow of their former colleges, in spite of being banished. Dr John Fell, son of Dr Samuel Fell and the subject of the familiar rhyme, having lost his place at Christ Church, moved to a house nearby where he conducted Anglican services privately and administered the Sacrament to many Royalists. With him were two other young Christ Church divines who had fought in the King's army before being ordained: Richard Allestree, a veteran of Edgehill, and Richard Dolben, who had been wounded in the defence of York. Dr Samuel Collins, having been turned out of the Provostship of King's which he had held for thirty years, as well as out of the Regius Chair of Divinity, lived quietly in Cambridge until his death in 1651.

In contrast to these stay-at-homes, there was Anthony Bockenham, who, having been deprived of his Fellowship at Pembroke, Cambridge, went to live in Constantinople. Dr Beale of St John's ended his days in Madrid as chaplain to Hyde when he was Charles II's representative there. His fellow-sufferer, Dr Martin of Queens', after escaping from prison, lived for a while in disguise in Suffolk, and then being recaptured and imprisoned again, eventually went to France. Crashaw also spent part of his exile in France, where he lived in extreme poverty. Feeling that the Church of England would be ruined by the 'unlimited fury' of the Presbyterians, he became a Catholic; after which he went to Rome, and on the recommendation of the Queen found employment as secretary to a Cardinal. Finally, he obtained a minor canonry at Loreto, where he died in 1649 while still in his thirties. His fellow-poet, Cleveland, also died young, before the Restoration, but never went into exile. After joining the Royalist army, he served as Judge Advocate at Newark, where he acted as propagandist for the King and defended the town against the Scots. During the Protectorate, he was imprisoned, but was released after appealing to Cromwell in a dignified letter. 'For the service of His Majesty,' he wrote, 'I am so far from excusing it, that I am ready to allege it in my vindication.'

After the Restoration, the Cavaliers of Oxford and Cambridge as a whole fared better than the rest of the Cavaliers. At worst, they recovered their places, but many of them were compensated for their sufferings during the war by generous preferment. Dr John Fell, aged thirty-five, succeeded his father as Dean of Christ Church. Of his two companions, Allestree became Provost of Eton and Dolben eventually became Archbishop of York, the place which, in the words of his epitaph, he had 'consecrated with his blood'. Sterne reigned as Archbishop of York before Dolben. Sheldon became Archbishop of Canterbury in 1663 after the death of Juxon; as an ecclesiastical statesman, he played a vital part in the restoration of the Anglican Church. Cosin was appointed to the princely See of Durham, where a cathedral and two splendid episcopal chapels, transformed by him according to Laudian precepts, more than made up for his broken angels at Peterhouse.

14

Sir Charles Lucas:
A Hero of the Second Civil War

The defence of Colchester during the summer of 1648 was an
epic struggle, bitter even by the standards of that year of Royalist
risings known as the Second Civil War, a year which engendered
more ill-feeling than the four years of the main conflict. But what
makes Colchester particularly memorable is that after the Cavaliers
had surrendered, two of their commanders, Sir Charles Lucas and
Sir George Lisle, were executed in cold blood by the victorious
Roundheads. There is a greater sense of tragedy about Lucas's
death than there is about that of his companion, for Colchester
was his home town; he died within a stone's throw of the house
just outside the walls by St John's Abbey where he had spent his
childhood and youth, and which had belonged to his family for
two or three generations. The Lucases were wealthy landowners
and exceptional among the gentry of that overwhelmingly
Roundhead part of the country in being staunch Cavaliers.
Charles Lucas and his brothers and sisters were brought up by
their parents—and in particular by their mother, who survived
her husband—to put loyalty to the King before all else.

While not in any way doubting the genuineness of this loyalty,
one suspects that it might have been furthered by some long-
standing feud between the Lucases and their neighbours which
made them go more than ever Cavalier as the rest of the neighbourhood went Roundhead. Certainly the way they were treated
by the local populace in 1642 suggests the paying off of an old
score, rather than mere Puritan indignation. Just as the eldest
brother, Sir John Lucas, was about to set off to join the King, a
mob of two thousand people led by the volunteers and trained-
bands invaded his house on the pretext of searching for arms and

hidden Cavaliers. They made havoc of the place, smashing windows, plundering the furniture and plate, tearing up the garden, killing the deer in the park; they even broke open the family vault and stuck their halberds through the coffins. Sir John Lucas, together with his wife, his mother and one of his sisters, was hurried off to gaol.

Sir Charles Lucas was not present when his family home was attacked, for he was already with the King's army. At twenty-nine, he was a seasoned veteran, with a knighthood and a high reputation as a cavalry officer; he had fought in the Low Countries where he was one of the first to enter the breach at Breda. Soldiering was his whole life, as it was for his elder brothers. His sister, Margaret, Duchess of Newcastle, tells us that when the brothers met they would spend their time practising swordsman-ship and marksmanship, or wrestling to keep fit; they seldom hawked or hunted, and seldom if ever danced or played music, 'saying it was too effeminate for masculine spirits'. One is reminded of those early-Victorian subalterns who told their hostess: 'The Tenth don't *daunce*.' Indeed, there is something of the nineteenth-century officer about Charles Lucas; his large dark eyes gaze out at us from his portrait with that melancholy expression one associates with heroes of Inkerman, Delhi or Kandahar—if the moustache beneath his massive nose were larger, or if, instead of wearing a Cavalier tuft he were fully bearded, the illusion would be complete. At the same time, one can picture him as a warrior in the antique mould, a Spartan.

Throughout the Civil War, Charles Lucas was one of the bravest and most effective cavalry leaders on the Royalist side. He was wounded at Powicke Bridge in September 1642, and in the following July he defeated a superior Roundhead force at Pad-bury, near Buckingham, killing a hundred of the enemy; a circumstance which cannot have afforded him much pleasure, for though a fierce fighter, he was compassionate and avoided un-necessary bloodshed. As Newcastle's Lieutenant-General of Horse, he charged with Goring in the Royalist left wing at Marston Moor, helping to rout the Parliamentary cavalry under Fairfax. Later in the battle, however, he was taken prisoner, and on the following day had the sad task of helping his captors to identify the dead: 'Unhappy King Charles!' he exclaimed, tears running down his cheeks, as he saw how many of his comrades were killed. After his exchange he became Governor of Berkeley Castle, where he was besieged by a Parliamentary force under Colonel Rainsborough. He replied to the besiegers' summons by declaring 'that he would eat horse flesh first, and man's flesh when that was done, before he would yield'—prophetic words, in view of what his garrison had to endure, three years later, at Colchester. But after nine days, he was obliged to treat, largely on account of disaffection among his troops. He was too stern a disciplinarian, too austere a character, to be much liked, least of all by men undergoing the drawn-out hardships of siege warfare; though on the field of battle he inspired great devotion, such was his courage and the gallant figure he cut.

Having been taken prisoner for a second time in March 1646, Lucas was released after giving Fairfax his word that he would not bear arms again against Parliament. When, in 1648, he led the Royalist rising in Essex, he was accused by Halifax of breaking his parole. He replied to Fairfax's accusation by claiming that he was no longer bound by his engagement, having been subsequently made to pay a heavy fine to regain his freedom and estate; he also argued that he was fighting in self-defence, for after he had, as he thought, purchased his freedom, the Parliamentary authorities put a price on his head. Neither of these arguments seems quite valid, since in the first place he had been obliged to give his word once again that he would not serve against Parliament as well as paying his fine; while his statement that he was acting in self-defence is hardly borne out by the knowledge that he almost certainly helped to persuade his fellow-Royalists of Essex to continue fighting.

The rising in Essex was the sequel to the rising of the Kentish Royalists under Goring's father, the elderly courtier and diplomat, Lord Norwich. When confronted with the might of Fairfax's army at Blackheath, Norwich ferried his forces across the Thames estuary into Essex, where he hoped to increase his strength and gain a few days' grace before Fairfax caught up with him. In fact, the Essex Royalists led by Lucas, Lord Capel, Sir George Lisle and other gentlemen, were already in arms, and about to join the Royalists in Kent.

The addition of the Essex Royalists increased Norwich's strength to four thousand. It was decided that the combined army should await Fairfax in Lucas's home town of Colchester, a place of great natural strength, situated on a hill protected on two sides by the Colne river. The main part of the town was surrounded by a wall six or seven feet thick; at one end stood the Castle with its immense Norman keep, of tawny stone banded with red brick taken from the ruins of the Roman city.

The Royalists reached Colchester on 12 June and found the gate closed against them and a body of armed citizens drawn across the road; for the town was no less Roundhead now than it had been in 1642. Lucas galloped forward, dispersed the party before the gate, and summoned those within. The gate was immediately opened and the Royalists took possession of the town, which, in the words of Clarendon, 'was not glad of their company'.

Knowing that they would be outnumbered by Fairfax's army, which after being joined by volunteers from Essex and Suffolk had a strength of six or seven thousand, the Royalists decided to stand a siege, confident that they would soon be relieved by the Scots, who had invaded England in support of the King. They had only a day in which to barricade the approach roads, and to get in provisions and other necessary stores such as pitch to pour on to the besiegers, for Fairfax's army arrived on the thirteenth. Lucas would not allow his soldiers to commandeer the cattle and sheep of anybody 'but those they should know to be actual enemies', being 'tender of his country'; which can be taken as proof that he had some friends in the locality, despite the hostility towards him and his family of so many of the inhabitants—unless it was simply that he did not wish his own or his brother's tenants to incur any loss. Whatever their cause, his scruples made it impossible for any effective foraging to be done in the short time that remained before the enemy approached.

Fairfax encircled the town and summoned it to surrender. Norwich refused the summons. He was nominally the commander of the garrison, but Lucas was from the first regarded both by his friends and his foes as the real Royalist leader. Similarly, on the Roundhead side, Fairfax was controlled by a group of Cromwellian hard-liners, in particular by Cromwell's grim son-in-law, Henry Ireton, whose duty was to watch Fairfax as much as to conduct operations. These men included Lucas's old adversary at Berkeley, Colonel Rainsborough. Following the refusal of their first summons, the Roundheads made a fierce assault on the gate, but were beaten off after hand-to-hand fighting in which a hundred or more were killed on each side. Fairfax then began his bombardment; and on 20 July he drove the Royalists out of all their advanced posts and into the walled town. Among the positions captured by the Roundheads that day was the Lucas family home, and they lost no time in plundering it of what was left after the previous visitation. According to Matthew Carter, the Quartermaster-General of Norwich's army, they also once again broke open the family vault, and dismembered the corpse of Lucas's mother, scattering her limbs and putting locks of her hair in their hats as trophies.

Having been confined within the town, Lucas set fire to the houses round the outside of the walls. This was a military necessity, for the enemy could have fired down at the defenders from their upper storeys; and indeed, they had time to throw down a 'hand grenado' from one of the houses which exploded a powder magazine, killing eighty Royalists. But Roundhead writers represented the burning as an atrocity: 'a terrible red dusky bloody cloud seemed to hang over the town all night . . . with such lamentable outcries of men, women and children.' Among other accusations made against the Royalists was the inevitable one of rape; it was reported that Lucas had himself 'ensnared a woman' and was about to have his pleasure of her when Norwich came in and asked him to go and inspect a gun emplacement, enabling his intended victim to jump over the wall and tell her story to the neighbours. On a more serious plane, the Royalists were accused by the Roundheads of poisoning their bullets. The Royalists, for their part, accused the Roundheads of using bullets that were 'chawed', or jagged, and therefore more lethal. They also complained of prisoners being maltreated. Whatever the truth of individual complaints, one can take it that as the siege dragged on, both sides showed less respect for the rules of war.

By the end of July, the defenders were reduced to eating horses, and even dogs and cats. The townspeople fared worse than the soldiers, and Roundhead reports made the most of their sufferings. The soldiers were alleged to have seized the civilians' bread rations; it was said that when a woman complained to an officer that she and her child had no food, he replied, 'God damn me, that child would make a great deal of good meat well boiled.'

Carter, on the other hand, tells us that when the poorer inhabitants made 'great clamours and exclamations of their illusage' Lucas persuaded his colleagues at a Council of War to spare them some of the army's supply of corn. When one of the horses of the besieging army was killed in the fighting, several of the townspeople lost their lives in an unsuccessful attempt to carry away its carcase.

Sickness followed hunger, and the garrison and townspeople were afflicted with dysentry. But as was inevitable in a siege, the besieging army suffered as much in this respect as the defenders; particularly as the weather was abnormally wet. The Roundheads were, however, well off as regards provisions and shelter, though they did not feel they had any to spare for the women and children who fled from the town. When five hundred women came hopefully towards the redoubtable Colonel Rainsborough, he told his men to fire over their heads so as to turn them back; then, finding that this did not have the required effect, he sent soldiers to them with orders to strip them, which made them run back to the town, only to be refused admittance.

The clamour of the townspeople for a surrender began to be echoed among the military. This was taken by Lucas's enemies as a sign of his unpopularity; even Clarendon speaks of how the soldiers found him 'more intolerable than the siege'. Yet the fact that they stood with him for as long as they did is surely to his credit. Even as late as the middle of August, when most of the horses had been killed and eaten and there was scarcely a dog or cat left in the town, Lucas was determined to hold out, hoping for the arrival of the Scots.

And then, towards the end of August, news came that the Scots had been utterly defeated by Cromwell at Preston. This was the end, and at last Lucas agreed to surrender. By now, Fairfax and Ireton were thoroughly angry and insisted that the Royalist officers should 'surrender to mercy', only allowing quarter to the men. These terms were rejected, and the Royalists planned a desperate rush through the enemy ranks. But the men refused to support the officers in this enterprise, and in any case, there were not enough horses left—it was sad that Lucas and his brother-officers should have ended by eating their horses instead of riding them to victory.

There was nothing for it but to accept the unsatisfactory terms which the Roundheads had offered. On 28 August after a siege of seventy-five days, the Royal Standard was hauled down from the Castle and the garrison surrendered. A few hours later, Lucas, Lisle and a third officer named Sir Bernard Gascoigne were taken to the Castle, where Ireton came to them and told them to prepare for death. Lucas asked by what law they were to die, to which Ireton replied that it was by the vote of the Council of War, Parliament having ordered that all who were found in arms were to be proceeded against as traitors. 'Alas!' exclaimed Lucas, 'you deceive yourselves; me you cannot; but we are conquered and must be what you please to make us.' Then, 'with a countenance cheerful as one going to a banquet rather than death, not showing the least symptom of fear, but as it were scorning death as much as he did the instrument that gave it,' he asked if he could have until next morning to settle his affairs and prepare his soul. When told that he must die that very evening before sunset, he said: 'Do not think I make this request out of any desire I have to live, or to escape the death you have doomed me to, for I scorn to ask life at your hands . . . Do your worst, I shall soon be ready for execution.'

When the Royalist officers realized that Lucas, Lisle and Gascoigne were to die, they were greatly distressed. Capel sent Fairfax a letter, signed by himself and others, requesting that they should all suffer the same fate, being equally guilty. The letter was ignored, and at seven that evening, the three were led out into the Castle yard to be shot. Lucas knelt for a few moments in prayer, then rose and stood erect. Smiling, he opened his doublet, bared his breast and called out to the firing party: 'See, I am ready for you. Now, rebels, do your worst!' Four shots rang out, and he fell dead.

Lisle was then led forward, and having knelt to kiss the lips of his dead friend, he stood up and faced death as bravely as Lucas had just done. It was now Gascoigne's turn; he was ready, with his doublet off, but before the shots were fired an officer came and told him that he was reprieved. Fairfax and his colleagues, in condemning him to die with the other two, were under the impression that he was an Englishman; but at the last moment they learnt that he was, in fact, a Florentine aristocrat who had entered the King's service and been knighted—his name was actually Guasconi. So they decided to spare his life, fearing that, if they killed him, 'their friends or children who should visit Italy might pay dear for many generations'. Even the Roundheads had an eye to the amenities of the Grand Tour.

The news that Lucas and Lisle had been 'in cold blood barbarously murdered' caused widespread indignation. Their death was remembered long after other more shocking episodes of the Civil Wars had been forgotten. The two Cavaliers passed into folk-lore and became popular heroes in and around Colchester—where Lucas and his family had once been the object of so much hatred. People believed that the grass would not grow in the Castle yard near the stone where Lucas had stood to be shot.

Some nineteenth-century historians, however, put forward the theory that the execution of Lucas and Lisle was not an act of vengeance as was traditionally believed, but a punishment according to military law, since they had broken their parole. In fact there was never any suggestion of breach of parole in the case of Lisle, or, for that matter, Gascoigne; and whatever view is taken of Lucas's failure to stand by his agreement not to bear arms against Parliament, this was not given as the reason for his execution. Lucas and Lisle were both put to death because the Roundhead commanders—and in particular, Ireton—felt that some 'examples' should be made from among the officers who had risen in support of the King and put up such a lengthy and 'obstinate' defence at Colchester. As knights, Lucas, Lisle and Gascoigne were the most obvious candidates, apart from the two peers, Norwich and Capel, who Fairfax declined to execute on account of their rank. Instead, he sent them to be tried by Parliament, which resulted in Capel's execution, and Norwich's reprieve thanks to the casting vote of the Speaker.

There were plenty of people who thought that Parliament was justified in trying and executing some of the leaders of the Royalist risings of 1648; after all, they could be held guilty of starting a new civil war, and of causing bloodshed. But the execution without trial of officers who had 'surrendered to mercy' was a very different matter; it was different, too, from the accepted custom of refusing quarter to the garrison of a town or fortress which had to be stormed. That was killing the enemy in the heat of battle;

the other was putting a vanquished foe to death in cold blood. To the average Englishman of 1648, who was as devoted to fair play as his descendants are reputed to be, it seemed 'a new and terrible thing'.

15

The Fantastic Lord Bellomont

The title of Bellomont has an air of fantasy about it which suited the man on whom it was conferred just as much as did his surname of Bard, for there was something of the troubadour about him; he was a picturesque adventurer who wandered to strange parts of the earth. Like so many unusual Englishmen, Harry Bard was a clergyman's son, his father having been Vicar of Staines in Middlesex. His family had been of some consequence in Lincolnshire for several generations, but he is said to have been in the habit of boasting that he was 'descended from that man in Norfolk who went to law with William and overthrew the Conqueror'—presumably an illusion to Hereward the Wake. Such boasting would have been part of his nature if Anthony Wood's description of him as 'a compact body of vanity and ambition' were true; but there was more to him than that. He had courage and ability, as well as being a fine figure of a man.

His love of travel first showed itself when he was a scholar of King's College, Cambridge: he went on a trip to Paris during one of the vacations, unbeknown to his family or the college. This, to his contemporaries, seemed a more remarkable feat than it does to us; not only because the nine weeks of the vacation was regarded as hardly long enough for such an expedition, but because the early seventeenth-century undergraduate was in age no more than a schoolboy. Having become a Fellow of King's in 1635 when he was twenty, he was able to give free rein to his wanderlust, and he spent the next few years travelling in France, Germany, Italy, Turkey, Palestine, Egypt and Arabia, mainly on foot, sending a lengthy account of his journeyings to his college friend, Dr Charles Mason. In Egypt he acquired a handsome Koran which he afterwards presented to King's; he is alleged to have stolen it from a mosque, and to have remarked, when told that it was only worth £20, that 'he was sorry he had ventured his neck for it'.

On his return home, 'he lived high, as he had done before, without any visible income'. It seems that he was paid for, both on his travels and after his return, by his elder brother Maximilian, a prosperous mercer of London. According to Wood, Maximilian greatly admired brother Harry's accomplishments, and was 'as much despised by him'. This shows Harry in an ungrateful light, but it is human nature for an adventurous spirit to look down on a solid man of business. And when the outbreak of the Civil War found Maximilian on the side of Parliament, which he served in the useful if unheroic capacity of a buyer of horses, it was only natural that Harry should have sided with the King. He joined the Royalist army, and the King took notice of him on account of his reputation as a traveller and a linguist. He became a colonel, and in the following year was knighted and received one of those honorary degrees which Oxford gave so open-handedly to the Cavaliers.

If Harry Bard's military career was helped by royal favour, he quickly proved himself, and won the confidence of Prince Rupert. In 1643 he was sent to Ireland to raise troops, and he returned with two regiments of foot, which fought at the battle of Alresford in March 1644 when the Royalists under Hopton were defeated by the Parliamentarians under Waller. In that action, Bard succeeded in bringing off a whole brigade which would otherwise have been destroyed; but later in the day he was taken prisoner, as well as being severely wounded, so that he lost the use of an arm.

After his release, he was put in command of a brigade, and then, early in 1645, he became Governor of Campden House, a great mansion in Gloucestershire which the Royalists garrisoned in order to cut off the enemy lines of communication between Gloucester and Warwick. Clarendon believed that the garrison in fact served no useful purpose other than 'enriching the licentious governor thereof, who exercised an illimited tyranny over the whole country'; he must have heard the story, printed in a Roundhead newspaper, of how when the Constable of Kineton failed to collect all the contribution money due from that town on the excuse that there was the plague in some of the houses, Bard exclaimed 'that if the plague were in one and the pox in the other, he would have all the money' and ordered the unfortunate Constable to be thrown into a pond.

In May 1645 the garrison was withdrawn from Campden and ordered to join the King's army which was then marching northwards. On leaving the great house, Bard burnt it to the ground in order to prevent it from being occupied by the enemy; an act for which he was universally condemned. The owner of the house, Lord Campden, was a Royalist; it had cost £30,000 when it was built during the previous reign, and was one of the wonders of the age, with its cupola and its Corinthian chimneys, its tiers of columns and its sculptured friezes. According to some reports, Bard burnt Campden by order of Prince Rupert; but whether or not he was acting on his own responsibility, it was in keeping with his spectacular career that he should have staged such a holocaust.

After leaving Campden, he accompanied the King northwards and distinguished himself at the capture of Leicester, where he and Sir Bernard Astley were the first to scale the walls, with only three ladders. At Naseby, he led a division with Sir George Lisle. In the month following Naseby, Bard was raised to the Peerage of Ireland as Viscount Bellomont; it seems that he was given his exotic-sounding title—which was nothing more than an attempted Latin rendering of Ballymount—with a view to his being sent on another mission to Ireland. He sailed for that country in December 1646, only to be captured at sea by a Parliamentary vessel. Having been brought back to England as a prisoner, he wrote to Parliament declaring 'that he had taken up arms neither for religion (for there were then so many that he knew not which to be of), nor for that mousetrap, the laws, but to re-establish the King on his throne; and therefore seeing that the time was not yet come, he desired leave that they would discharge him.' Thanks to this remarkable missive—and also, perhaps, to the good offices of the worthy Maximilian—he was released and ordered to leave the country, being allowed to take his wife, children and servants with him.

All that we know of Bellomont's years on the Continent is that some time then he managed to decide what religion 'to be of', and became a Catholic; and that in May 1649, while at The Hague, he was arrested on the charge of having assisted in the murder of Isaac Dorislaus, the Dutchman who had prepared the evidence against the King at his trial. Dorislaus had come to The Hague as the envoy of the Commonwealth, and shortly after his arrival had been stabbed to death by a party of Cavaliers in disguise. The charge against Bellomont was soon dropped, and is regarded by most historians as having been unfounded; for while the Dutch authorities arrested nobody else in connection with the murder, it was generally believed to have been the work of Scots, followers of Montrose. According to the Parliamentarian, Bulstrode Whitlocke, however, the murderers of Dorislaus were English; and in any case there is no reason why some of them should not have been English, even if the majority were Scots. So we cannot rule out the possibility that Bellomont assisted in what most of his contemporaries would have regarded not as a crime but as the just punishment of a regicide.

In 1650 Bellomont was commissioned by the young Charles II to embark on what must surely have been the craziest venture which any Cavalier was asked to undertake for his Sovereign. This was to go as ambassador to the Shah of Persia, the King of Morocco and the Prince of Georgia, and endeavour to obtain money from them for the Royalist cause. Later, it was decided to abandon the visits to Morocco and Georgia, and to concentrate on the Shah, who of the three potentates seemed the most likely to be of help since he was believed to owe the King of England a debt for the part played by English ships in the capture of the Portuguese settlement of Hormuz in 1622. Even if the Shah proved unwilling to part with any money himself, there was the hope that he could be prevailed upon to expel the factors of the Roundhead East India Company, enabling certain customs dues which the Company enjoyed to be collected on behalf of the King.

Needless to say, the East India Company got wind of this scheme, and ordered its servants abroad to seize the Royalist ambassador and send him back to England as a prisoner. So as well as the other hazards of his journey, Bellomont had always to beware of the machinations of his English enemies. He sailed from Venice in disguise towards the end of 1653, aboard a small single-masted ship. On the voyage, he befriended a Venetian boy named Niccolao Manucci, who had stowed away in order to see the world. Bellomont offered to take Manucci to Persia

188

with him as his personal servant and the boy accepted with delight. In the account which he afterwards wrote of his travels, Manucci tells us that Bellomont loved him as if he had been his son.

After four months, Bellomont and his few followers reached Smyrna, and set out from there with a caravan on an adventurous journey through Turkey. There was snow on the ground; they had their money and valuables stolen at Brusa, though the Armenian Governor kindly gave them what they needed; they were attacked by robbers in the mountains and had their luggage examined with great severity by 'dishonest boors' at the frontier. They found the Persians much more friendly and respectful than the Turks. The Khan of Erivan, hearing that Bellomont was an ambassador from Charles II, gave a banquet in his honour, presented him with horses and silks and sent an armed guard to accompany him as far as Tabriz. Here Bellomont stayed a month and bought new clothes to wear at the Shah's court; those which he had with him being of Turkish style.

The Shah, Abbas II, was then at Kazvin, which Bellomont reached thirteen days after leaving Tabriz, and about nine months after setting sail from Venice. Here, according to his own report, he was treated 'right royally'; a house was put at his disposal, he was given a cavalry escort, he was showered with compliments, congratulations and offers of help. But though he stayed for two months, he came no nearer to achieving his mission. The Shah's minister, Azamat-ud-daula, received him in audience, mainly, it seemed, for the purpose of finding out his rank and what presents he had bought. Having heard from some Armenians that Bellomont was 'of great family', the minister sent to Smyrna to check if this were true.

A week later Bellomont was summoned to the palace, and in a hall of many pillars, entered through a courtyard in which two lions were tethered with golden chains, each with a golden drinking bowl, he met the Shah and presented him with some fine French armour and a letter from Charles II. The Shah seemed pleased, asked after the English King, and sent the letter to be translated. When this had been done, there came a second summons to the palace, to a sumptuous banquet. Bellomont was regaled with pilaus served off golden dishes and sweetmeats in jewelled boxes, but there was not a word about business. He had to console himself with the prospect of meeting the Shah again at Isfahan; attributing his lack of success to the fact that he only had eight or ten followers, instead of the retinue of two or three hundred which Oriental ambassadors usually affected.

Isfahan was then at the height of its glory. The vast square, the mosques of turquoise blue, the frescoed palaces, the avenues of plane trees, the gardens heavy with the scent of roses and jasmine, the pools edged with onyx, the arcaded bridges, the endless covered bazaars filled with merchandise from all over the world, combined to make it a city more splendid than any European capital of the time. Bellomont was comfortably housed, and Mr Young, of the English factory, unlike most of his colleagues in the East India Company, showed him great kindness. But it was six months before he saw anything more of the Shah or his minister; for they ignored him until they had heard from Smyrna that he was indeed what he purported to be.

Only then did Azamat-ud-daula receive him. The minister listened attentively to what he had to say, and promised to pass on his request to the Shah. A week later, the Shah entertained him to another banquet, but said nothing of his request, merely enquiring whether the Persian climate suited him, and asking if he would give him Manucci, who stood behind his chair; to which Bellomont tactfully replied that he would willingly have given him the boy had he been his own son, but that he could not part with him as he was responsible for him to his parents. The next week brought a present of brocades and carpets from the Shah, but still no answer. Bellomont went again to the minister and spoke to him more stiffly. Still nothing happened, except that the Shah invited him to a review of troops in the great square.

Bellomont continued to press Azamat-ud-daula, reminding him that he had been in Isfahan for nearly a year. After more prevarications, the minister sent for him, and told him that the Shah greatly desired to help the King of England, but could not think of how he could do so. It was impossible to send a Persian army to his assistance, because he was too far away. As for helping him by sea, to send a great fleet was extremely difficult, and in any case Persia had no ships, nor the materials with which to build them.

Bellomont listened to this long-winded speech with growing impatience, then, in half-mocking tones, he told the minister that he had 'a much easier method of remedying all this, without giving trouble to the Persian monarch, and without fatiguing the Persian soldiers, so famous throughout Europe'. This was that the Shah should pay, cash down, the money he owed to the King of England, but which clearly he had no intention of paying. Azamat-ud-daula, smiling graciously, said that the Shah did indeed wish to pay, but that the amount demanded was so large it would require too many beasts of burden to carry it, and might be robbed on the way; while if it were sent by sea, it might be lost in a shipwreck, or captured by pirates. To which Bellomont retorted that 'if they gave him the money, he knew quite well how to take care of it'.

As a last resort he asked if the Shah would banish the Round-head factors from his kingdom, but the minister replied that the Shah declined to banish anyone who was not guilty of an offence, while adding that Bellomont was at liberty to eject them with his own forces, if he so wished. Bellomont said heatedly that 'he had not looked for such an answer from a king of such fame in the world'. The minister continued to smile, murmuring that 'such events were sent from above'.

A week after this interview, Bellomont was invited by the Shah to a farewell banquet, at which he was ceremoniously presented with a letter for Charles II. He took it and handed it to his interpreter, giving the impression that if the man did not take it quickly, he would throw it at him. Then, 'without any civility, or any sort of bow', he turned his back on the Shah and stalked out. Manucci was sure they would be killed; but this snubbing of the Great Sophy in his own palace brought no retribution, and they were allowed to leave for Shiraz on their way to India. Having failed with the Shah, Bellomont resolved to visit the Mogul, Shah Jehan, in Charles's cause, though this does not seem to have been part of his instructions. The English at Bandar Abbas, who had feared that he would put the Shah against them, were only too pleased to give him a passage to India in one of their ships.

The ship reached Surat, then one of the busiest ports in the East, early in 1656. Bellomont went ashore secretly, on the advice of the captain who had heard that the English were planning to seize him and put him aboard a homeward-bound vessel, according to the orders from London. Indeed, during the two months which he spent here, the English offered him 'a thousand civilities' in order to get him into their clutches, even trying the stratagem of inviting him to a banquet on board one of their ships. But he remained aloof from them, and when he fell ill with a cancerous sore on his cheek, he was attended by the Dutch Company's surgeon, who, contrary to what Wood tells us of his character, found him 'very well-informed, modest and courteous'.

The surgeon was unable to heal Bellomont's sore, and he valiantly set out for Delhi with his cheekbone exposed. His caravan made its way slowly to Burhanpur, then along the Narbada river and across the mountains to Gwalior. At length he came to Agra, where the Taj Mahal was just about finished. The Governor accommodated him in a handsome house and the local English made him all kinds of offers, which he resisted, though he did consent to attend a feast at their factory. During the meal, he complained greatly of the heat, for it was now the middle of June; but he was determined to reach the Mogul's court at Delhi as soon as possible and so resumed his weary journey a few days later. Towards the evening of the third day after his departure from Agra, he suddenly cried out to Manucci 'in great pain', asking for water, and before it could be given to him, he died. His death seems to have been caused by heat-stroke; of all the Cavaliers who laid down their lives for their King, he did so furthest from home and in the most unlikely manner.

Bellomont's widow, and his son and three daughters—the youngest of whom was suitably named Persiana—were left in great poverty. The Restoration brought them little in the way of relief; it does not seem to have occurred to the King that Bellomont's services gave his family a claim on the Royal bounty. Prince Rupert, however, may have been motivated by some such sentiments when he took the second daughter, Frances Bard, as his mistress. According to a document of uncertain authenticity, she and the Prince were actually married. In which case their son, Dudley Bard, might have succeeded to the throne, had he not been killed fighting the Turks at Buda; a thought which adds a final touch of fantasy to the story of Lord Bellomont.

Conclusion

After the execution of the King, England was governed by a Council of State, which formed the majority in the so-called 'Rump'—what remained of the Long Parliament after Pride's Purge. By 1653 this form of government had failed and Cromwell, who, having defeated Charles II when he invaded England with a Scots army, was by now far and away the strongest man in the country, dissolved the Rump and replaced it with a nominated Parliament which was equally unsuccessful. So the Commonwealth was superseded by the Protectorate, with Cromwell as Lord Protector, which endured until Cromwell's death in 1658. Cromwell was succeeded as Protector by his son Richard, but 'Tumbledown Dick' was quite unequal to the task of governing and retired into private life. There followed a period of uncertainty, and then, in 1660, with the support of the Presbyterians and the army under General Monck, Charles II was restored to the throne.

The Restoration established the reforms for which Hyde and the other moderates had worked in the early months of the Long Parliament; it was a return to the situation which existed in the summer of 1641, when the controversy between King and Parliament appeared to have been peacefully resolved. There was no question of a restoration of Charles I's Prerogative rule. On the other hand, the Laudian Church was very much restored; and despite the promise of religious freedom made by Charles II at Breda, the victorious Anglicans in Parliament passed a series of penal laws against Catholics and Dissenters, as nonconforming Protestants came to be known. Even the Presbyterians, who had played so important a part in the King's restoration, suffered. The King tried to counter this legislation by his two Declarations of Indulgence but was obliged to withdraw them owing to the strength of Parliament. Only during the brief reign of his brother and successor, the Catholic James II, was there the religious toleration which had been promised at Breda; for James, who has gone down to history as a Catholic bigot, granted freedom of worship to the Dissenters as well as to his own co-religionists. After James had lost his throne, there was toleration for Dissenters—except for Unitarians—but not for Catholics.

While there is no excuse for the breaking of Charles II's promise of religious freedom, it is hard to see how the putting to death of the surviving regicides, which is regarded as the other black mark against the Restoration, could have been avoided. The killing of a king was held to be so heinous a crime that Charles II would have been disgraced in his subjects' sight, as well as in the eyes of the world, had he allowed the men who were instrumental in putting his father to death to go unpunished. It was not really within his power to pardon them; had he done so, he would have appeared to have betrayed his own kingship.

Apart from the regicides and the Dissenters, the former Roundheads were treated very well at the Restoration. During the years that followed, they were on the whole more prosperous than the former Cavaliers, who received virtually no compensation for their losses during the war. Although the prevailing atmosphere in the reign of Charles II was strongly Royalist and the Civil War became known officially as the Rebellion, there was little if any victimization of those who had fought on what was now regarded as the rebel side. In fact, the aftermath of bitterness left behind by the Civil War in England was remarkably slight; the rift between Cavaliers and Roundheads healed quickly. Only in Scotland and Ireland did the hatred linger on. In Scotland, under the harsh rule of the Duke of Lauderdale, the Restoration was followed by the 'Killing Times', those years of warfare between the government and the Covenanters in which Montrose's kinsman, John Graham of Claverhouse, played a leading part. In Ireland, the harm done by the Civil War and the Cromwellian Settlement caused a new and no less violent conflict before the century was out; though, thanks to Ormonde, there was peace for as long as Charles II was King.

For a country which had recently been torn by civil war, Restoration England was not only well integrated, but flourishing. The country continued to grow richer through overseas trade; and if the emergence of England as a world power was speeded up under Cromwell, the Restoration at any rate did not slow down the process. Admiral Blake won his great victories under the Commonwealth and Protectorate; but the navy of Charles II won a no less resounding victory against the Dutch in 1665. Charles's secret negotiations with Louis XIV may have been a shameful chapter in the history of British diplomacy, but it was not so very long afterwards that British arms beat *Le Grand Monarque* at Blenheim and Ramillies; in fact, Marlborough himself served with the troops sent by Charles to the assistance of the French King under the terms of the secret Treaty of Dover.

Just as Restoration England is believed to have been politically corrupt, so is it thought of as having been morally degenerate. However, the image of the bawdy England of Charles II is just as much a caricature as that of the austere and joyless England under Puritan rule. The popular view is coloured by the amours of the King himself and by the excesses of the more notorious libertines of the court, such as Rochester; there seems little reason for believing that the average morals in the reign of Charles II were any different from those in the reign of Charles I. Most people were still profoundly religious. The Restoration Church may have persecuted the Dissenters, but at the same time it enjoyed a period of great spiritual vigour, the reign of Charles II being the age of Tillotson, Stillingfleet and the other 'Caroline Divines'.

If the court of the 'Merry Monarch' is thought of as having been rather too frivolous, it should be remembered that Charles II also took an interest in the Royal Society, which, ten years after receiving its charter from him, elected Isaac Newton as a Fellow. Charles II's contemporaries included Wren, Dryden, Halifax and Sir William Temple; his reign was a golden age just as much as that of Charles I. Or rather, the flowering of the national genius which began under Elizabeth was not cut short by the Civil War but continued right through the seventeenth century; the war did no good, but in the long run it did surprisingly little harm.

Select Bibliography

AGAR ELLIS, HON. GEORGE, *Historical Inquiries respecting the Character of Edward Hyde, Earl of Clarendon*, London 1827.

ARNOLD, MATTHEW, article on *Falkland* in *Nineteenth Century*, March 1877.

ATTWATER, AUBREY, *Pembroke College, Cambridge, a Short History* (ed S. C. Roberts), Cambridge 1936.

AUBREY, JOHN, *Brief Lives* (ed Andrew Clark), Oxford 1898.

AYLMER, G. E., *The King's Servants, the Civil Service of Charles I, 1625–42*, London 1961.

BANKES, VIOLA, *A Dorset Heritage*, London 1953.

BARWICK, JOHN, *Life*, London 1724.

BARWICK, JOHN, *Querela Cantabrigiensis*, Part 2 of *Mercurius Rusticus*, Oxford 1646.

BONE, QUENTIN, *Henrietta Maria, Queen of the Cavaliers*, London 1973.

BUCHAN, JOHN, *Montrose*, London 1928.

BULSTRODE, SIR RICHARD, *Memoirs*, London 1721.

BURGHCLERE, LADY, *Life of James, First Duke of Ormonde*, London 1912.

BUTLER, THEOBALD FITZWALTER, *James Butler, First Duke of Ormonde*, in *Journal of the Butler Society* 1, Kilkenny 1968.

CAMBRIDGE COLLEGE HISTORIES, *Clare*, by J. R. Wardale; *King's* by Rev A. Austin Leigh; *Magdalene*, by Edward Kelly Purnell; *St John's*, by James Bass Mullinger, London 1899–1904.

CARNARVON, EARL OF, Speech delivered at unveiling of monument to Falkland, 9 September 1878, reprinted in *Fortnightly Review*, 1 November 1882.

CARTE, THOMAS, *History of the Life of James, Duke of Ormonde*, London 1786.

CARTE, THOMAS (ed), *Original Letters*, London 1739.

CARTER, MATTHEW, *A Most True and Exact Relation of That as Honourable as Unfortunate Expedition of Kent, Essex and Colchester*, NP 1650.

CARTWRIGHT, JULIA, *Sacharissa*, London 1901.

CHOLMLEY, SIR HUGH, *Memoirs . . . addressed to his two sons . . .* Taken from an original MS, London 1787.

CLARENDON, EDWARD, EARL OF, *History of the Rebellion and Civil Wars in England* (ed W. Dunn Macray), Oxford 1888.

CLARENDON, EDWARD, EARL OF, *The Life of Edward, Earl of Clarendon . . . Written by himself*, Oxford 1827.

CLARENDON STATE PAPERS, Calendar of Clarendon State Papers, preserved in the Bodleian Library, Oxford 1919–32.

CLARK, ANDREW (ed), *The Colleges of Oxford*, London 1891.

CLIFFE, J. T., *The Yorkshire Gentry, from the Reformation to the Civil War*, London 1969.

COLCHESTERS TEARES, *London 1648* (Clarendon Historical Society Reprint 1884).

COLE, WILLIAM AND OTHERS, *A Catalogue of all the Provosts, Fellows and Scholars that have been either elected or placed into King's College in Cambridge*, 1748–9 (BM Add MSS 5816).

COLLETT, HENRY, *Little Gidding and its Founder*, London 1925.

FALKLAND, LUCIUS, VISCOUNT, *A Letter sent from the Lord Falkland . . . unto the . . . Earle of Cumberland, at York, 30 September 1642*, London 1642.

FANSHAWE, LADY, *Memoirs*, London 1905.

FERGUSSON, BERNARD, *Rupert of the Rhine*, London 1952.

FITZGERALD, BRIAN, *The Anglo-Irish*, London and New York 1952.

FULLER, THOMAS, *Church History of Britain*, London 1655.

GARDINER, S. R., *History of the Great Civil War*, London 1891.

GORING, GEORGE, LORD, Anon, *A True Relation of the Several passages and proceedings of Colonell Goring at Portsmouth*, London 1642.

GOUGH, RICHARD, *Antiquities and Memoirs of the Parish of Myddle*, Shrewsbury 1875.

HAMILTON, COUNT ANTHONY, *Memoirs of Count Grammont*, London 1793.

HARTMANN, CYRIL HUGHES, *The Cavalier Spirit*, London 1925.

HAZLITT, W. CAREW, *The Poems, Plays and other Remains of Sir John Suckling*, London 1892.

HEATH, JAMES, *A Brief Chronicle of the Late Intestine Warr in the Three Kingdoms of England, Scotland and Ireland*, London 1663.

HENRIETTA MARIA, QUEEN, *Letters* (ed Mary Anne Everett Green), London 1857.

HENRIETTA MARIA, QUEEN, Anon, *A True Relation of the Queenes Maiesties Returne out of Holland*, York and Oxford 1643.

HERBERT, SIR THOMAS, *Memoirs of the two last years of the reign of Charles I*, London 1702.

HINDERWELL, THOMAS, *History of Scarborough*, Scarborough 1798.

LEAHY, SHEILA, *The Duke and the Poets*, In *Journal of the Butler Society* 5, Kilkenny, 1973 and 1974.

LISMORE PAPERS (ed A. B. Grosart), privately printed 1886-8.

LLOYD, DAVID, *Worthies*, London 1670.

LYTTON, EDWARD BULWER, LORD, Review in *Quarterly Review*, vol 108, 1860.

MANUCCI, NICCOLAO, *Storia do Mogor* (trs William Irvine), Indian Texts Series, London 1907.

MARAH, REV WILLIAM HENNESSY, *Memoirs of Archbishop Juxon*, Oxford 1869.

MARRIOTT, J. A. R., *The Life and Times of Lucius Cary, Viscount Falkland*, London 1907.

MATHEW, DAVID, *The Age of Charles I*, London 1951.

MERCURIUS AULICUS, 1643.

MERCURIUS BRITANNICUS, 1645.

MERCURIUS PRAGMATICUS, 1648.

MERCURIUS RUSTICUS, 1642-43.

MERCURIUS RUSTICUS, *or the Countries Complaint of the barbarous out-rages committed by the Sectaries of this late flourishing Kingdome*, Oxford 1646.

MODERATE INTELLIGENCER, 12 September 1645.

MOTTEVILLE, FRANÇOISE BERTAUT, MADAME DE, *Memoires sur Anne d'Autriche et Sa Cour* (ed M. F. Riaux), Paris N.D.

MULLINGER, JAMES BASS, *Cambridge in the Seventeenth Century*, London and Cambridge 1867.

MURDOCK, KENNETH B., *The Sun at Noon*, New York 1939.

NALSON, JOHN, *An Impartial Collection of all the memorable Events from the Scotch Rebellion to the King's Murther*, London 1682-3.

NAPIER, MARK, *The Life and Times of Montrose*, Edinburgh 1840.

NEWCASTLE, DUKE AND DUCHESS OF, Anon, *The First Duke and Duchess of Newcastle-upon-Tyne*, London 1910.

NEWCASTLE, MARGARET, DUCHESS OF, *The Life of William Cavendish, Duke of Newcastle, to which is added the True Relation of my Birth, Breeding and Life* (ed C. H. Firth), London 1907.

NEWCASTLE, WILLIAM, EARL OF, *Answer to six groundlesse aspersions cast upon him by the Lord Fairfax*, York and Oxford 1642.

OMAN, CAROLA, *Henrietta Maria*, London 1936.

ORMEROD, GEORGE (ed), *The First Siege of Lathom House, from a contemporary MS* (Harl MSS 2074), printed in Civil War Tracts, Chetham Society 1844.

PERRY, HENRY TEN EYCK, *The First Duchess of Newcastle and Her Husband as Figures in Literary History*, Boston and London 1918.

ROBINSON, MAJOR EDWARD, *A Discourse of the Warr in Lancashire*, Chetham Society 1864.

Select Bibliography

ROUND, J. H., *The Case of Lucas and Lisle*, Transactions of Royal Historical Society, New Series, vol VIII, London 1894.

RUPERT, PRINCE, *Prince Rupert his reply to a pamphlet entitled The Parliaments vindication* . . . London 1642.

RUPERT, PRINCE, Anon (by I.W.), *The Bloody Prince*, London 1643.

RUPERT, PRINCE, Anon, *Prince Rupert, His Disguises*, London 1642.

RUPERT, PRINCE, Anon, *Observations upon Prince Rupert's White Dog, called Boy*, NP 1643.

RUSHWORTH, JOHN, *Historical Collections*, London 1692.

SCOTT, ROBERT FORSYTH, *St John's College, Cambridge*, London 1907.

SEACOME, J., *House of Stanley*, Manchester 1767.

SKELTON, ROBIN, *The Cavalier Poets*, London 1970.

SMITH, GOLDWIN, *Falkland and the Puritans*, In *Contemporary Review*, April 1877.

SOPHIA, ELECTRESS OF HANOVER, *Memoirs* (trs H. Forester), London 1888.

STANLEY PAPERS, printed by Chetham Society 1867.

SYMONDS, RICHARD, *Diary of the Marches of the Royal Army*, Camden Society 1859.

TANNER, J. R., *English Constitutional Conflicts of the Seventeenth Century*, Cambridge 1928 (reprinted 1948).

TULLOCH, JOHN, *Rational Theology and Christian Philosophy in England in the Seventeenth Century*, Edinburgh and London 1872.

VARLEY, F. J., *Cambridge during the Civil War, 1642–1646*, Cambridge 1935.

WALKER, JOHN, *An Attempt towards recovering an Account of the Numbers and Sufferings of the Clergy* . . . *in the late time of the Grand Rebellion*, London 1724.

WARBURTON, ELIOT, *Memoirs of Prince Rupert and the Cavaliers*, London 1849.

WARWICK, SIR PHILIP, *Memoires of the reigne of King Charles I* . . . London 1701.

WEBER, KURT, *Lucius Cary, Second Viscount Falkland*, New York 1940.

WEDGWOOD, C. V., *George Goring, Soldier and Rake*, in *Sussex County Magazine*, March 1935.

WEDGWOOD, C. V., *The King's Peace*, London 1955.

WEDGWOOD, C. V., *The King's War*, London 1958.

WEDGWOOD, C. V., *Montrose*, London 1952.

WHITLOCKE, BULSTRODE, *Memorials of the English Affairs*, London 1682.

WILLIAMS, RONALD, *Montrose, Cavalier in Mourning*, London 1975.

WISHART, REV GEORGE, *Memoirs of James, Marquis of Montrose* (trs Rev Alexander D. Murdoch and H. F. Morland Simpson), London 1893.

WOOD, ANTHONY À, *Athenæ and Fasti Oxonienses*, London 1691 and 1692.

199

WOOD, ANTHONY À, *Life and Times* (collected by Andrew Clark), Oxford 1891.

WORMALD, B. H. G., *Clarendon, Politics, History and Religion*, 1640–1660, Cambridge 1951.

YOUNG, G. M., *Charles I and Cromwell*, London 1935 (New Edition 1950).

Index

Elizabeth of Bohemia, Queen, 49, 50, 153

Erle, Sir Walter, 133, 134

Essex, Robert Devereux, 3rd Earl of, 17, 52, 53, 55, 90, 93, 130, 169

Evelyn, John, 84

Exeter, 97, 130

Eythin, James King, Baron, 28, 31, 58, 59

Fairfax, Ferdinando, 2nd Baron, 27, 28, 29, 30

Fairfax, Sir Thomas, 3rd Baron, 18, 19, 21, 96, 137, 183; in Yorkshire, 27, 28, 29, 30, 60, 92, 161; at Marston Moor, 58, 92, 177; besieges Oxford, 60, 169; besieges Bristol, 61; besieges Colchester, 178-82

Falkland, Henry Cary, 1st Viscount, 37, 38, 39

Falkland, Lucius Cary, 2nd Viscount, 36-48, 51, 67, 79, 108, 143, 167; upholds constitutional liberty, 14, 36, 41, 44-5; his circle of poets, wits and scholars, 36, 38, 39-41, 107; religious beliefs, 37-8, 39; in 'Short' Parliament, 41; friendship with Hyde, 41, 42, 44, 45, 47, 48, 75; in 'Long' Parliament, 41; condemns Strafford, 42; supports Episcopacy, 42-3; opposes extremists, 42-4; in triumvirate, 44-5, 78; depression over war, 45-7; at Edgehill, 46; peace efforts, 46-7; death at Newbury, 47-8, 80

Falkland, Lettice, Viscountess, 38-9, 40

Fanshawe, Lady, 88, 98, 169

Farnham, 94

Fell, Dr John, 174, 175

Fell, Dr Samuel, 170

Ferabasco, Henry F., 10

Ferrar, Nicholas, 166

Fiennes, Colonel Nathaniel, 55

Finch, Sir John, 41, 75

Finmore, William, 170

Five Members, attempted arrest of (1642), 5, 13-4, 16, 44, 78, 80

Forth and Brentford, Patrick Ruthven, Earl of, 59

Frederick, Elector Palatine, 49, 50

Fuller, Thomas, 69

Gascoigne, Sir Bernard, 182-3

Gassendi, Pierre, 33

Glamorgan, Edward Somerset, Earl of, 117, 120

Glamorgan, Lady, 120

Gloucester, Henry, Duke of, 123

Gloucester, siege of (1643), 47

Go, lovely Rose (Waller), 105

Godolphin, Sidney, 40, 47

Gondibert (Davenant), 108

Gordon of Ruthven, Patrick, 141

Goring, George, Lord, 16, 28, 60, 81, 87-99; at Marston Moor, 57, 59, 92-3, 177; military genius, 87, 89; unfavourable reputation, 87-8, 90-1, 92, 94-5, 98; in Dutch service, 89; governor of Portsmouth, 89, 90, 91; betrays Army Plot, 90; surrenders Portsmouth, 91; raises forces in Holland, 91-2; captured at Wakefield, 92; Lancashire and Yorkshire campaign, 92-3; success in south, 93-4; failure of grand design, 94; mixed fortunes in south-west, 95-8; life abroad, 98-9

Goring, Lettice, Lady, 88

Grand Remonstrance (1641), 5, 6, 14, 43, 77, 160

Great Tew, 36, 39-41, 75

Greville, Fulke, 102, 104

Hales, Sir Matthew, 36

Hamilton, James, 3rd Marquis of, 140, 144, 145, 146, 151

Hampden, John, 4, 6, 42, 43, 45, 107

Harvey, Colonel Edmund, 71

Hayward, Richard, 67, 71, 72

Helvoetsluys, 62

Henrietta Maria, Queen, 10, 13, 24, 25, 29, 32, 62, 65, 120, 145, 165; Catholicism, 3, 12, 82, 123; influence on Charles I, 11-2, 14-5, 16, 19, 56; in Holland, 14, 89, 90, 91-2, 108, 127-8; Goring's support for, 89, 90, 91-2; work for Royalist cause, 127-31, 159; return to England, 128-30; and Yorkshire campaign, 129-30; in France, 130-1; Cholmley's 'surrender' to, 159-60

Herbert, Thomas, 70

Herrick, Robert, 011

Hertford, William Seymour, 1st Marquess of, 52

History of the Rebellion (Clarendon), 26, 73, 81, 86

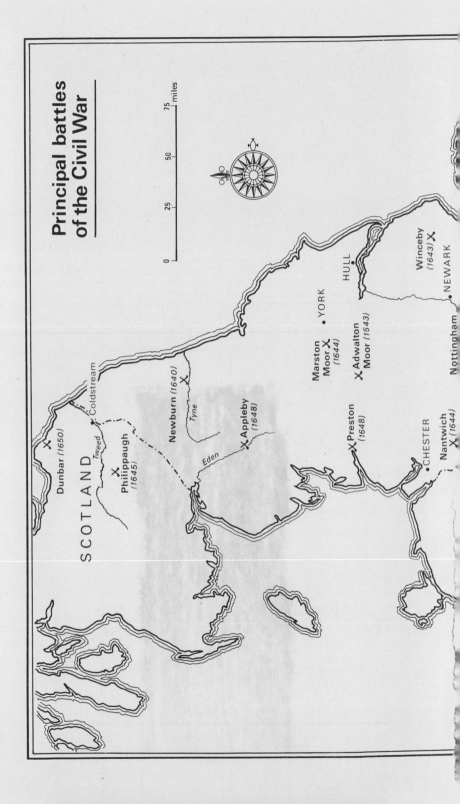

Principal battles
of the Civil War

0   25   50   75 ⌐ miles

SCOTLAND

Dunbar (1650) ✗

Tweed

Coldstream •

Philippaugh (1645) ✗

Newburn (1640) ✗

Tyne

Eden

✗ Appleby (1648)

York •

Marston Moor ✗ (1644)

✗ Adwalton Moor (1643)

Hull •

Winceby ✗ (1643)

• Newark

• Nottingham

✗ Preston (1648)

Chester •

Nantwich (1644) •